Linking
Cultural and
Natural Heritage

Edited by John Marsh and Janice Fialkowski

Linking Cultural and Natural Heritage

The Proceedings of a Conference at
Trent University, Peterborough, Ontario
June 11-13, 1992

Edited by:
John Marsh and Janice Fialkowski

Published by:
The Frost Centre for Canadian Heritage Development
Studies, Trent University 1995

Linking Cultural and Natural Heritage
The Proceedings of a Conference at
Trent University, Peterborough, Ontario
June 11-13, 1992

Edited by John Marsh and Janice Fialkowski

ISBN 0-9693790-4-8

Copies available from:
    The Frost Centre for Canadian Heritage
    and Development Studies
    Trent University
    Peterborough, Ontario K9J 7B8

Contents

Acknowledgements ....*viii*

Introduction
John Marsh ....*ix*

Welcome Address
Karen Haslam ....*xi*

Natural and Built Heritage *1*

The Greening of Heritage:
Historic Preservation and
the Environmental Movement
T.H.B. Symons *3*

Sustainable Development
Sylvia Sutherland *17*

Resources and Energies
Hamish Wilson...*19*

Natural and Cultural Heritage Planning,
Protection and Interpretation: From Ideology
to Practice, a Civics Approach
J.G. Nelson *33*

Integrating Natural and Built Interpretation:
Two Case Studies, Rideau Hall, Ottawa and
the MacKenzie King Estate, Gatineau Park
Edwinna von Baeyer *45*

The Built and Natural Environments:
Forging a Link: The New England Experience
Tom McMillan..*49*

Landscapes of Gain/Landscapes of Loss:
A Bioregional Model for the Analysis of
Cultural and Natural Heritage
John Wadland *61*

Linking Natural and Cultural Heritage on
The Alexander Mackenzie Voyageur Route
Peter Labor *65*

Closing Address
Michael Valpy *69*

Rural Heritage...**81**

Heritage Awareness at the Country Roadside
Thomas F. McIlwraith *83*

Rural Landscape Heritage Resources of the
Peterborough Area
Alan Brunger *87*

Ontario's Landscape Legacies: A Model for a
Province-wide Inventory
Nancy Pollock-Ellwand..............................*91*

The Heritage of Uxbridge Township
Ian K. Woods...*117*

Rural Heritage Conservation Districts:
A Case Study of Rainham Township
David McClung...*119*

Recreational and Tourism Heritage...............**123**

The Bigwin Inn
Douglas McTaggart...................................*125*

The "Chateau" at Wanapitei on Lake Temagami
Bruce and Carol Hodgins...........................*133*

The Chippewa Park Carousel, Thunder Bay
Michele Proulx *135*

Cultural Tourism **145**

Tourism: Niagara-on-the-Lake
Jim Alexander...*147*

Cultural Tourism: Port Hope
A. K. Skulthorpe *151*

Urban Heritage.......................................**153**

The Peterborough Armoury
Thomas H. B. Symons...............................*155*

London's Talbot Block - What Did We Learn?
Nancy Tausky *157*

London's Talbot Block - What Did We Learn?
Mark Gladysz..*163*

A Restoration Project By Heritage
Sault Ste. Marie Inc
Wilhelm Eisenbichler................................*167*

Relocation of Threatened Heritage Structures
To A Municipally-Owned Subdivision:
Markham Heritage Estates
Regan Hutcheson *171*

Facadism or Partial Retention
   William N. Greer..*177*

Salvaging Heritage: The Non-Profit Way
   Matthew F. Schultz...*179*

Construction Management:
The Team Approach to Restoration
   J.D. Strachan...*183*

Architectural Integrity and Human Needs.......*191*

Architectural Integrity vs Human Needs
   Lois Harte-Maxwell *193*

Architectural Integrity vs Human Needs
   John Ota..*197*

Handicapped Access to Historic Courthouses
   Doug Wilson *203*

Archaeological Work...*209*

Archaeological Ethics
   Susan Jamieson *211*

Municipal Responsibilities for Archaeology
   Heather Broadbent...*213*

Other Papers *217*

Heritage and The School Room
   Su Murdoch...*219*

Motivating the Volunteer Committee
   Georgette Houle *221*

A Global Perspective:
World Heritage Sites
   John Marsh..*227*

Biographies of Other Speakers *235*

Conference Programme...*241*

Listing of Participants..*257*

The Frost Centre, Trent University *273*

Frost Centre Publications.......................................*274*

Acknowledgements

The help of the following with the conference is gratefully acknowledged:

Ontario Ministry of Culture and Communications

Ontario Heritage Foundation

Ontario Historical Society

Corporation of the City of Peterborough

Louis Taylor, George North Studios

Ground Zero

Trent Valley Navigation Company

Liftlock Cruises

Liftlock IGA

Louis Taylor

Conference Committee:
Paul Wilson, Blair Armitage, Nan Belfry, Andrea Bonner, Ken Doherty, Glenda Hunter, John Marsh, Jackie Tinson, Mary Lou Evans, Janice Fialkowski, and special thanks to T.H.B. Symons

Conference Volunteers:
David Blanchard, Wayne Bonner, Brian Buchardt, John Callender, John Fisher, Christopher Greene, Ron Haley, Kathy Hooke, Art Hutchison, Jean Kyne, Jeff Leal, Kim Reid, Ray Willis, Ken Yates and the countless others who gave so much of their time.

The help of the following with the conference proceedings is gratefully acknowledged:
Melody Armitage, Nan Belfry, Janice Fialkowski, John Marsh.

Introduction

John Marsh
Director, Frost Centre for Canadian Heritage and Development
Studies, Trent University, Peterborough
John grew up in England where he learned to appreciate its rich his-
tory and attractive countryside. He gained a Ph.D. from the
University of Calgary with a thesis on the historical geography of
Glacier National Park. He has since undertaken teaching, research
and consulting on natural and cultural heritage conservation,
tourism and interpretation in Canada and abroad. He is now Director
of a research centre and graduate programme at Trent University
dealing with Canadian Studies, and heritage management.

THIS VOLUME PRESENTS A SELECTION OF PAPERS most of which were based on the presentations made at "Green Gutters and Gargoyles", the Annual Conference of the Local Architectural Conservation Advisory Committees of Ontario, held at Trent University in Peterborough, from June 11 to June 13, 1992. It is a selection because not all presenters submitted papers. However, other papers not presented at the conference, but consistent with its theme, have been included.

The main aim of the conference was to explore linkages between cultural and natural heritage, linkages unfortunately often neglected. Cultural and natural heritage may be linked in the physical sense, few natural areas having no cultural attributes, and most cultural or built heritage sites having a natural context, even if only with respect to topography. Cultural and natural heritage may also be linked in an institutional way, for example, when they come under the same legislation, policy or agency. They should be linked conceptually so that we can consider if the approach to valuing, inventorying, protecting, using and interpreting one is relevant to the other. We should also be considering if the means used to gain public, financial and government support for natural heritage protection could be used to gain support for cultural heritage and vice versa.

The first papers in this book include the keynote addresses of the conference. They extol the values of cultural and natural heritage, demonstrate links between them, express concern about threats to such heritage, and call for action to protect it.

Cultural and natural heritage are integrated, perhaps more than anywhere, in the countryside. So in section two we have several papers on appreciating, inventorying and saving rural heritage.

Cultural and natural heritage are also entwined, often in a particularly appealing fashion, in many recreation and tourism landscapes. This is revealed in the papers in section three which discuss a resort, a rustic "chateau", and an historic urban park. The following section discusses the cultural tourism that may be developed in, but also threaten heritage areas, case studies being provided of Niagara on the Lake and Port Hope.

Section five provides insight on the problems, progress and methods of conserving our urban heritage. There are general papers, technical papers, and case studies of places such as London, Markham and Sault Ste. Marie.

Subsequent sections of the book, reflecting other themes of the conference, deal with a wide variety of heritage topics. There are papers on making heritage sites accessible to the disabled, archeological sites, volunteers and heritage education.

The papers have been published largely as submitted, hence the variations in length and style. The names of the authors, their positions and biographies are given as indicated at the time of the conference. Likewise, most of the papers refer to conditions at the time of the conference, that sometimes may have changed.

The text has been illustrated with line drawings by Louis Taylor that were used at the conference on the invitations to dine at heritage homes in Peterborough.

Following the papers, the conference programme and list of participants are provided.

I hope this book, therefore, will constitute a substantial and suitable record of the conference, extend its impact and prove of interest and benefit to all those with an interest in cultural and natural heritage and the important links between them.

Welcome Address

The Honourable Karen Haslam
Minister of Culture and Communications

IT IS AN HONOUR TO BE WITH YOU THIS MORNING. On behalf of the Ministry of Culture and Communications, and its agency, the Ontario Heritage Foundation, I welcome you to the Provincial LACAC Conference.

I am pleased the ministry was able to support this conference, and to help bring together so many representatives of the heritage community from across the province.

Heritage is an issue close to my heart. In Stratford, where I live, we have a love of history. This comes from a long tradition of respecting the past and our rural roots. And so, when travellers come from around the world to take in the Festival, we have much to share with them. Right beside the Festival is the Avon River, and our riverside park. There are many more sites where architectural history runs side-by-side with natural history.

It is a personal pleasure to share my concern for heritage with you. As delegates, municipal representatives, architects, developers and environmentalists, you share your talent and knowledge with your community. You show great concern for heritage resources, and for the life of the community. Many of you volunteer a great deal of time, in doing so.

The citizens of Ontario appreciate your contribution, not only because of the expertise you bring, but because you represent and respect their own interests.

Your efforts guide municipal leaders, and help save and preserve our heritage... architectural and natural. We can live the beauty of the past. I am sure that you have all noticed the impact that our host, PACAC, has made, here, in Peterborough. Some very handsome buildings - such as the George Street United Church and the Pump House... to name only a few - live on because of the PACAC's commitment.

LACACs play a leading role in heritage, encouraging all communities to know about their own heritage - and to protect it - so that we may all know who we are as a community, as a province, and as a nation.

This conference gives us a chance to renew our passion for heritage, and to see conservation in an ecological light. The theme of this year's conference, "Green Gutters and Gargoyles", brings into focus the strong relationship between heritage conservation and environmental, and urban, ecology.

The partnership of the built and natural heritage movements is something we need to work toward. The Brundtland Report underlines the importance of this partnership. The report calls for "...sustainable development to meet the need of the present without compromising the ability of future generations to meet their own needs". It stresses that growth can be sustained only through the conservation of natural and human assets.

This call needs to be answered within the community, and our communities must have the power to take action. Conservation decision-making needs to be grounded in the knowledge, experience and values of local communities. As LACAC members, you are a critical part of the conservation network, because you work so closely with your communities.

The answers must be backed up by policies.

To reinforce the work you do, and to protect our heritage in perpetuity, we must have new heritage legislation. Municipalities must be given clear-cut responsibilities and direct guidance on heritage issues. We need to open up the channels for local citizens to give their input into heritage-related decisions within their own communities. And, we have to define clearly the provincial role in a way that supports community-based decision-making.

These principles need to be entrenched in legislation, so that we may make claim to our own past... and have the authority to protect it.

We need heritage legislation with teeth.

No doubt all of you know about the work of the advisory committee on the new heritage legislation. LACAC members are a definite presence on the committee, and have already made a tremendous contribution to the committee's recommendations.

In February, the committee released a working paper on the proposed legislation. The paper underlined the urgency of heritage conservation, and the social and economic benefits that flow from it. These recommendations have come out of the contribution of LACAC members. I know that LACACs have waited to see the development of the new Heritage Act. For those of you who have not looked over the working document, our Heritage Policy Branch will be more than happy to furnish copies.

I can't tell you how much I appreciate the work of the committee members. They have worked closely with heritage groups, and in doing so created a hard working and inspired forum.

I am pleased that my parliamentary assistant, Gary Wilson, is continuing to chair the committee.

The committee is now completing its deliberations and is drafting the final report. I expect to have it in hand by the middle of August... but you will see it before I do. I understand that the committee is circulating it in draft, for comment, to provincial heritage organizations.

If you are not yet aware of the preliminary recommendations of the committee, or if you want to know the latest developments, contact Allen Tyyska and Dan Schneider, from Heritage Policy Branch.

The committee wants to hear your ideas. It has worked hard to reflect your concerns, and we all need to know if it has succeeded. Participatory planning will create an Act that encourages the widespread preservation of our heritage. I am committed to this process, and as your minister I will devote myself to achieving our mutual goals. We will get our teeth, and they will be strong.

Natural
and Built
Heritage

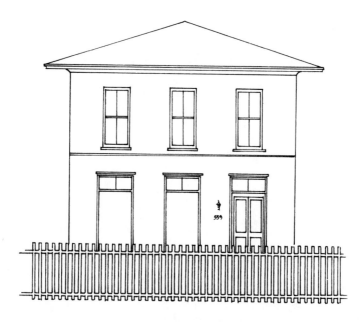

565 Harvey Street

The Greening of Heritage: Historic Preservation and the Environmental Movement

Dr. T. H. B. Symons
Vanier Professor, Trent University, Peterborough

> *Dr. T. H. B. Symons was the founding President and, until his retirement in 1994, Vanier Professor of Trent University. His distinguished career has involved him extensively in Commonwealth university affairs, human rights, Canadian native issues, and matters relating to Canadian culture and heritage. Among many other appointments in Canada and abroad, Professor Symons is currently Chairman of the National Historic Sites and Monuments Board of Canada.*

IT IS A PLEASURE TO PRESENT THIS OPENING PAPER to a conference to do with heritage which has been named, so aptly and lyrically, **Green Gutters and Gargoyles**. May I join in welcoming the Conference to Peterborough which has been my home now for more than 30 years. This historic community, with its equally handsome and historic environs, offers a particularly appropriate setting in which to explore the theme chosen for the Conference: that is "The relationship between our built and natural environments, and the care of both".

The programme that has been developed by the Steering Committee, under the chairmanship of Councillor Paul Wilson, is well designed to illuminate the Conference theme. If I may, I would like to congratulate Mr. Wilson; the Committee; the Co-ordinator, Janice Fialkowski; and the others who have helped to conceive this programme; as well as the many volunteers who have made its implementation a reality.

We should commend, too, those who have given support to the Conference, including the Ontario Ministry of Culture and Communications, the Ontario Heritage Foundation, and the City of Peterborough.

As this Conference progresses, it should, indeed, as the promotional material proclaimed, enable us "to discover how a desire to retain our architectural heritage has had heritage preservationists **Reducing, Recycling,** and **Reusing** for many years".

Certainly, the Conference has been well planned. It offers a remarkably broad, diverse, and yet detailed programme, within which there are opportunities for novices to learn and for older hands to refresh and to up-date their knowledge and skills. It is an occasion for all participants to expand their perceptions and understanding, to hear and to develop new ideas and approaches, and to discuss the ongoing business of heritage conservation. The Conference should, in short, be a great forum for mutual education, and that is very much how I hope it will develop.

I noted with particular interest that the Conference has been preceded by two workshops. The first of these was on *Conflict Resolution*, surely a down-to-earth, practical, and helpful subject, and not just for LACACs! I rather hoped you might go on to offer it, for example, in Ottawa to the good people on Parliament Hill - who are dealing with our never-ending constitutional crisis.

Perhaps the subject of the second workshop, *Cemetery Preservation*, followed naturally from the first dealing, as it does, with the tranquillity that comes from the ultimate conflict resolution? However, I wondered if the enthusiasm, even for this good cause, was not perhaps a bit excessive or at least open to possible misunderstanding, when your programme urged participants to "Join us in one of Peterborough's cemeteries (for on-site participation)". In this regard, I wish you all not only a most successful Conference, but also a safe trip home.

I noted, with some concern, that my remarks have been billed as a keynote address. Usually, as I understand it, a keynote address is full of élan, uplift, sunshine and exhortation. With your permission, I do not propose to follow that route. Rather, what I would like to do in the next brief while is simply to think out loud with you about a number of issues involved in your Conference theme, and then to raise a few questions, in hopes that such a course of action might possibly be of assistance in your ensuing deliberations.

First, let us look realistically at the place of heritage in our society today. The attention of the nation in 1992 is on many things, but I think it is safe to say that heritage is not near the top of the list. The environment is. And this is because the environment has been made relevant to the average Canadian (that mythical but useful person); whereas heritage has not. The environmentalists have delivered clear, popular, well-understood messages. Heritage preservationists have not. The well-being of the environment is now an accepted and fundamental concern to a great many thoughtful citizens, while heritage conservation is still seen as a fringe activity by many of those same people.

Yet environmentalists and heritage preservationists share the common concerns, the common goals, and the common values that arise from their mutual commitment to a Conserver Society. They have a near identity of interests. Surely, then, they should make common cause?

Why, then, one must ask, is heritage not part of the environmental movement? Or, perhaps we should reverse the question: Why should the environmental movement embrace heritage? One reason this has not occurred is that for many years a goodly number of our historic sites and commemorations seemed to mark environmental exploitation, as we celebrated the ugly side of material achievement. Or, in similar vein, such sites have often marked the military and economic subjugation of indigenous peoples. But heritage sites and structures can also illustrate good cultural and natural conservation practices, and, increasingly, they do so.

Nor does the environment occupy quite the pre-eminent place amongst our public concerns that it held not so long ago. It is noteworthy that both heritage and the environment are virtually absent from the current Canadian constitutional discussions.

Do these observations suggest a plan of action? I think they do. I would suggest that the arguments for environmental protection can and should be extended to include heritage conservation and historic preservation, and that this could be more readily done, to the mutual advantage both of the environment and of the historical heritage, if such arguments were cast in eco-ethical terms. Good conservation practices, whether for the natural environment or for the built environment, should have both ecological and cultural integrity.

To this end, I think it will be important for heritage conservationists often to give more attention, and support, to the environmental dimensions and consequences of their activities than is now the case. And the heritage movement must now actively work for the integration of heritage values into the environmental ethic. Just as the environmental issues have been made relevant to our everyday life in the past decade, so should heritage concerns be made part of our everyday value system in this current decade.

It may be said now, in these difficult and acutely sensitive times of constitutional and cultural tension for our country, it is not wise or possible to push for greater attention to heritage and to heritage values in public policy.

I do not agree with this view for one moment!

I would argue, on the contrary, that now, more than ever before, we should be paying attention to heritage in our country. It is what we have in common, what we share - and if we had paid more attention to this fundamental aspect of our national life for the past 125 years, we might now be able to feel some greater confidence, and enthusiasm, about the prospects for a continuing Canadian heritage during the next 125 years.

Threats surround us: threats to our heritage, threats to our environment, threats to our national unity, threats to our national sovereignty. By addressing the threats to our heritage - that is, threats to the elements of our culture that we value - we can address many of the threats to our national unity and sovereignty.

What we choose to save, or destroy, reveals our values as a people. In the words of Professor Robin Winks of Yale University, "Our cultural resources ought to be inviolate, for they tell us about ourselves". What is our heritage, if not the aspirations of the people who made it, and, one might add, the aspirations of the people who have chosen to preserve it?

If we are to know ourselves, if we are to serve well both ourselves and others, then we must understand and care for our heritage in all its diversities - yes - and imperfections. We must know and use well our heritage, in order to convince policy makers that it matters, that it has significance, that heritage is not merely an isolated and marginal activity. We will have to develop the arguments, and demonstrate in clear and unmistakable terms, why heritage conservation is important to the health and vitality of our country. Further, we will have to convey effectively the twin message that the cultural world is part of our environment and that the natural world is part of our heritage.

In this situation, there is a clear role and responsibility for our educational institutions, at all levels. If we do not know and use our heritage, if we do not respect the environment, it is in large part because we have not been taught these things.

The educational system is an iceberg that moves slowly. There is certainly now some motion on the teaching and study of both heritage and the environment. But the iceberg is still moving too slowly on these urgent matters. The need is now, and it is acute. In this regard, may I commend to you the example and experience of Simcoe County educators who are pioneering in their presentation of heritage and its linkage to environmental issues?

Beyond curriculum reform, there is much that schools can do, of a broader nature, by the values they foster and represent.

Educational institutions may also have a direct role in heritage and environmental matters by the way they manage the buildings, properties, and artifacts for which they have responsibility.

In this arena, universities have often a special responsibility because of their extensive property holdings, and the many buildings and sites of heritage interest that still stand on many university campuses. Think, for example, of Laval's fantastic first site in the heart of old Quebec; of McGill's many heritage buildings in downtown Montreal; and, in our own province, of Queen's campus in the heart of historic Kingston, of the University of Ottawa in the midst of the capital city, of the really immense heritage holdings still remaining on the University of Toronto campus, and so on.

The sorry fact is that many of the educational institutions, at all levels, which ought to be in the vanguard of an enlightened concern for heritage, have often been despoilers, insensitive to heritage values as they destroyed significant and re-usable buildings. In so doing, they provided an appalling example for others in society, who might make a more believable plea of ignorance.

In this regard, I would like to pay tribute to the founding governors, faculty, and staff of Trent University, who, from the outset, showed a deep concern and respect for heritage values that is reflected in the many historic houses that have been preserved and incorporated into the life of the University, as well as in the respect shown for cultural landscape and the environment. Trent's is by no means a perfect record, but it is one of the best in sight.

May I point also to the example of a number of schools, both secondary and elementary, that have taken such steps as the creation of a Heritage Council to recommend policies and programmes to ensure the preservation of those things which constitute their physical and cultural inheritance?

Lastly, in regard to public education, may I point to the scope and need for serious educational programmes for the general public that will provide information and raise awareness about the value of the built heritage and its relationship to the environment? Money spent on such programmes could make a genuine contribution to Canadian affairs in these critical years. And they might free us from the pathetic, feel-good blarney about Canada that we are being spoon fed at the moment in paid federal government advertisements.

Hand in hand with education goes research. I need not tell this audience how important research is to the proper identification and conservation of heritage. This research aspect of heritage needs far more recognition and support than it has been receiving. It is research, and the informed knowledge resulting from research, that will bring scholarship, and the assurance of standards and integrity, to every aspect of the work of the heritage movement.

Heritage research can take many forms. There is, for example, much to be done in research of a material nature - in how to identify materials and techniques from another time, and how best to preserve or support them.

There are all the questions arising from the welcome swing to the three Rs - **Reducing, Recycling, and Reusing.** What are the limits to sensible recycling? and what are the constraints on re-use? The materials of existing buildings are, indeed, a great bank of stored materials. But it requires knowledge, money, time, and energy to release and re-use them. Demolition is often wasteful of all these; but not always.

Researched knowledge is the key in the frequent and difficult task of weighing up the comparative merits of recycling or using new materials in heritage conservation work. How do they compare as to costs and efficiency? What are the real costs?

As this will suggest, there is need also for extensive economic research in the heritage field. Across the board, and for each project, one must ask: What are the economics of building re-use? of materials re-use? and of site dispositions? What are the economics of job creation and the development of skills? Are the appropriate economic impact studies of the impact of heritage and of heritage conservation being undertaken, as communities move further in this direction?

The economics of heritage is, or ought to be, an important emerging field of specialization. Jobs, livelihoods, marketing, and the community tax base are all going to be affected by any extensive programmes of heritage conservation.

Research is needed, as well, into the public policy aspects of heritage work. What are the most appropriate legislative and regulative arrangements for heritage identification and conservation? at the municipal level? at the provincial level? at the federal level? What are, or will be, the impacts of an increasingly conserver society on political processes, on public policies, and on the political framework? Thus, in political science, too, the impact of heritage activity suggests the emergence of a new field of specialization.

Demographic research into the scope and nature and consequences for heritage of population change and population movements requires increasing attention. So does the interplay of geography and history as they have shaped and affected heritage in the different communities and regions, across the country.

And, in the midst of the many environmental and other arguments for architectural conservation, let us not forget what is perhaps the simplest and most important: a prime reason for preserving architecture is that it is a route to the discovery and appreciation of accurate and meaningful history. Heritage conservation and historical research are each other's handmaidens.

The cultural and economic impacts of tourism, as it flows to heritage sites, need study. You are here, in part at least, because Peterborough and the historic Valley of the Trent embrace so much of heritage significance.

In a few weeks' time, an important and unusual international conference will be held here. The meeting of the International Association of University Professors of English will draw to this community distinguished scholars from around the world. Other gatherings will occur here throughout the year, and in every case the quality of the heritage of Peterborough - its buildings, its style, its cultural landscapes, its natural setting - will have played a part in their decisions to come here.

The cultural pluralism and many diversities of Canada pose a particular challenge for researchers in the heritage field. A knowledge of the country's ethnic and cultural pluralism is basic to any real understanding of Canadian society, its history and its future prospects. Much of this knowledge and understanding can be best derived from research centred on the historic sites and artifacts that mark the often distinctive experiences of the diverse Canadian peoples.

Research is not just an abstraction. It depends on people. It is done by people. This, too, is a field for research. We need to know more about those who are involved in the work of historic preservation and, also, to know more about those who are not and why they are not. We need to know more about the concept and practice of voluntarism as applied to heritage work. What are its strengths and its limitations? Which professional groups are involved and which are not, and why not? What is needed to facilitate the closer interaction of planners, architects, contractors, public officials, and many others in the field of historical preservation? And how might a new and more productive relationship be brought about between such people and the skilled craftspersons and workers on the job?

Questions of perception also need research. One of the most powerful concepts in our society is the concept of public service. To what extent has this concept so far come into play in regard to heritage? To what extent is work in the area of historic preservation seen a service in the public interest? In what ways is it not so perceived, and why not?

There is need, as well, for more conceptual research, or reflective research as Alex Corry called it, in regard to the nature of heritage. What is heritage? Clearly, it is a changing and evolving concept.

Only a decade or so ago, heritage was seen as being simply the older buildings and what went with them. Now, we view heritage as the total environment inherited from the past. It includes our tangible legacy of physically touchable things: buildings and structures of every sort; archaeological sites; archives; artifacts; and material items; and, also, cemeteries, gardens, landscapes, and natural resources. Marinescapes and underwater sites, too, are of special importance to Canada with its frontage on three great oceans and its remarkably extensive freshwater in tens of thousands of lakes and rivers. It includes, as well, our intangible legacy of customs, values, knowledge, and beliefs. It is the sum of all we have and are, of the total historical experience of our society to this moment. It is the context into which we have been born and in which we now live. It provides us with our sense of identity and our bearings for the next journeys into coming generations.

When one reflects upon this concept of heritage, one must be struck not merely by its great importance but by its transcendent importance. Why, then, has it received so little attention from our political leaders? And, let it be said, from our educators? These are questions that cry out for researched attention. The answers will tell us a lot about ourselves and about our country.

When I speak of research in the heritage context, I am sure that you will realize that I am speaking of something more than the footnote scholarship concept of research that marks, and often inhibits, the purely academic world. The focus of academic studies often excludes critical or creative studies, so that matters of taste are out of sight and out of mind.

Heritage belongs in the field of art as well as in the field of academe. Heritage is concerned with life and life is an art. It needs to be seen, therefore, in the context in which the arts are studied and where the values of imagination and creativity are safeguarded, lest our view of life, past or present, become the product of exclusively logical analysis. Research needs to embrace imagination, as well as intellect, if it is to fathom the meanings of heritage.

But there is one form of heritage research in which the task is not only scholarly and reflective, but also numerical. We need inventories and registers of heritage buildings, sites, and objects - national, regional, provincial, and local. We need to know what we have - to know what is there - in order to be able to get on with its conservation and interpretation.

Many communities are well-advanced on this task. You will, for instance, be receiving a report on the admirable heritage inventory commissioned by the Township of Uxbridge. None the less, most of Canada's countable heritage is uninventoried and, indeed, unknown.

Much of heritage is, however, uncountable. And many of those heritage items that are countable have heritage dimensions that are uncountable. In this regard, we need to give thought to heritage in culture and to heritage as culture. It is in this area that we will find the greatest significance of heritage; and our concern for historic buildings and artifacts belongs in that context.

Having spoken of context, may I make the point that it is important to see our heritage activities here in Ontario in a wider context - both Canadian and international. There is much to be gained from comparisons, and from trans-national and international co-operation. One has only to look, for example, at the Matrix System developed by ICOMOS which will systematize the recording of buildings through drawings and photographs to be reminded of the value of international co-operation and participation in heritage. The perspective that comes through external associations is helpful and often essential. When, for example, we criticize the Ontario Heritage Act, and the shortcomings of the present LACAC system, we should bear in mind that the legislation (and the resulting LACAC system) was the first in Canada, that it broke new ground, and that it has encouraged and inspired similar developments in the years since 1974 in a number of other provinces - and, indeed, in a number of other countries.

We learn from one another's ideas and experiences, and it is always important to be in touch with those who share our interests in other jurisdictions, within Canada and beyond. At the Ontario Provincial LACAC conference, it is natural to think in limited and provincial terms. But, provincial terms must not become blinkers. We need also to think about heritage in national terms.

Some of you may recall the Speech from the Throne in the Parliament of Canada on 1 October, 1986, when Her Excellency was caused to declare that: "The preservation of historic properties is important in fostering a sense of history and national identity among Canadians", and went on to note that the Government of Canada is "the largest owner of heritage sites and properties in the country", and to pledge that it would "assume a leadership role in their restoration and preservation".

Alas, that was the high water mark in the federal government's commitment to the built heritage. Since that time, there has been an appreciable diminution in that commitment. Despite the hard work and best efforts of an immensely dedicated staff in National Historic Sites at Parks Canada, and in several other Departments concerned with material heritage, you will all be familiar with heritage buildings and structures in the federal care that are in need of attention. There are a great many such, all across Canada. And, beyond them, there are many more buildings and sites of national significance which ought to be in the federal care - or in somebody's care - but are not.

In your daily focus at the municipal and provincial levels, I hope you will not forget your role as citizens of Canada and the need to prod, to encourage, and to support the Government of Canada towards the fuller discharge of its responsibilities for the national heritage. We must all work together, at all three levels of government, in the cause of heritage. It is time to review and to take stock of just where we are in the field of heritage conservation and historic preservation. What is going well and what is not? What are the areas of little progress? How adequate are the legislative tools currently available to assist in this work? It is time, for example, to revisit the Ontario Heritage Act which is now two decades old. The Act deserves acclaim for its pioneering role. But events have moved quickly and it is now seriously outdated. It deals only with buildings and archaeological sites. It focuses narrowly on protecting heritage resources, rather than on making such resources available, to the extent possible, for the use and enjoyment of the full community. The Act fails, also, to recognize and to accommodate and sustain, the cultural diversities within the Ontario heritage, including the francophone dimension, the aboriginal peoples, and the growing multiplicity of ethnocultural groups. Even more basically, the Act does not provide for adequate powers and resources to conserve the province's heritage. In consequence, day by day, year by year, there are steady and irreparable losses.

The Act provides no province-wide standards to guide the municipal role. Thus, different communities often have very different ground rules for heritage conservation. A new act should also provide greater opportunities for interested citizens to participate and to make their views known. Such criticisms are not meant to speak negatively about those now engaged in the LACAC system. On the contrary, they are meant to draw attention to their need for more support.

But, in all jurisdictions, the greatest need at present is for the promotion of a much more positive relationship between the historic preservation and heritage-minded movement and the environmental and ecology-minded movement. Together they constitute a wider movement towards a conserver society that will preserve and build appropriately on what we have and that will put a halt to the despoilment of our heritage, whether natural or man-made. In this context, architectural preservation is much more than simply an aesthetic and historical movement. It is part of such wider environmental concerns as sustainable development, waste management, and the whole range of quality of life issues. It takes its rightful place in the inter-connectedness of things.

Preservationists and environmentalists need to collaborate. They are natural allies. They share a responsibility to prove that non-renewable resources, whether built or natural, are truly irreplaceable and deserving of conservation. They share a concern to preserve and protect the world's special places, both historic and ecological. They share interests that are fundamentally similar and frequently identical. The resources of each should reinforce the work of the other.

That does not mean that the interests of preservationists and environmentalists will always be a neat fit. On occasion, their specific projects may differ and may sometimes even be at cross purposes. But, at bottom, there should be a common cause.

As the thinking of heritage preservationists broadens from an original concern with single historic sites and buildings to a wider concern with streetscapes, with historic districts, and with entire cultural landscapes, there is a growing realization that historical resources and environmental resources are very often inextricably intertwined, that historic preservation is a significant part of environmental conservation and vice-versa. They have a shared concern for context, for the surrounding environment, whether historical or ecological. The importance of the conservation of natural habitats and of ecosystems is parallelled by the need to preserve the context of historic sites which can lose their meaning and something of their authenticity when their adjacent environment of buildings and landscape is destroyed. Similarly, heritage tourism and eco-tourism share a common interest in ensuring that tourism does not damage the natural and historic environment.

Preservationists and environmentalists must co-operate to discover, to invent, to develop, and to improve a full array of tools, both technological and political, to preserve and protect the world's natural and historic sites. They must share, too, in the long range planning required to assure today's heritage in future generations.

In short, preservationists and environmentalists should come together for the stewardship of finite natural and cultural resources. Such a concept of heritage stewardship must become a fundamental value of our society.

Our society now finds itself engaged in a perilous balancing act. We are engulfed in the mad rush and uncertainty of technological change, of an abandonment of values, of the atomization of what was once a shared community of beliefs. In these circumstances, it is difficult to know who we are and to decide what matters. Now, more than ever, we need to draw on the accumulated folk wisdom of the generations and to benefit from past experience. In this situation our heritage has a crucial role to play. We may well lose that balancing act and fall into a rootless condition like the tumbleweed if we do not, soon, rediscover our sense of history and our sense of purpose.

May I suggest that we need a sense of urgency as we go about our heritage work. We are involved in a race against time, and it is not a race that we are presently winning. Every day, our cultural amnesia becomes a little more pronounced. Every day, the list of heritage desecrations and of opportunities lost, sometimes forever, grows longer.

Everything about which I have spoken calls for co-operation, a great deal of co-operation, within institutions, between institutions, with the public, and with government. But for co-operation we need more than the old refrains about avoiding duplication and promoting coordination. We need a new conceptual framework, one that sees the treatment of heritage as a totality, embracing both the human and man-made heritage and the natural heritage, both the built environment and the natural environment. We need a holistic approach to heritage concerns.

In this vein, I strongly support the proposal, made by the Ontario Museums Association in its brief to the Ontario Heritage Policy Review, for the establishment throughout the province of Local Heritage Committees to draw together representatives of museums, art galleries, architectural conservation, historical groups, genealogists, archaeologists, and natural history groups. To these categories, I would add interested community organizations of whatever sort and, surely, archivists, librarians, and in fact many more. Such an approach is very much in keeping with the recommendations of the Applebaum-Hébert Federal Policy Cultural Review Report in its chapter on Heritage. We need almost a new definition and perception of heritage, one that pries it loose from the sometimes dead hand of antiquarians and professional historians and other groups who have tended to monopolize the field, however good their intentions. Heritage must become the business of everyone.

Despite years of advocacy, the cause of heritage in Canada has not yet become a national movement. The heritage cause requires a total national effort, a combined operation in which all who care about it are joined together and make common cause. That is the level of co-operation that is really, and urgently, needed.

In all your work, it is time, I think, for a less reactive and more pro-active stance. It is time for your LACACs to take a stronger leadership role in their communities and in the broader Ontario and Canadian society.

May I conclude, as one citizen, and as Chairman of the Historic Sites and Monuments Board of Canada, by thanking each of you for your participation in the heritage preservation movement. The work on which you are engaged is of immense importance to our society, if Canadians are to know and to understand themselves. You are engaged in an enterprise that is of great value to Ontario, to Canada, and beyond. It is fundamental to our sense of community and identity, and to our distinctiveness and diversity. It is fundamental to our heritage. It is fundamental even to our sovereignty and independence as a people, and to our ability to contribute intelligently to our own and to world affairs.

I wish you continued success with all your future endeavours.

The Weller-Boucher House
548 Weller Street

Sustainable Development

Sylvia Sutherland
Administrator for the Peterborough Downtown Business
Improvement Area.

As the former Mayor of Peterborough, Sylvia Sutherland brings to the
conference a wealth of experience in a variety of areas. Sylvia has
taken a keen interest in both heritage preservation and environmen-
tal issues. Responsible for the founding of the Peterborough
Committee on Sustainable Development (the first such committee in
Canada), Sylvia has also served on the Ontario Round Table on
Environment and Economy and been appointed to the
Environmental Advisory Committee to Ontario Hydro.

T HIS PAPER DEALS WITH THE CONCEPT of sustainable development as it
applies to the built environment. Sustainable development is
usually thought of in terms of the economy and the natural environment, ignoring the importance of the built environment to the
basic definition of sustainable development: "development that
meets the needs of the present without compromising the ability of
future generation to meet their own needs."

The premise of this paper is that the built environment, as much as
the natural, shapes our thoughts and forms our character. Our surroundings, built as well as natural, influence how we feel and act, as
well as our health and intelligence. It is therefore important that we
preserve the best of our physical landscape to afford future generations
the same sense of place, of identity, of pleasure that we have had.

This means that we must handle change very carefully. Change
will happen. Buildings will disappear. Landscapes will change.
Given those realities, how do we direct that change so that it will be
beneficial rather than detrimental? How do we preserve successful
public spaces? How do we build new public spaces that will be used?
How do we maintain the connectedness between the urban and the
rural environment?

We must deal with the issue of standards and taste, and resist the
pressure to adopt "popular" values. Venice is superior to Las Vegas,
Michelangelo to the graffiti "artists" of the New York Subway,
Mozart to the Top of the Pops. These realities must be recognized in
our buildings as well, if future generations are to have the same
opportunity to develop as ours.

I challenge you to think about the national landscapes, built and natural, that you know and care about, and to consider how secure these places are at this point. Consider what changes would damage your sense of connectedness to these landscapes.

Let us also think about our favourite nearby places, rural and urban, private or public, and examine why these places are important to us. How changeable are they with time and season? Are they missing anything? Are they neglected? How vulnerable are they?

We should also consider our regional environment, built and natural, and examine our sense of connectedness to it. We should identify those features that make it special, and note how far afield we have to go to reach a place that feels different from our own neighbourhood.

In conclusion, the experiences these places have made available to us are an inheritance entrusted to our care, they are vital to the opportunity of future generations to develop with a sense of excellence, a sense of place.

Sources for this paper included the Brundtland Report, Tony Hiss's The Experience of Place, and Michael Middleton's Man Made the Town.

Resources and Energies

Hamish Wilson

HERITAGE COMMUNITIES CAN CREATE POSITIVE GAINS by emphasising the environmental benefits of building conservation in addition to the traditional architectural and historic reasons. In fact, given the appalling length of time to revise an already weak Ontario Heritage Act, the environmental arguments may well have more of an impact than the legislation with the exception of within the City of Toronto. Bill 57, a demolition control bill for designated structures, requires that there be a building permit in hand prior to the issuance of a demolition permit.

I have been interested in both environmental and heritage matters for many years and recently, under the auspices of the Toronto Region Architectural Conservancy, I've been attempting to link both interests. My interest in heritage preservation has expanded beyond landmark preservation. I am greatly interested in a general preservation of buildings. Many environmentalists would likely be more broadly supportive of general preservation than the preservation of only the monuments of the patriarchal and rich imperialists. When recognizing that all the materials of our cities and towns come from some environment somewhere, we can develop a concern about the use, maintenance and eventual fate of all of the materials of buildings and cities.

There are three major benefits to the environment from heritage conservation: the conservation of embodied energy and resources consumed in past decades, the avoidance of further resource demands on a currently more fragile environment and thirdly, the reduction in waste.

The materials of buildings are varied but they share a common thread: they are taken from some environment somewhere; there is energy consumed in the extraction: energy consumed in the refining or manufacturing or processing, energy consumed in the transportation to market and energy consumed in the placement of the materials (hauling to site) as well as the working of the materials onsite. Building maintenance and preservation thus promote the conservation of natural environments and reduce energy consumption and attendant effects, as well as helping to solve the waste disposal problem. By conserving a building, we can ameliorate the environmental degradation of the past century (often in our back-yard), we can reduce the amount of landfill (often significantly) and, as many building sites are rebuilt, we can reduce the environmental impact of new building materials.

Let us progress from general principles to some specifics of the embodied energy of some materials. Figures come from Richard Stein's *Architecture and Energy* (1979, Doubleday), and a CMHC report (not yet released) called *Optimize*, which begins to assess life cycle costing for new materials (including environmental impact). The embodied energy in the materials of a house can represent as much as 30 years' worth of operating energy.

The most obviously and understandably energy-intensive materials are brick and masonry. Every brick weighs about five pounds and, because it is a fired product, has about 15,000 BTU in it. Inefficiencies of early combustion are difficult to assess, but older bricks probably have a higher embodied energy content than new ones.

Concrete is calculated at 25,000,000 BTU per cubic yard. It is certainly heavy - a cubic yard can weigh over 2,000 pounds, which converts to approximately 12,500 BTU a pound.

Wood is calculated at 7,600 BTU per board foot and the *Optimize* report found that the wood of a house could have the largest total of embodied energy. The milling and transporting of softwoods (fir and spruce) from B.C. is no doubt part of the problem. The recycling of older wood from buildings when possible makes better use of forests, past and present. Shingles per square foot have 25,000 BTU.

Oil paint can have nearly 500,000 BTU per gallon. Metals are a refined product and energy intensity varies but aluminum was calculated to have 92,000 BTU per pound.

Plastics are high in embodied energy, as are carpets and other synthetics. As they are essentially oil resources that have had further energy in their refinement, this is not a surprise.

Although insulation absorbs energy to manufacture, the *Optimize* report indicated that the embodied energy of an R2000 building design was recovered in 1.5 years of operating energy.

We should be careful not to use the figures from the *Optimize* report for existing buildings. One consultant was surprised at some of the figures but it is a complicated and new field. The figures are a good guide but they are for new materials and may not reflect the inefficiencies of older production. Some values are appearing higher than they might otherwise. Another consideration is that by reducing the processes to numbers without reflecting on what they represent, combustion, for example, becomes an abstraction rather than plumes of black smoke.

In the course of production of a small brochure outlining the environmental benefits of heritage conservation, we hit upon adapting the Mobius loop and changing the 3Rs to a hermit preservationist's 3Rs: Retain, Renovate, Repair - all in situ activities. This is an important point - the greatest heritage value is derived from existing fabric, best maintained and preserved. The greatest optimization of the embodied energy and resource tends to derive from the preservation and re-use of the existing materials, largely in place. The destruction of older buildings can reduce, recycle and reuse but they can involve a loss of heritage value and imply a removal and grinding up of materials and reconstitution. The fourth R - that of recession - which while troublesome, does allow us pause for reconsidering our wasteful ways.

Reconsideration of our activities can include learning what is called the Third Law of Ecology, articulated by Patrick Moore, a co-founder of Greenpeace, which states that "all resources (food, water, air, minerals, energy) are finite and there are limits to the growth of all living systems". These limits are dictated by the finite size of the earth and the finite input of energy from the sun. (In regards to the latter comment about energy, most environmentalists don't regard nuclear power as a viable option for many reasons: expense, hazard and cancers from the nuclear fuel chain and the daunting task of keeping the radwaste out of the biosphere for up to 90,000 years.)

We must also bear in mind that matter is neither created nor destroyed; we merely collect, re-arrange, and dispense it with energy involved in each step.

Ecologists often concern themselves with what our economic theory calls externalities. Often private consumption involves a degrading of a collective resource but there is no charge to the user for any harm caused by the end product. A classic example is that of air pollution; much water pollution also stems from a lack of charge for the common resource being debased. Garbage disposal is now less of an externality and is now much more interesting to all with increasing costs being paid by the garbage producer in the ever-decreasing landfill site.

Ecologists are also concerned with systems as a whole, synergistic effects and not defining everything in dollar terms, which heritage preservationists know a little about when arguing for the aesthetic benefits of architecture and the "softer" benefits of preservation. What is the true value of clean air and clean water and clean land? We should not quickly acquiesce when told that something is not "economic" because the real bottom line is we have to have an environment to do business in.

When we view our activity more in environmental terms, i.e. material and energy flows, and land use and abuse, we can see there is a need for not simply accepting the displacement of materials in the name of progress or placing some limits on current private consumption for the sake of future generations who will not have the same heritage as we enjoy.

So why do materials become displaced? Why do materials become waste? Sometimes materials wear out. Our activity, or the elements result in removal. Uncontrolled water, through lack of maintenance or faults of workmanship or design, creates premature disposal. Style changes, face-lifting or the imposition of designs in a shell result in waste and changes in regulations and building standards also incur disposal.

So how much resource is being wasted? It is very challenging to present accurately the extent of the problem. There have been numerous attempts at snapshots of the waste stream, more in the US than in Ontario, but the variety of sources and the nature of disposal makes it very hard to delineate precisely how much. The commercial and institutional sector are major players, homeowners and do-it-yourselfers are a major source, and renovators, contractors, and speculators another. Each of these sectors is more active at some time, and dormant at others. Currently, there is more dormancy than activity, but given the interests that exist in the housing industry and market, there is a need for speaking up now to ensure we have wiser use of heritage resources.

American studies have indicated Construction and Demolition (C and D) wastes are about 25% of the waste stream. Canadian studies don't show such proportions - an estimate of the waste of the Metro C and D waste proportions is about 11% only. However, a federal department indicated the national total was as high as a third, and an excavation of a Metro dump from the 1950s found about a 28% C and D. This was the result of a dig by American garbologist, William Rathje, who in the July/August Garbage magazine, indicated that several other excavations have indicated that the often overlooked C and D component is in fact consistently 28% by weight and volume. A 20% figure is thus likely conservative.

The discrepancies between Metro statistics and others can be explained somewhat by: the tendencies of homeowners to dispose of their building debris with household garbage, by cities which don't often include themselves thereby sending materials directly to the dump and by the lack of any measurement of waste haulage to the States. And sometimes construction materials just aren't counted in. An oil tank was once found at curbside by a measuring team. A discussion ensued about whether or not to include it in the composition study. Because it wasn't deemed to be part of an everyday process, it was discounted as it would have skewed the statistics. But such unusual items do become surplus. So again a 20% figure is conservative. We're more interested in existing materials than with new construction. Metro Toronto's waste composition study found that 52% of demolition waste was wood/rubble, 25% was aggregate, 5% plaster/drywall, 5% ferrous materials and 13% other materials. Other statistics indicated that the tonnage of wood from demolition sites in Southern Ontario was substantial - up to 369,000 tonnes in 1988 with little recycling.

Purist preservationists must decide in advance how much ground they wish to give when they begin talking about building conservation for environmental reasons. The recycling of materials is good, but deconstruction should be avoided; the emphasis must be on building conservation in situ as being the best use for heritage. It's not OK to rip it down if you're recycling it. Recycling is better than waste but why does it have to be dismembered in the first place? It is a very basic question that is seldom asked.

In the "Preliminary Study of Construction and Demolition Waste Diversion Constraints and Opportunities Report" of MacViro Consultants for the Waste Reduction Office (W.R.O.), the reduction of waste through building conservation was not explored. Consider two quotes:

> *"Reduction is generally not feasible in the demolition sector and materials reuse opportunities are constrained by limited markets, project economics and schedules. (5-1)*

> *"The major opportunity for at-source waste reduction exists in the construction sector as opposed to the demolition sector."*

This is frustrating isn't it? On one hand, we have agencies and statistics telling us how much of our building stock is going to be around for the next while, and our eyes can see that the proportion of new to older, existing buildings may be one in ten. There has been too much accepting of the status quo and development and demolition industry input.

It isn't always easy to incorporate the conservation of materials and heritage into a building or development plan, but it is not impossible. Yes, there are constraints upon time and money, but a rough analysis of the time of a development and the planning and approval process is often longer than the construction process and usually far greater than the deconstruction process. Taking some extra time to deconstruct more carefully is neither onerous nor expensive. If it takes so long, why is it coming down in the first place?

The Contract Record of August 1929, contained some interesting comments about just how much salvaging was occurring with buildings being taken down in the City of Toronto. It was estimated that between 65% and 80% of the materials of buildings were re-used or recycled. A recent American reference indicated that under some conditions, up to 90% of a building could be recycled. Clearly, if the will is not there in the first place, then not much will happen.

This point is coming out in discussions within the Strategy Team for Waste Reduction in the C and D sector of the W.R.O. While much focus is on the design end, it is as much the assumptions of owners and the capital of owners which are providing a great deal of the impetus for waste. We've had a waste economy for a long time and we're beginning to shift - so slowly it seems - to a conserving economy that the inertia of waste in such a tradition-bound setting as property ownership and development is great.

There are signs of changes. Both the Ontario Roundtable on the Economy and Environment and the City of Toronto's new Official Plan addresses the resources of buildings. However, it does take a lot of energy to promote these concerns; many good ideas don't come to fruition and collect dust somewhere or are over-ridden by more practical concerns, i.e. those of business interests.

A concept of native Canadians is worth mentioning simply to contrast with our ways of doing things. Most natives believe that we don't own the earth, that we are merely stewards. But our way is focused on private ownership and disposal, and we don't tend to think beyond a few years or our lifetimes, let alone our children's children. While there are many interested in wise stewardship, it is not encoded.

This doesn't mean that every building is so well built that it will last a century more, or that there won't be some change in urban environments. There is the constant challenge of getting to the place before it gets to you, and deconstruction can be a more expedient and financially efficient route. Standards have changed for reasons and age does affect the integrity and bonding of materials.

Which leads to the next point. There is a lot of work to be done in educating those who work on buildings to emphasize careful taking apart with an eye to reuse. Destruction is unwise and organised de-construction can be safer, cleaner and cheaper. Taking the time to remove old mouldings carefully and pulling the nails out through the back could mean that no new tropical hardwoods are used for door trim.

We have in Toronto (Scarborough) a new used materials yard, Reuze, where materials are simply dropped off to be sold. We all know the difficulties of dealing with existing materials onsite - where to safely store them, where they aren't in the way. We certainly could use more careful disassembly as well as a place nearby to trade our treasures.

There is often another advantage in older materials - less toxicity. For the most part, older buildings have materials which are less toxic and less hazardous than new materials, which tend to be made of synthetic compounds which emit gas. Older buildings may have problems with dust, moulds and insects, but the most serious old house environmental trouble spot is the lead in older paint. Lead paint can be found on brick, on plaster and on the wood used in floors and external trim. This is a major problem. (See the *Old House Journal* of July 1992.) CMHC is working on a brochure outlining the ways of dealing with older lead-based paint, however it continues to be a persistent, vexing problem.

Interestingly, the house repair and maintenance activities of the middle class produce the most toxic substances for the middle class. Maintenance demands will increase with acid rain damage. The ozone depletion won't just increase cataract rates and skin cancers, fry the phytoplankton and scorch the plants which feed us, it is also going to increase the degradation rates of many materials - which contain or use CFCs or HCFCs in their manufacture: polyurethane insulation boards; sprayed polyurethane insulation, phenolic foam insulation; extruded polystyrene insulation; polyethylene sheet; and refrigerators and heat pumps. Yet there is a big conflict between building owners/occupants and the environment: we don't want total biodegradability - at least not while we're living in it or owning it. We want buildings that resist water. The challenge is to do it in a way which isn't too poisonous, and which steps as lightly on the earth as possible. We are moving in that direction, but faster steps can be taken with the re-use of our existing buildings.

Heritage can use environmental arguments for building preservation. There are strong arguments for keeping heritage materials in place: it saves resources extracted in the past and can prevent new resources from being taken out of an environment; the energy involved in all processes is conserved; there is less demand on the dumps. The waste from the materials of cities is, if not a quarter of the waste stream, then about a fifth. This still is very high and we have the right to ask those who exhort us to recycle our tin cans and bottles to practise what they preach and promote the recycling of structures - preferably in place. It probably will cost a little bit more in the short run, but our thinking has to go beyond the short term to think of our children's children. Many of us can see the degradation of the commons in our own lifetimes and it is getting worse, not better.

We are nearly at a point where we can ask for demolition control based on the energy and resource intensity of existing buildings relative to the zoning. If a current building is say two-thirds density and well-built, renovation occurs. For a building between one-third and two-thirds density, and a mixed intensity, with a price or premium then de-construction with recycling becomes mandatory. Cases below one-third density, landmark status or building movement on site or off-site or recycling and reuse of components would be required.

Heritage communities can also point to the great job creation potential for further support for building preservation. A CMHC study in 1986, *The CAN REN MARKET*, stated that job creation in renovation is twice that of new construction, per dollars spent. There are some caveats in promoting too much job creation through renovation, as there are hackers who don't have training in respectful rehabilitation and bureaucrats and officials who don't really care about their heritage. A current provincial job creation program on heritage buildings is sacrificing the heritage for the jobs.

The greening of our heritage can really help to save our world. We can't throw it all out and must learn to reduce and reuse and recycle in our building activities. We don't want our buildings to rot out though, and we must attempt to use benign substances for the care and maintenance of the fabric. The waste of the solid buildings of our past must surely be over now but we all have stories, I'm sure, where heritage resources have become heritage rubble. The waste must stop.

TABLE 1:
Top 20 Commodities in Standard House Sorted by Total Weight

Code	Commodity	As-built Total (kg)	% of Total
379	Ready-mix concrete	192,289	64.2
49	Sand and Gravel	45,140	15.1
191	Lumber and Timber	15,036	5.0
386	Plasters & other gypsum basic products	10,945	3.7
380	Bricks and Tiles, Clay	10,276	3.4
195	Veneer and Plywood	7,443	2.5
196	Millwork (Woodwork)	2,870	1.0
216	Building Paper	2,524	0.8
375	Cement (Mortar, etc.)	2,223	0.7
387	Min.Wool & Thermal Insul.Mat.Nec.	2,112	0.7
377	Concrete Basic Products	2,028	0.7
283	Metal Pipes, Fittings & Sidings	1,182	0.4
390	Glass, Plate, Sheet, Wool	949	0.3
409	Paints & Related Products	936	0.3
308	Pipe Fittings, Not Iron & Steel	877	0.3
170	Carpeting, Fabric Rugs, Mats, etc	407	0.1
135	Plastic Pipe Fittings & Sheet	315	0.1
401	Asphalt & Coal Oils, Nes	303	0.1
250	Steel Pipes & Tubes Nes	234	0.1
	Other	1,603	0.5
	Estimated Total House Weight	299,691	100%

The top 20 commodities sorted by embodied energy for the Standard House is presented in Table 2. The embodied energy is for materials in the as-built house and does not include life cycle factors, such as installation, repair and replacement.   OPTIMIZE/CMHC 1991pg 26

TABLE 2:

Top 20 Commodities in Standard House Sorted by Total Embodied Energy

Code	Commodity	As-built Total (MJ)	% of Total
191	Lumber & Timber	*110,896	13.1
195	Veneer & Plywood	*108,831	12.9
379	Ready-Mix Concrete	103,151	12.2
283	Metal Pipes, Fittings & Sidings	80,408	9.5
135	Plastic Pipe Fittings & Sheet	59,474	7.0
386	Plasters & Other Gypsum Basic Products	49,024	5.8
387	Min Wool & Thermal Insul. Mat. Nes	38,747	4.6
409	Paints & Related Products	37,752	4.5
216	Building Paper	30,317	3.6
170	Carpeting, Fabric Rugs,Mats, etc	30,278	3.6
196	Millwork(Woodwork)	28,330	3.4
308	Pipe Fittings, Not Iron & Steel	25,763	3.1
380	Bricks and Tiles, Clay	22,019	2.6
390	Glass, Plate, Sheet, Wool	20,456	2.4
353	Small Elec.Appliances, Domestic	16,822	2.0
250	Steel Pipes & Tubes Nes.	9,113	1.1
301	Heating Eq, Warm Air Ex.Pipes &E.	7,122	0.8
355	Refrig, Freezers & Comb. Domestic	7,028	0.8
304	Com.Appliances, Cook & Warming Fo	6,926	0.8
511	Tiling, Rubber, Plastic	6,537	0.8
	Other	45,174	5.4
	Estimated Total Embodied Energy	844,169	100%

* Lumber use may over-state consumption relative to many Canadian houses, since it includes one-time use only of timber for form work.

OPTIMIZE/CMHC 1991pg 27

TABLE 3:
Top 20 Commodities in Standard House Sorted by Lifecycle Embodied Energy

Code	Commodity	Life Cycle Total (MJ)	% of Total
170	Carpeting, Fabric Rugs, Mats, etc	*152,985	11.7
195	Veneer & Plywood	*124,837	9.5
191	Lumber & Timber	122,657	9.4
379	Ready-Mix Concrete	122,514	9.4
283	Metal Pipes, Fittings, Sidings	86,370	6.6
409	Paints & Related Products	82,044	6.3
353	Small Elec.Appliances, Domestic	70,830	5.4
135	Plastic Pipe Fittings & Sheet	65,741	5.0
386	Plasters & Other Gypsum Basic Products	61,287	4.7
387	Min Wool & Thermal Insul.Mat.Nes	51,120	3.9
196	Millwork (Woodwork)	42,506	3.2
216	Building Paper	35,171	2.7
308	Pipe Fittings, Not Iron & Steel	32,346	2.5
355	Refrig, Freezers & Comb.Domestic	29,591	2.3
380	Bricks and Tiles, Clay	29,297	2.2
304	Com.Appliances,Cook & Warming Fo	29,162	2.2
511	Tiling, Rubber, Plastic	27,525	2.1
390	Glass, Plate, Sheet, Wool	24,618	1.9
301	Heating Eq, Warm Air Ex.Pipes & E	21,365	1.6
306	Gas Ranges & Elec. Stoves, Domestic	19,779	1.5
	Other	78,568	6.0
	Estimated Total Lifecycle Embodied Energy	1,310,313	100%

OPTIMIZE/CMHCpg 28

TABLE 4:
Embodied Energy of Materials and Construction Per Square Foot of Construction

	1000's BTU/SQ FT
Residential - 1 family	700
Residential - 2-4 families	630
Residential Garden Apt	650
Residential - High Rise	740
Hotel/Motel	1,130
Dormitories	1,430
Industrial Buildings	970
Office Buildings	1,640
Warehouses	560
Garages/Services Stations	770
Stores/Restaurants	940
Educational	1,390
Hospital Buildings	1,720

TABLE 5:
Demolition Energy of Construction Materials for Existing Buildings

Construction Type	Small 5,000 to 15,000 sq.ft.	Medium 50,000 to 150,000 sq.ft.	Large 500,000 to 1,500,000 sq.ft.
Light eg: wood frame	3,100 BTU/sq.ft.	2,400 BTU/sq.ft.	2,100 BTU/sq.ft.
Medium eg: steel frame	9,300 BTU/sq.ft.	7,200 BTU/sq.ft.	6,300 BTU/sq.ft.
Heavy eg: masonry, concrete	15,500 BTU/sq.ft.	12,000 BTU/sq.ft.	10,500 BTU/sq.ft.

Neighbourhoods Committee City of Toronto April 27, 1982

TABLE 6:
Energy Embodiment of Primary Materials

Material Category	Embodied Energy per Material Unit
Wood Products	9,000 BTU/BDFT
Paint Products	1,000 BTU/sq.ft (450 sq.ft/gal.)
Asphalt Products	2,000 BTU/sq.ft
Glass Products	15,000 BTU/sq.ft windows 40,000 BTU/c.ft plate
Stone & Clay Products	9,600 BTU/c.ft concrete 400,000 BTU/c.ft brick
Primary Iron & Steel Products	25,000 BTU/lb
Primary Non-Ferrous Products	9,500 BTU/lb

The values indicated in the above tables are from *Energy Use of Building Construction*, published in 1976. Since that time certain of these values have been changed, but not so substantially as to make them obsolete. The changes are the result of two factors:

1. The increased cost of energy has affected the technology, making it possible to produce many building materials with less energy per unit.

2. The more recent studies have further refined some values and aspects of the methods indicated above. Particularly regarding operating energy for buildings, a very extensive research study was carried out. The effort was primarily to develop a data base to support the proposed Building Energy Performance Standards (BEPS) in the U.S.A. Only a small part of this research effort has been published.

References

Energy Expenditure Associated with the Production and Recycle of Metals, J.C. Bravard, H.B. Flora II, and Charles Portal, Oak Ridge, Tenn., Oak Ridge National Laboratory, 1972.

Energy Use of Building Construction, B.M. Harmon, R.A. Stein, B.Z.Segal, D.Suber, C.Stein, Energy Research Group, Centre for Advanced Computation, University of Illinois; Richard A. Stein and Associates, Architects, New York, NY, December, 1976.

Assessing the Energy Conservation Benefits of Historic Preservation, Booz, Allen and Hamilton, U.S. Govt. Printing Office, Washington, DC. Stock No. 024-000-008-56-8.

593 Weller Street

Natural and Cultural Heritage Planning, Protection and Interpretation: From Ideology to Practice, A Civics Approach

J. G. Nelson
Heritage Resources Centre, University of Waterloo
Dr. Nelson is currently a Professor of Geography and Urban and Regional Planning, and Chairman of the Heritage Resources Centre at the University of Waterloo. Dr. Nelson has authored numerous publications and has been involved in a number of nationally and internationally important projects, including: Consultant to Parks Canada, Department of Environment, Economic Council of Canada; Director of the Renewable Resources Project, Inuit Tapirisat of Canada; and a member of the non-government Canadian Advisory Committee for the Stockholm Conference on the Environment.

A GROWING NUMBER OF PROFESSIONALS and actively involved citizens no longer view heritage as largely a matter of artifacts and the protection or preservation of historic buildings, old growth forests, and other aspects of cultural and natural heritage. These people advocate a new concept of heritage which, among other things includes:

- thinking holistically, notably by combining the natural and the cultural through linking concepts such as landscape;

- focusing as much on maintaining valued cultural and natural processes such as festivals, building construction techniques or forest succession as on structures such as the walls of buildings or special species of plants or animals;

- thinking more in terms of large areas and the connections among them rather than isolated historic sites or nature reserves;

- thinking more in terms of a pluralist approach involving many ethnic or indigenous perspectives rather than the predominantly Anglo or French-Canadian ones of the past; and

- thinking in terms of using and working with heritage in a dynamic and evolving way, for example, in hiking trail development, or in community planning as manifest in some of the recent visioning exercises conducted in Eramosa township or Halton Region.

Growing interest in this new concept of heritage arises from a number of sources. Witness the conclusions about the need for a more holistic and dynamic view of heritage put forward by the Ontario Heritage Review as a result of public hearings and other activities in the 1980s. Witness, also, the work of Heritage Canada, the national office and institution in Ottawa which has taken a very active interest in clarifying and furthering the holistic and dynamic approach for example, through its mainstreet and regional landscape programs notably in the last ten years. Witness, also the recent work of the Ontario Heritage Foundation in establishing and supporting a natural heritage program within the context of its emphasis on human heritage over the last several decades. Witness, also, the attempts to promote a more integrated approach to natural and cultural heritage at the federal level through the Conference on Heritage in the 1990s *Towards a Government of Canada Strategy*, Edmonton, October, 1990.

It is not being argued here that these recent changes in viewpoints of heritage are entirely new. For decades, consciously or unconsciously, individuals and groups have followed the elements of the emerging model in Ontario. One example is the St. Jacobs canal which was built to carry water from the Conestogo tributary of the Grand River, to provide power for nineteenth century mills still standing in the town today. The mill and surrounding buildings have been modified in appearance and are now used for commercial and other different purposes. But they retain over a fairly large area the essential character and utility of the past. The canal itself still carries running water to the mills and then back into the river, but it is now paralleled by an excellent community-maintained walking trail lined with trees and shrubs providing habitat for warblers and other migrants in spring and summer and other animals throughout the year. The trail is enjoyed by many walkers and visitors at all seasons. Some of the visitors are tourists who come to St. Jacobs to stay in hotels that also are located in historic buildings and to enjoy the surrounding urban and rural character of what for more than a century and a half, has been a Mennonite landscape. In many of these respects then, the St. Jacobs area fulfils the elements of the new heritage model.

Another example of a comprehensive and dynamic approach is the "living levee" area in downtown Cambridge. Here planning to adapt to floods and also to protect historic buildings and areas, resulted in a unique recreational area. This area - the living levee - combines the characteristics of a historic and a natural park and a learning area where nineteenth and early twentieth century tunnels, power wheels and other technology, have been protected for the edification of present and future citizens.

But such examples seem uncommon amid the many changes going on around us. Many places, agencies and groups seem to neglect the socially and environmentally beneficial elements of the holistic heritage model. In this regard it would be useful at this conference to try and identify more good examples or "success stories" - known to those in attendance - as a basis for making more people aware of the opportunities.

Other instructive examples of a holistic and dynamic view of heritage could be given for my home area, the Grand River Valley, which has been nominated for Canadian Heritage River Status on the basis of its outstanding historical and recreational resources. A list of places reflecting the interaction of natural and cultural heritage would include the Luther and Dunnville Marshes in the northern and southern extremities of the valley and the Grand River forest in the centre, between Cambridge and Paris. In these areas large marshes and forests, apparently relatively little affected by humans, are actually the product of a long history of human activities including dam construction and agriculture as well as conservation and recreation management by agencies such as the Grand River Conservation Authority (GRCA).

But such examples seem uncommon in Ontario and the question naturally arises as to why we continue to fragment our heritage ideas and efforts given growing advocacy for a more integrated, holistic, and dynamic approach.

It has been suggested that one fundamental reason is the continuing tendency for many people to portray heritage as some kind of romantic frill which does not really have the power to guide us into the future as realistically as the utopian development thinking of the last five decades. More specifically, it has been suggested that many leaders as well as people generally do not sufficiently appreciate the many roles that a full view of heritage can play in our lives.

A list of natural heritage uses would include:

1. Conservation of wildlife, vegetation, soils, water, air, and other resources for economy, society and different ways of life.

2. Conservation of gene pools for agriculture, medicine and other uses.

3. Conservation of nature for its own sake independent of any value for humans.

4. Conservation of nature for aesthetic purposes, for stimulation of thought and emotions, and of poetry, literature, music and art.

5. Use for learning generally, for formal education by schools and other educational institutions as well as for informal individual or group learning by naturalists or citizens generally.

6. Use for research and scholarly activity, for under-standing and benefitting economically and culturally from the world around us.

7. Use as benchmarks or as place to monitor land use and other changes in local, national and international environments, for example in measuring acid rain, global warming, sea level rise, or other changes induced in part by industrial and other human activity.

8. Use as places where archaeological sites or other evidence of past human use, technology, and industry can be conserved and interpreted in a context relatively close to that in which they originally occurred, thereby enhancing our understanding of what we have done and are doing to the world around us.

9. Providing multi-functional green spaces in urban areas, "oases" of purer water, marshes and wetlands to reduce floods and protect valued wildlife, plants and scenery, and indeed, to provide in the city for many of the individual functions noted previously.

10. Also providing the foregoing functions in a larger regional context, amid the residential, commercial, industrial, communications, and other development that has for decades been our principal concern and which now increasingly threatens quality of life and prospects for sustainable development.

A similar list could be prepared for human heritage. Thus archaeological and historic sites could be seen as valuable for their own sake, as well as for aesthetic, artistic, recreational, tourism, economic, social, cultural, and learning purposes. Holistic attention to the past also provides a window to Canada as a multicultural society and nation.

To appreciate the power of a combined approach to heritage we need only think about the potential so widely neglected in respect of archaeology. An archaeological site has both a natural and human side, although it is the human side which usually receives emphasis in terms of what it tells us about the people of the past, their technology, their economy, and their culture. Yet, a little thought will show that the natural side also has a story to tell of the character and evolution of climate, wildlife, plants, and other aspects of the total environment. Interpretation of this natural side of our archaeological and historic past is especially significant today at a time when we are thinking more and more about the implications of global warming and other changes largely due to the industrial and urban activities of humans.

Another reason for the failure to move more vigorously toward a holistic and dynamic approach to heritage is difficulty with the institutional arrangements that we use to plan, protect, and interpret heritage. These difficulties have been recognized most forcefully in regard to the role of governments. Thus, at the Edmonton Conference on "Heritage in the 1990s", the following actions were put forward as helpful:

1. With federal support, Heritage Centres should be set up in urban areas across Canada as citizen information places and as catalysts for a greater recognition of heritage in the broad natural and cultural sense.

2. More co-operation should be fostered among governments and private groups especially through means such as heritage institutes and centres in universities and colleges.

3. The federal government should provide leadership in these efforts as it clearly has the basic responsibility and the mandate for heritage on a national basis. Thus every effort should be made to complete the national park system in co-operation with the provinces by the year 2000. Efforts should also be made to complete the representation of historic themes in the historic parks system. Planning should also begin on moving from a park centred natural heritage system to a network of interconnected nodes and corridors and a green framework for sustainable development in Canada. The recent reports of the Crombie Commission on the Toronto metropolitan area reflect some of these ideas. Studies of the Grand as a Canadian Heritage River and concerns about the Oak Ridges Moraine north of the City of Toronto manifest a similar perspective. This move will necessarily involve more extension of outreach and more facilitation of the work of private groups and of private as well as public stewardship.

4. A federal program comparable to the Canadian Landmarks program set forth in the 1979 Parks Canada policy should be established to provide the impetus for co-operative heritage efforts among governments, corporations and citizens. A Canadian Landmarks program could form the nucleus for the recognition and appropriate management of unique and outstanding landscapes in Canada, landscapes which would be an expression of the interaction of both natural and human heritage.

5. The federal government should continue to lead in monitoring change in environment or natural heritage but should extend this

monitoring to include land use change and associated changes in landscapes and human heritage. In this respect ongoing initiatives such as *State of the Environment and State of the Parks* reports need to be strengthened and broadened to include changes in land use, landscapes and human and natural heritage.

6. The outreach activities of Heritage Canada in linking heritage with community development through main street and regional heritage programs should be strongly encouraged. The Man and Biosphere program (MAB) should also be more strongly supported as a major means of co-ordinating stewardship activities on adjoining public and private land.

At the time that they were presented the foregoing recommendations were thought of as applying primarily to senior government. But their spirit and intent certainly applies at the provincial, regional, and local levels as well.

It has been suggested that another significant barrier to the implementation of a more holistic and dynamic approach to heritage is that we do not possess the methods or means of doing so. A glance at the program for this conference suggests that this may be an exaggerated difficulty. Witness the ideas in the conference program in regard to *integrating concepts* such as heritage regions and landscapes as well as parks and other types of *reserves*; zoning, and other *regulations*; and, easements, subsidies, tax-relief measures and the other *fiscally oriented tools* available to us. Nodes and corridors, "green" hiking trails, and other networks, as well as bioregions, are also among the newer approaches known to concerned agencies, groups and persons, although discussion of them at meetings such as this is most important in advancing their use.

The foregoing does lead, however, to what many believe to be the most fundamental challenge to a more holistic and dynamic approach to heritage and that is that the message has not reached the many people - *the private citizens* - who must become more actively involved in thinking about planning, protecting, and interpreting heritage if a more holistic and dynamic view is to prevail. To recognize this we need only reflect on a few facts. Thus any government park or protected area reserve, must have the support of the people to be established, planned, and managed in sustainable ways. Any zoning or other regulations must also be generally acceptable to citizens and to businesses in order to work well. And most important at this time of declining government financial power, the economic, social and environmental effects of any heritage policies and programs will have to be generally acceptable to the people of Ontario.

Furthermore, most of our heritage in the holistic and dynamic sense is outside the immediate domain of government. Thus many heritage lands, waters, and activities will continue to be privately owned and controlled. And, the spiritual and cultural aspects of life - ways of thinking and acting as they are informed by heritage - will continue to lie to a great extent beyond governments, although subject to heavy influence by them as well as by professional and educational policy practice.

It is to this fundamental challenge of the informing and activating of the citizen which I wish to direct my final and most important comments. My first point is that while governments will have a strong role in advancing a more holistic and dynamic view of heritage, in future this will not be done so much through the previously preferred science-based rational planning and management model as through what might be termed a civics approach. Some details on the management and the civics approaches are presented in Tables 1, 2 and 3 for your detailed study.

The rational planning and management model has achieved some good things. However, because of its reductionist and specialized character it has contributed in a fundamental way to the fragmentation problems that plague us today. One need only look at the way government is divided into specialized sectors and departments to recognize this. Even at the regional and the local levels heritage is often divided up into environmental and human heritage units which do not work together regularly or well. Universities and other educational systems also are divided up in the same specialized manner. They therefore encourage citizens to think in a compartmentalized way in their working, social and environmental activities.

Under the foregoing circumstances it is **not** likely that either governments or the universities will be the main source of the synthesizing or cross-sectoral view that is needed to promote a more holistic and dynamic view of heritage in the near future. To the extent that they wish to move more quickly in the holistic direction, governments are severely handicapped by funding problems. Governments are generally in debt and financial difficulty at national, provincial and local levels. They cannot deliver existing or any new programs as they did in the past when money was more plentiful. Yet the challenges to heritage are more complex and stronger than ever.

Under these circumstances governments are increasingly attempting to work through partnerships and volunteer programs to achieve their objectives, which do not generally involve a strong holistic and dynamic approach. Government programs could have these characteristics, however, if citizens steered the overall effort more vigorously in that direction. It is in this context that the value and role of the civics model becomes clear (Tables 2 and 3). A fundamental characteristic is that the civics model is pluralist. It respects and works with many different views and approaches. It is also interactive and involving. It builds on the strengths of various agencies and groups. It encourages and relies heavily upon private initiative and stewardship. It merits much more attention by governments, academics, interest groups, and citizens interested in working toward a more holistic and dynamic view of heritage in the years ahead.

TABLE 1:
Management Model

World View	specialized, sectoral, disciplinary, systematic, viz. geology, vegetation, wildlife, economy, society, culture, resources, environment, development.
Goals	progress, economic and technical development, wealth, leisure, a universal or global economy and social system, nation building, and international co-operation.
Means	science, technology, education, technical and other training, separation of objective and subjective elements of world.
Mechanism	management, namely command and control with consultation and participation and compensation to affected parties, driven by government funding.
Planning Approach	rational, setting goals, identifying alternatives and selection of best alternative, research by experts, professionalism, cybernetic, tempered by satisfying and the like, public participation, co-ordination among agencies and groups.
Implementation Processes	governments and corporations, through systems involving identification of mandates, roles, responsibilities, authority, funding.

Criteria for Judging Success	efficiency, effectiveness, growth, technical, progress.
Current Situation	disarray, some successes, some failures, in terms of goals, criteria and other factors. Often inefficient (e.g. long time periods and costs for assessment and implementation), fragmented view of world, struggle for holism and comprehensiveness, desire to understand connections and interrelationships (for example between natural and cultural heritage), economic difficulties and inequities locally, nationally and internationally, failure of government to deliver through funding and other traditional means, literacy and learning failures, voluntarism, call for strong community role, movement of government from rational command and control model to one of facilitating grassroots or community approaches.

TABLE 2:
Civics Model

World View	comprehensive, holistic, cross sectoral, multidisciplinary, systematic and eclectic, thinking in terms of spectra more than specialties, viz. ecology, human ecology, heritage (both natural and cultural, dynamic and living), environmentalism in the broad human and natural sense, deep ecology, bio-regionalism, whole economy, community.
Goals	sustainability, maintenance and enhancement of economy, society and environment, economy and environment as opposite sides of same coin, meeting basic human needs, multi-culturalism equity.
Means	mutual learning, use of local or indigenous knowledge as well as science, trans-disciplinary, scholarship, critique, dialogue, integration.
Mechanism	pluralist, government, corporation, citizen, public and private co-operation, self-reliance and voluntarism.

Planning

Approach   transactive, participatory, interactive, adaptive, integrative mixed scanning.

Implementation

Processes   preparation for understanding and participation, learning (demonstration, experiment), monitoring, assessment, implementation, adaptation.

Criteria for

Judging Success   meeting basic needs, level and kind of involvement, equity, level and kind of social skills and aptitudes, a strong sense of heritage and civics.

Current

Situation   difficult to foresee, possibly stronger informal economy to meet basic needs, stronger communities, but perhaps more competition among communities and countries, difficulty in achieving sustainability, problems of over-work and "burn-out" through multiple calls for a civics approach from many sectors, difficulties posed by growth in population and resource consumption, possible balance among various government levels and private groups in maintaining and enhancing environment, economy and society, problems of so-called Third and Fourth Worlds or multi-culturalism.

TABLE 3:
Basic Processes in the Civics Approach

Understanding	Broadly informing; comprehensive; selective in terms of significance, assessment and action, focusing on preparedness for decision.
Communicating	Understanding and using varied means and media; personal and group communication skills; technical understanding and skills; inter-group or cross-cultural understanding and skills.
Assessing	Understanding of and ability to evaluate and select on the basis of principles and standards, pluralist in orientation; awareness of various kinds of social, economic and environmental assessment; understanding of trade-offs; importance of understanding and assessing institutions both as resources and as obstacles to desired change.
Visioning	Ability to think systematically and interactively about time and change; historical as well as a futuristic perspective; understanding a time in both natural (geologic, biologic), and human (historic) senses; a human ecological perspective.
Implementing	Understanding how to decide and act; ideas and models of co-ordination; integrating the technical and socio-economic, the scientific and the humanistic; understanding and use of bridging institutions, of demonstration, of a research and experimental approach, of mixed scanning and transactive planning.
Monitoring	Understanding and use of auditing and follow-up procedures as part of all aspects of civics; understanding of different kinds of monitoring and the pluralist nature of monitoring; regular, periodic, and technical monitoring and assessment.
Adapting	Understanding that continuous adjustments to turbulent and changing circumstances are part of the civics model; objectives and activities frequently change among individuals, groups and nations in a dynamic world; capacity to foresee and adapt; evolutionary, interactive, competitive and accommodating; tolerance for ambiguity.

469 Weller Street

Integrating Natural and Built Interpretation: Two Case Studies, Rideau Hall, Ottawa and the Mackenzie King Estate, Gatineau Park

Edwinna von Baeyer
Landscape Historian
   Edwinna has been contributing to Canadian landscape history for over 14 years. Her work has appeared in numerous publications and has covered subjects from railway gardens and the rise of the horticultural society to specific sites such as Rideau Hall, Ottawa. Her latest full-length landscape history, Garden of Dreams: Kingsmere and Mackenzie King, presents a lively picture of the prime minister's horticultural enthusiasms and the influences that shaped his life.

IN RECENT YEARS, INTEREST IN PRESERVING and, in some cases, restoring cultural landscapes has been further stimulated by two major influences - the environmental movement and the heritage preservation movement. Combining the interpretation of landscape and its built components is not only essential for proper management of many historic sites, but also adds layers of meaning and of interest for the site visitor. In many cases, the landscape history is inseparable from the architectural history.

Cultural landscapes are on a continuum from wilderness to farm yards to highly altered landscapes such as city gardens. It is with designed landscapes that I deal primarily in my work and which I have been invited to discuss here.

Designed landscapes have much in common with natural landscapes - one has to deal with soil, topography, climate, plant material in either case. On the other hand, designed landscapes are intimately connected to their allied architectural elements. Since the late 18th century, one of the strong tenets of the landscape designer's belief was that house and garden must be united.

So, I will not be presenting here the theory and philosophy behind the protection or interpretation of cultural landscapes - I'll leave that to the theoreticians. I will be presenting two case studies where the integration of the interpretation of architectural elements and their surrounding landscape is essential to the proper management of the sites, which gives the fullest interpretation and the deepest meaning of the sites for site managers and for the public. For me, landscape gives meaning to, and is usually inseparable from architecture. A landscape history highlights the evolution of the site, the lives of the people connected with it, and, of course, adds to the history of the house or other building.

However, I recognize that there are problems with this type of interpretation. The main problem is that we do not have a visiting public in Canada who are knowledgeable about the styles of different periods, the standard components of historical gardens, and so on. There is not a single body of references which brings together all the styles, components and so on. We do not have a national data base, and as yet we do not have a national inventory of historic gardens. This all adds to the task of interpretation.

Let's turn now to the two sites I will be briefly discussing: Rideau Hall (Government House), Ottawa and the William Lyon Mackenzie King estate in Gatineau Park outside Ottawa. Both sites are administered by the National Capital Commission (NCC).

On the surface, both sites seem to be quite similar: both are laid out as country estates, both have famous people connected with them, neither were professionally designed. However, once one begins to delve into the history, the personalities and the function of the two sites, they begin to diverge radically. Why this is so, lies in the nature of the personalities connected with the landscape and the type of source materials available for interpreting the sites.

The Rideau Hall landscape was a product of many vice-regal and bureaucratic inputs. However, its form, function and meaning are all the same - the landscape reflects the presence of the monarch in Canada and was a symbol of the British empire. It is a ceremonial landscape which serves a state function and derives its main meaning from this. It is a tightly centralized landscape, unlike the far flung layout of the King estate. The reference sources used were less personal, more factual, more budgetary, than the emotive King diaries.

The sources used included:

Rideau Hall papers, RG 7 - which included household accounts, work orders, letters, memos - held in the National Archives

Auditor General annual reports

Ottawa Improvement Commission and Federal District Commission (both precursors of the National Capital Commission) annual reports

Department of Public Works annual reports - DPW had charge of the site from the 1860s up into the 1920s

Archival photos, especially aerial photographs, were especially helpful in discovering the evolution of the landscape.

We now move from Rideau Hall, into the Gatinau Hills to the King estate. It is not a great physical distance, but an enormous psychological distance. The King estate had a multitude of deeply personal meanings and symbols for Mackenzie King. In King's mind, his country estate landscape reverberated with the voice of God, the spirits of his departed loved ones, the power of antiquity, overlaid with a thick layer of King's love of all things British and concern over his social status. It was a stage-set where King acted out a number of roles: cottager, country squire, gentleman farmer, forester, protector of wildlife and parkland, and a sensitive, cultural, powerful politician. Landscaping his estate and improving it in other ways was the passion of his life and allowed him also to play the role of the gardener as hero. It has a more farflung layout, more like a typical English estate.

The sources used included:

The fantastic King diaries which he kept from age 18 to the day of his death, held at the National Archives of Canada.

King papers, another rich source - a mountain of material including letters, memorabilia, memos, etc.

Kingsmere papers - bills, memos, plant lists, plans, gardening articles, etc.

Numerous secondary sources on the history of cottaging, gentleman farming, resorting, rise of the national park, etc.

Photos from King's enormous collection

Now, I would like to outline briefly the interpretation process for both sites. The Rideau Hall project was a team effort supported by two government departments - Public Works Canada and the National Capital Commission. The goal was to produce a report, the findings of which would be integrated into the NCC's master plan for the site.

It was interesting to see that the estate could be divided into functional zones - the parkland, the ornamental gardens, the operations area, the sugar bush, etc. I discovered that they were "dynamically static" for over 100 years. That is, the function stayed the same, but the components in each went through a number of changes.

My partner on the history side of the team, Mark Laird, is a conservation landscape architect. He made assessments of all the estate components - the paving, structures, plantings, buildings, etc. Then, based on the history of the site, and the present-day details, he made recommendations on how to better blend in components, on restoring some, destroying some, etc. He made drawings of the gardens at different historical periods. Interestingly, he took pictures from the same viewpoints as the historical photos we collected to show changes and as a basis of analysis. At the same time, the NCC team members, both landscape architects, were interviewing Rideau Hall personnel on how the site is used and to probe and find out their wish list. From these, we learned of many serious pressures on the site such as building a number of structures in the middle of the cricket field.

The result of the study is the report: *Rideau Hall Landscape Conservation Study,* published by the two departments.

On the other hand, the King estate interpretation was mainly a solo effort, although a number of small projects have been done for the NCC and they have based a certain amount of interpretation on my book, *Garden of Dreams, Kingsmere and Mackenzie King.* I organized the research on the sequence of King's acquisitions - cottage, country home, farm, ruins - for each one gave rise to a new role for King to play, new perceptions for him to view his landscape. I also branched out into a number of secondary and primary sources in order to place King's country life into historical context - the history of cottaging, estate landscaping, gentleman farming, rise of national parks, and so on.

Finally, I want to conclude by noting that even though these full interpretations are important for many sites, I know that it is not easy to find the funding for this research, and moreover it is often difficult to find the necessary, primary historical material to do a proper history of a site landscape. Rideau Hall and the Mackenzie King estate were unusual in the amount of available, relevant material with which a landscape historian could work. In the best of all possible worlds, this integrated interpretation will educate the public, sensitize site managers to wider interpretations, and hopefully prevent insensitive intrusions on the site.

I invite you to step out of your buildings and into the garden and discover the interesting stories it has to tell.

"The Built and Natural Environments, Forging a Link: The New England Experience:

The Honourable Tom McMillan
Canadian Consul General to New England
Born and educated in Canada, Tom McMillan was first elected to
the House of Commons in the general election of 1979. He was re-
elected in 1980 and served as Environment Critic, and then Deputy
House Leader, for the Progressive Conservative Party in Opposition.
Following his re-election in 1984, Tom served as Canada's first full-
time Minister of Tourism. He became Minister of the Environment in
August 1985, and served in that position until December 1988.
During Tom's tenure as Envirionment Minister, the Government of
Canada created five new national parks, reformed the country's
parks and pollution laws, launched a major program to combat acid
rain, hosted land-mark international conferences on global pollution
problems like ozone depletion and climate change, and slashed
allowable exhaust levels for motor vehicles, among many other
achievements. Mr. McMillan received the prestigious Edgar Wayburn
Award from the U.S. Sierra Club and the Canadian Governor
General's Conservation Award. In 1990, Outdoor Canada magazine
named him one of the three people who, in the previous decade, did
the most to protect Canada's natural environment. He was also a
special visitor to Yale University as Graves Lecturer and Hoyt Fellow
and addressed the United Nations' General Assembly.

LET ME BEGIN BY SAYING HOW DELIGHTED I was to be invited to address the plenary session of this, the 1992 Provincial Local Architectural Conservation Advisory Committee Conference - *"Green Gutters and Gargoyles"*.

It is a particular pleasure to return to Peterborough, where I worked for almost a decade and where many of my closest friends live. Since moving to Boston three years ago, I have not been able to visit Peterborough as often as I would like. But I still consider this city a second home, after my native P.E.I.

The smart-looking program for *Green Gutters and Gargoyles* says the conference theme is the close relationship between the built and the natural environments and the need to care for both. The theme is an excellent one. The public too frequently view the built and natural environments as separate and distinct. In the real world, the two are inextricably linked. I wish to develop that point in this article.

Recently, I had the honour to serve as the Master of Ceremonies for Canada's 1992 Environmental Achievement Awards. The ceremony was held on the spacious grounds of the Guild Inn, overlooking the famous Scarborough Bluffs, on the shores of Lake Ontario. Back in 1932, two visionaries - Spencer and Rosa Clark - purchased that beautiful site to encourage people to earn a living in the arts and crafts at what they called "The Guild of all Arts". Spencer Clark also used the site to fulfil his passion for preserving Toronto's heritage by assembling architectural fragments from buildings being demolished throughout the city. In the gardens of The Guild, he created a veritable outdoor museum of office and bank building fragments, lovingly transported and painstakingly re-erected as reminders of the magnificent old structures that once stood in Canada's largest city.

I think it was highly appropriate that the national awards for achievement in preserving the natural environment should be presented in a setting designed to celebrate the built heritage.

Today, sixty years after Clark began his quest, one can wander through the grounds of The Guild Inn, admiring the classical columns and portals and arches and stones and carvings saved from some sixty of Toronto's finest old buildings demolished by the wrecker's ball over the years. All of us should feel indebted to Spencer Clark for salvaging bits and pieces of our country's built heritage and for presenting them in an outdoor museum setting that, in this province, only Mackenzie King's "ruins" at Kingsmere can rival in natural beauty and majesty.

But a much deeper sentiment that every Canadian should feel is outrage that the original buildings from which Clark's architectural fragments were salvaged no longer exist. And they no longer exist because so-called community leaders were too short-sighted or greedy or just plain dumb to realize the inherent cultural, aesthetic and even spiritual value of what they were destroying. Indeed, Toronto, Canada's largest city, now has fewer pre-Confederation buildings than Peterborough, a community ten times smaller.

Lest we think I am picking on Toronto, a practice that comes naturally to a Maritimer, let me assure you I am just as appalled by the callous destruction of the built heritage in my own part of the country. My hometown, Charlottetown, P.E.I., calls itself "the Cradle of Confederation," having hosted the first meeting of the Founding Fathers of our country in September 1864. Province House is where the Fathers of Confederation drew up the Seventy-two Resolutions that formed the 1867 British North America Act, Canada's first constitution. It is arguably the most historic building in all Canada.

One would think that a city that takes such obvious pride in its association with the founding of our nation would treasure every part of its built heritage, especially that which enhances its status as the Confederation City of Canada. To some extent the community does do so, and many splendid buildings in Charlottetown have, in fact, been restored. But nothing can compensate for what happened just a few years ago to a stately three-story neo-classical bank building that completed the fourth corner of the principal intersection of Charlottetown, only a few feet from the very building where Canada was born. This Greek revival building, a fine prototype of 1920s bank architecture, was reduced to rubble by the Canadian Imperial Bank of Commerce in an act of architectural vandalism decidedly more imperial than Canadian. In the building's space now squats, within eye-sight of Province House, a two-story mediocrity that would fit perfectly in Cleveland, Tulsa or the darkest cranny of the West Edmonton Mall.

The role played by the country's leading institutions in Canada's appalling neglect of its built heritage is nothing less than shoddy. The sorry stewardship of the three segments of society that have controlled our major Canadian heritage buildings, the churches, government and the banks, could most aptly be described as The Good, The Bad and The Ugly.

Let us continue with the banks for a moment. In return for their protected place in Canadian society, which gives them near-monopoly powers over the financial affairs of every one of us, they have, with a few shining exceptions, discarded, ignored or desecrated much of the cultural property under their control. All too often, bankers treat conservationists as though they were derelicts demanding million-dollar lines of credit.

The case of the Canadian Imperial Bank in Charlottetown is hardly unique. Toronto's war of the banks has been going on longer than the War of the Roses and just as inconclusively. In 1913, the Bank of Toronto opened its head offices in an imposing structure that had been inspired by the Paris Bourse, a grey marble magnificence the like of which we will not see again. When the Toronto-Dominion Bank was putting up the T-D Centre in the middle 1960s, it casually destroyed the old building. While the T-D Centre, taken as a whole, is important modern architecture, there is little doubt that the destruction of its predecessor was entirely gratuitous. All that was needed to save it was a little imagination and a dose of community spirit, sadly lacking in the case of the Bank.

Fortunately, some Canadian companies combine those qualities and, while doing good for the community, do well for themselves. Seven years ago, with Lord Thomson of Fleet, I had occasion to dedicate a Markborough property on the Sparks Street Mall in Ottawa; it comprises the facade of a late 19th-century store that has been wrapped within a fascinating glass-skinned tower. It is now home to a Zeller's store and has proven a strong magnet for the community. Moreover, the company knows that it has a property that cost a lot less than if the old structure had been demolished and a new one erected in its place. The company got great value, and considerable public relations advantage, for its heritage leadership. As to the extent of the savings, true to Zeller's own advertising slogan at the time, only they know how little they paid.

In fairness, I am not suggesting that banks are unrelenting villains. But they are as capricious as the emperors of Rome: this building is permitted to live, that one is fed to the bulldozers. For example, at almost the same moment the Bank of Commerce was smashing its Charlottetown branch building, it was saving its own head office in Toronto, which is now the centrepiece of Commerce Court. Ominously, there is no consistent pattern to which we can point and say, "Well, at least the banks are becoming more sensitive to conservancy issues". Astonishingly, even as we sit here today, there are other major bank battles shaping up, including in my hometown. But the banks are not the only specially treated sector of Canadian society that has failed to provide leadership on heritage issues.

While accepting all of the factors that persuade churches to sell to developers, one is free to reject a defence often raised about such sales. Sometimes it is claimed that churches are exempt from usual community awareness of heritage conservation because they need not concern themselves with what is often referred to as "mere bricks and stone". First, a heritage building is not mere anything: if it is deemed important, it has value in its own right. Second, churches do enjoy tax-exempt status, which places additional tax burdens on the rest of us. They cannot, therefore, act without reference to the goals of the general community, as happened back in 1983 in Ottawa, with the destruction of Clegg House. That incident, with its aura of deliberate lawbreaking, leaves a permanently foul taste. Whatever the consequences for the church group involved, the sad reality is that one of Ottawa's few pre-Confederation stone buildings wound up as a heap of rubble. The fact that the Clegg House site continues to be a parking lot nine years later simply underscores how senseless the destruction was.

I daresay that many of you might wonder how a former politician, now masquerading as a diplomat, has the effrontery to criticize either banks or churches. After all, when the book is written that defines hare-brained insensitivity to the built heritage, long chapters will be reserved for all levels of government. Among the dumbest ideas, I suppose, was U.S. President Ulysses Grant's suggestion that Venice could be made a much nicer city, if its canals were drained. Closer to home, on Parliament Hill in the nation's capital, there was the pillage of the West Block's interior and the fortunately-frustrated plans to vandalize the East Block. At the provincial level, one of the loonier plans was to tear down a substantial part of the northern section of Ontario's Parliament Buildings, to make room for the latest high-rise office towers.

Unhappily, another provincial scheme, this time to destroy a building of major historic and architectural significance, was successful. I'm referring to the Provincial Lunatic Asylum that stood on Queen Street in Toronto. The way it was treated, incidentally, sheds light on governments' tendency to see buildings as responsible for the uses to which they are put. In the Queen Street case, that was an injustice, a mindless misreading of history. Whatever its later problems of overcrowding and inefficiency, the fact is that the Asylum, when it was built, was an extraordinary humane attempt to treat the mentally ill. Tearing down that building robbed future generations of the right to learn about their historical and architectural roots and to learn from past mistakes.

The same is true of the destruction, at a municipal government level, of the Van Horne mansion in Montreal. The mansion was not an arrogant U.S. railroadman who came North to exploit a fast-developing society; it was his home, a gem of its time, one that would have informed and delighted Canadians for years to come.

No discussion of municipal attitudes to buildings is complete without mention of Toronto's city halls, old and new. When citizens organized and demonstrated against Eaton's plans to destroy their old city hall, the family must have thought Torontonians were, in equal parts, crazy and ungrateful. As we now know, that fight resulted in a better deal for everyone, including the Eatons. It is intertwined, of course, with the way Toronto built its new City Hall. Looking back, the decision to hold a major international competition and to accept a breathtaking and innovative design was the first step in making Toronto a world-class city.

At the federal level, a major relatively recent disaster was the near-destruction of the Royal Mint. The fact that it was possible to begin demolishing a building that had been given the highest protective classification should haunt all of us. It is a bitter lesson in what can happen when our vigilance flags even for a short time. Despite the most valiant efforts of government-hired architects and designers to reverse the damage once the incident became a cause celebre, the painful truth is that something irreparable was lost.

Our communities need to do more than preserve the best of their older buildings. They need to encourage the erection of striking new structures that future generations will view as part of their heritage. Most of our communities continue to engage the wrong people to build the wrong buildings in the wrong places.

At one time, the word "urban" had a positive ring to it. It implied refinement and culture. Cities were born of the desire and necessity of people to live and work close to one another. As architect Webb Nichols of Cambridge, Massachusetts, has written, proximity inspires, creates and requires what is physically and spiritually unique to cities - the public space, the streets, the squares, parks and other meeting places and the communications, acceptance and civility of the inhabitants. A rational city street speaks of our aspirations and values, says Nichols. "It is a measure of our commitment to each other. It can be evidence of our desire for beauty and self-expression."

The key to fostering wider interest in heritage issues lies with those of us who are already committed conservationists. American anthropologist Margaret Mead once said, "Never doubt that a group of committed people can change the world. Indeed, it is the only thing that ever has." In our case, yours and mine, we must not only act but we must act together. And we must speak clearly and loudly to society as a whole about the importance of Canada's past, as expressed in her buildings.

The built environment is a part of Canada's family album, a way in which we learn who we are by understanding who we were. Even in a society that prides itself on how quickly it can rid itself of "things", throw away bottles, pizza boxes or bathing suits, no one throws a family album away and re-invents reality every day. Those of us who are conservationists know that instinctively. Our job is to ensure that we are heard above the din of those who equate the future with anything that is new and who do not understand that confidence in that future comes from knowledge and appreciation of the past.

For Canadians, the Conservation Ethic must become civic religion. The conference material called that ethic the three 'r's'; reduce, reuse, recycle. I would add a fourth 'r' - reclaim. New Englanders express this same four 'r's' ethic in a distinctly New England way: "Use it up, wear it out, make it do, or go without." I am not convinced we Canadians really possess the Conservation Ethic, at least insofar as the built heritage is concerned. Perhaps, because we see ourselves as a young country, that which is old is considered, perversely, of little value.

All of us who have ever lost a particular heritage battle, or who simply feel a deep sense of loss every time any part of our built heritage is demolished, need to ask ourselves: Why is it that, even though public awareness of the issue seems at an all-time high, it still requires an almost super-human effort to preserve what's left of the country's built heritage? I think the answer is that, despite a marked improvement in public attitudes in recent years, the Canadian heritage cause has yet to become a genuine national movement.

Since I am among friends, let me be extremely frank. To save the built heritage, it is not enough to be on the side of the angels; with so many other worthy causes these days, that space is badly over-crowded. The heritage movement needs clout. We live today in a society of vested interests. More and more decisions are being made by powerful governments wielding great authority in favour of strongly organized groups. Government in most Western democracies is less a matter of leadership than a matter of brokerage politics. Politicians are reduced to distributing public spoils based more on who shouts the loudest than on who speaks the most sense. As a former politician, I regret the trend. As a political scientist, I am appalled by it. As a heritage champion, I think the movement needs to reconcile itself to it. Two choices face us: either the heritage cause uses the system to its advantage or it ignores the rules of the game and ensures its continued failure.

More than angels, the heritage movement needs an army of combatants, a strong, well-funded lobby, equipped with the most modern and sophisticated means of pressing its case in the power centres of the land. And, yes, when the need arises, it must be capable of throwing its weight around. Those at the Cabinet table or in the City Council chamber who are committed to the cause need a potent constituency to back them up.

Environmental groups have demonstrated the might of such an approach. Today, groups like the Sierra Club in the U.S. and Friends of the Earth in Canada have mobilized public opinion to the point where environmental issues are now near the top of the political agenda of both countries. Indeed, the massive amount of public and media attention showered on the Earth Summit in Rio de Janeiro has as much to do with the skilful orchestration of the event by environmental NGOs as it has with the import of the issues being debated.

I am well aware of the valuable role local Architectural Conservation Advisory Committees perform in the 200 or so municipalities throughout Ontario that have the benefit of their advice on built heritage issues. Provincial organizations like the Ontario Heritage Foundation also do a lot of good work. At the federal level,

I think the Historic Sites and Monuments Board, under the able leadership of Peterborough's own Tom Symons, is more effective now than ever before. But all such groups can do only so much to stop the steady loss of our country's rich built heritage.

At the heart of the problem is the fact that heritage has been viewed too narrowly. We are fishing in too small a pond. Specifically, we have failed to recognize the seamless mesh between the splendours of what humanity has created and the wonders of what nature has wrought. The built environment and the natural environment have been treated as two solitudes. In the process, the opportunity has been missed to mobilize a vastly larger constituency. That constituency embraces every single person and group committed to preserving the very best features of the total physical milieu that shapes a community and that is shaped by it.

Much can be learned from the Australian Heritage Commission. Established in July 1975, the Commission is responsible for "all those places which have been identified as worth keeping and handing on to future generations, (including) wildlife habitats, natural ecosystems, landscapes of great beauty, grand buildings and structures, humble dwellings, workplaces, ruins, sites of historic events..."

Australians rightly view nature and human creation as a seamless web, a vision captured by their use of the felicitous term "National Estate" to refer to anything worth preserving. In the dictionary, "estate" means "total possessions". And that, after all, is what the natural and built heritage, together, should mean to Canadians, your groups included. In fact, the Australian National Trust, the private sector equivalent of Heritage Canada, treats the built and natural environments as inseparable. So does the UNESCO World Heritage Site Program.

Based on such a broad vision, our own built heritage cause can become a true national movement. How can we make it happen? We must, first, engage the nature environmentalists in common cause, for they have a lot to contribute. They will have to be persuaded that the reduction of a historic building to rubble is as great a loss to the commonwealth as the pollution of a lake. Both forms of vandalism diminish the very qualities of life that make Earth more than a place to serve time.

A sense of wonder, of pleasure, of excitement can be as strongly elicited by Victoria Hall in Cobourg as by Mount Rundle in Banff. A fine old building and a majestic mountain are no less linked to a common national heritage because one is the creation of humanity, the other is the work of nature.

Nowadays, the link between the built and the natural heritage is tightened by the fact that both are threatened by acid and toxic rain and by other pollutants that corrode architectural treasures and historical waystations as assuredly as they destroy lakes, kill fish, devastate forests and harm human health.

The close kinship between the built and natural heritage was formalized in the federal government through the Minister of the Environment, for he was responsible for both fields at the Cabinet table. When I became Environment Minister, I tried to knit my Department's built heritage program tightly into the fabric of the entire ministry. I think some of my officials thought this perspective was eccentric, if not bonkers. But I remain convinced that there is an inherent logic to it.

After all, the wrecking ball is not the only danger to the built environment. Concern about the effects of pollution must encompass our buildings, not just our lakes and forests, our lands and wildlife. In fact, conservationists must remember that the fight to reduce air-borne pollutants, in particular, is also a fight for the built environment.

Indeed, priceless cultural properties around the world are at the mercy of acidic and toxic precipitation in all its forms. For example, the Lincoln Memorial in Washington, Marco Polo's home in Venice, and the Parthenon in Greece are all at serious risk. In the case of the Parthenon, what people and nature could not destroy in 2500 years is being threatened by pollution in our own lifetime.

I have now been living in New England for nearly three years. In that time, I have not become totally enamoured of American society, I assure you. But I am struck by how relatively successful New Englanders have been in saving their built environment. It is not because their heritage laws are so strict, for hardly any exist. Rather, it appears to be because the Conservation Ethic is genuinely part of the total culture. So, laws in this area appear unnecessary. A Maine antique dealer once told me that New Englanders never throw anything away. Certainly, they don't seem to have thrown away much of their architectural heritage.

I live in Weston, a small picture-perfect New England town eighteen minutes from down-town Boston. Within minutes of my home in either direction, on the fringes of that American metropolis, are countless towns and villages that, together, accommodate tens of thousands of people. I doubt that there is a heritage-conscious person in this room who would change hardly a thing about many of those towns.

One of my favourites, in the near-perfect category, is Concord, Massachusetts, about thirty minutes from downtown Boston. Like many of the villages and towns outside London, England, in the Cotswolds, Concord has retained its essential charm and simple elegance over the generations. Concord has done so because the local people have been confident enough in their own good taste and values to reject the vulgar fashions, fads and fancies that have ruined other communities. Rigorously enforced commercial signage policies are part of the approach. But, with or without heritage by-laws, heritage sensitivity is so ingrained in their community culture that a shopkeeper would no more blight the streetscape with an oversized or crassly executed storefront sign than he or she would appear naked at a civic function.

Laws can play an important role in saving the heritage of Canada, whether one is talking about the natural or the built environment. And I'm a firm believer in heritage laws. But, just as strong laws rigorously enforced cannot ultimately prevent an unscrupulous electro-plate company from disposing of toxic chemicals down the toilet, so also zoning laws, signage policies, height restrictions and the like, necessary though they are, cannot alone save the built heritage of a community. Heritage must come second nature to the people. It cannot be imposed on a hostile culture and be expected to work.

Sound heritage laws **reflect** the Conservation Ethic; they are not a substitute for it. If that ethic does not yet come naturally to Canadians, as I fear it does not, those to whom it does come naturally can do much to foster it in the population as a whole. I believe many potential zealots are to be found in the traditional environmental movement, if only a greater effort were made to identify and enlist them. If the traditional heritage movement and the traditional environmental movement were to join forces in common cause, both causes, which are essentially the same, in any event, would be virtually unstoppable.

Allow me to conclude on this note. We Canadians are currently going through a period of profound soul-searching, about the Constitution and, more fundamentally, about keeping our country from self-destructing. I am convinced that certain things about a society reveal what it values, indeed, whether the people who make up that society hold any strong beliefs in common and, thus, are capable of living harmoniously together as a united nation. Surely, one such window to the soul of a nation is its treatment of those natural and created features that define a country as distinct and, yes special among nations.

A people that says no to slash-and-burn logging in the mystic isles of South Moresby in British Columbia, so that not just Canadians but all other citizens of planet Earth can bask in nature's glow, is a nation that signals to itself and to the world that it possesses a set of core values that cannot be easily smashed by the transient forces of politics or provincialism. The same holds true when a society, through its national and local leaders, comes together, as it did, to commemorate the Peterborough Armoury. Like any other time we Canadians celebrate our built heritage, the designation of the Peterborough Armoury as a national historic site expressed our collective sentiments that we love and want to save the finest examples of our cultural property because we love and want to save the community, our country Canada, to which those physical things give glorious expression.

For us Canadians, the preservation of our natural and built environments, therefore, is the noblest cause of all. That is your mission. That is our common cause. I congratulate you for your commitment to it. Good luck with this vital work on behalf of our country, all Canadians and, indeed, Canadians yet unborn. It is a pleasure to be in your company.

515 Hunter Street West

Landscapes of Gain/Landscapes of Loss: A Bioregional Model for the Analysis of Cultural and Natural Heritage

John Wadland
Canadian Studies Program, Trent University, Peterborough.

John is a historian and Chair of the Canadian Studies Program at Trent Univeristy. Jointly with Tom Whillans, a biologist in Trent's Environmental Studies Program, he offers an interdisciplinary research course on Bioregionalism, focused on the Haliburton area. This course attempts to marry the sciences, social sciences and humanities in an investigation of the relationships between cultural heritage, environment and economy.

FOUR YEARS AGO MY COLLEAGUE, TOM WHILLANS, and I introduced at Trent an honours seminar premised on the theory of bioregionalism. Etymologically bioregion means "life-place":

> Geographically, bioregions are areas having common characteristics of soil, watershed, climate, native plants and non-human animals, and common human cultures. Culturally and psychologically, bioregionalism seeks the integration of human communities with the non-human world. Consistent with the tradition of the ecological community, bioregionalism emphasizes decentralization, human scale communities, cultural and biological diversity, self-reliance, cooperation, and community responsibility.[1]

Professor Whillans is a biologist and I am a historian. Through this course we combine our interests in natural and built heritage, attempting an interdisciplinary analysis of the relationships between them.

The course is focused on the Haliburton bioregion, an area bounded in the north by Algonquin Park, in the south by the boundaries of Peterborough and Victoria counties and including the towns and villages of Minden, Dorset, Haliburton, Wilberforce, Gooderham, Kinmount, and Donald, among others. The population of this area is approximately 12,000 full-time residents. The cultural history and folklore of the bioregion is richly complex.

Economically it is regarded as a dependent hinterland where most of the merchantable pulpwood and timber has been logged out, where mines, farms and railways are abandoned and where industry is all but non-existent. In the eyes of most people, Haliburton is a summer playground for middle-class Torontonians and American tourists who abandon the heat of the city for the myriad lakes and rivers which characterize its shield landscape.

Our course has been shaped in part by the imperatives of the Brundtland Report and of the Earth Summit in Rio, in part by the literature of the new school of environmental history headed by scholars like Donald Worster, Carolyn Merchant, Alfred W. Crosby and William Cronon in the United States. Our object, as students and faculty, is to contribute to our immediate community in the course of pursuing a research focused pedagogical agenda. Participants in the course come equally from the humanities, social science and science disciplines. Each student undertakes a primary investigation which addresses a need defined by the local community. The object of the exercise is the cross pollination of ideas, the sharing of findings and the education of all by each. The research projects, in both method and content, are informed by a bioregional theory which understands that all cultural activity has environmental implications. The land is not merely the stage on which the human drama is enacted; it is the leading player in the play. The land is the place where all the effects of human activity play out their long-term relationships. To quote the American environmental ethicist, J. Baird Callicott:

> relations are "prior to" the things related, and the systematic wholes woven from the relations are prior to their component parts. Ecosystemic wholes are logically prior to their component species because the nature of the part is determined by its relationship to the whole.[2]

Within these parameters a number of stimulating papers have already emerged. It is anticipated that by the end of our tenth year, all student research will be synthesized into a comprehensive document which will explain the Haliburton bioregion, proposing socioeconomic options which build upon sustainable relationships between culture and nature.

As an example of the interesting work that students are undertaking, especially in the analysis of built heritage, I wish to say a few words about the derelict chemical plant at Donald which captured the imagination of Andrew Hamilton.[3] This skeletal monument is neither beautiful, nor architecturally distinctive. It is a giant, rectilinear concrete and steel factory, an aberration abandoned in the wilderness.

The plant was built in 1906 by R.A. Donald of Markham, Ontario (and eventually purchased by E.P. Taylor's Standard Chemical Company) to supply charcoal for the smelting of iron. Between the wars, as coal replaced charcoal for this purpose, the byproducts of the charring process - acetate, used in the manufacture of explosives, and wood alcohol, used in cleaning solvents and as anti-freeze - were more highly valued. The Donald chemical plant was eventually by-passed by technology (specifically petro-chemicals) and by time. As it settles back into the ground the ghosts of its 300 man workforce are recalled in the stories of the remaining community. Its attractiveness as a site was its propitious location at the end of a CNR branch line, in the middle of a dense hardwood forest, adjacent to a river, and surrounded by a labour supply of farmers and loggers. "The Chemical" (as it became known) transformed an informal economy into a wage economy, introduced quantities of Italian and Finnish immigrants to augment the cheap labour force and cut, in concentric circles out from the plant, and beyond, virtually every living maple tree on Crown and private land in the bioregion. The company owned and operated all the stores in town; it built and rented all the houses, to which it supplied electricity and hot water from the steam generator in the factory. The plant witnessed many transformations in technology besides those affecting demand for its products. For example, the hauling of wood was originally a job for teamsters, conducted only in winter. But horses were replaced, first by a huge Lynn caterpillar tractor, and ultimately by trucks, which encouraged year round cutting farther afield. Winter roads were replaced by all-weather roads. Mobility within the bioregion increased.

Until its closing in 1946 the chemical plant at Donald, built and managed by wealthy Toronto industrialists, functioned like a maple tree vacuum in Haliburton. Only the descendants of those few far-sighted farmers who refused to clear cut their woodlots to sell to the company are able to produce maple syrup today. A once mixed forest is now predominantly coniferous, birch and poplar. The Burnt River, essential to the distilling and generating capacities of the plant, also carried its effluent the length of the bioregion. While this waterway appears to have returned to "normal," anglers are warned to minimize their consumption of fish.

Torontonians and Peterburians who prettified their urban dwellings - the very buildings celebrated at this conference - often depended for the wealth to build them upon plants, like that at Donald, which exploited immigrant workers, preserved for the children of the Haliburton bioregion as a metaphor for Canada and for the place of their home in its history. The landscape of loss which is their heritage is explained by complex chemical processes which required the consumption of a forest in the production of weapons to make the world safe for democracy. Donald is a history lesson, a chemistry lesson, an economic lesson and an ecology lesson rolled into one.

Notes

1. Robyn Eckersley, *Environmentalism and Political Theory: Toward and Ecocentric Approach.* (Albany: SUNY, 1992), pp. 167-68.

2. J. Baird Callicott, *In Defence of the Land Ethic: Essays in Environmental Philosophy* (Albany: SUNY, 1989), pp. 110-111.

3. Andrew Hamilton, "Modernity, Metaphor and Maples: The Landscape Created by the Wood Chemical Plant in Donald." Unpublished Paper, April 6, 1992.

Linking Natural and Cultural Heritage on The Alexander Mackenzie Voyageur Route

Peter Labor
Frost Centre for Canadian Heritage and Development Studies
Trent University, Peterborough, Ontario
Peter has pursued a career immersed in outdoor recreation, tourism and adventure travel. He has managed outdoor programs in Nova Scotia and Ontario and travelled to four continents on board the 47m tall ship Pogoria as a midshipman and instructor for an educational adventure program at seas for Canadian youth - Class Afloat. He has taught and facilitated courses in expedition management, outdoor skills and social statistics at the School for Outdoor Recreation, Parks and Tourism at Lakehead University. Peter shared responsibilities for the planning and managing of the four-year project which retraced, by canoe, the 13,000 km. journey of Alexander Mackenzie. He is currently pursuing a M.A. at Trent University with research on historic waterway routes and education.

THE ALEXANDER MACKENZIE VOYAGEUR ROUTE is a heritage waterway route which traces the path taken by Alexander Mackenzie in becoming the first European to successfully record a crossing of North America from sea to sea. Supported by proclamations from the six provinces through which it passes, the route recognizes a physical cross-section of the Canadian landscape and a cultural history upon which the country was established. Named after Alexander Mackenzie, the first European to record a crossing of the North American Continent north of Mexico, the heritage and historic value of the route far exceeds its use by Mackenzie or even prior use as a trading and transportation corridor by explorers and Natives. The rivers, lakes and drainage basins of this intricate network of water constitute a physical wonder, but when combined with a rich cultural history beginning with thousands of years of Aboriginal use and continuing to the present, they represent a heritage resource of considerable importance.

The initial concept of the Alexander Mackenzie Voyageur Route came in 1975 after the Nature Conservancy of Canada received a proposal to preserve the 350 kilometre "Grease Trail" which

Alexander Mackenzie followed from the Fraser River to the Bella Coola Valley on the Pacific Coast. The Alexander Mackenzie Trail Association was formed, and there is now a protected corridor, The Nuxalk-Carrier Grease Trail / Alexander Mackenzie Trail, reaching from the Fraser Valley, across the Chilcotin Plateau to the Pacific. The dedication of a sea-to-sea waterway route which would stretch from "Canada" (Ontario/Quebec) to the Pacific Ocean seemed the next logical step. In 1993, the Alexander Mackenzie Voyageur Association was formed from the earlier Trail Association to continue its efforts for national commemoration.

Of great importance to the national efforts was the Canada Sea-to-Sea Bicentennial Expeditions. On the 200th anniversary of Mackenzie's crossing, groups of students from Lakehead University recreated the voyage across Canada by canoe. In doing so, the groups visited hundreds of communities and shared a view of a human history of the fur trade through reenacting the fur trade era.

Canada's inland waterways are part of an important heritage which begins with the First Nations' spiritual bond to the land and continues through a legacy of economic and political growth and change as a result of European based expansion and resource demands from fishing to furs to forestry. Many of the communities located along the route were settled because of the adjacent waterway, and others are now closely linked to their waterway by industry, recreation, or transportation.

Heritage is seen as a reflection of culture, in which one may find intrinsic value, and a sense of self which may be passed on to future generations. Heritage provides a link between history and culture in establishing a grounds for recognition and preservation of those things which provide identity. Each individual's relationship to the natural world of land and water defines that individual's heritage, and through recognition of values which are held in common with others, a shared heritage is born.

By examining the links between culture, heritage and history during the fur trade in Canada through the common theme of the Alexander Mackenzie Voyageur Route, an integrated view of the country may be gained. The physical landscape on which history acts out its evolving story provides a setting within which different cultural realities may reach a common point of understanding in establishing a shared history with common heritage ties.   There are many federally and provincially protected areas located along the Alexander Mackenzie Voyageur Route, including National and Provincial parks, World Heritage Sites, National Historic Sites and Heritage Rivers. Although the protection of such physical heritage is important, the role of the government can extend beyond land acquisition and protection to include the recognition, and protection of non-tangible heritage resources associated with the route. By establishing a support system through which community groups can operate, new and creative partnerships are forged within communities, amongst communities and between communities and government agencies such that the shared aspects of heritage will be addressed without neglecting community specific needs. In the end, the recognition, celebration or education offered through working on a shared heritage resource may open a dialogue on history and aid communities and individuals in better understanding themselves.

The future of the Alexander Mackenzie Voyageur Route is yet to be decided, but several initiatives are exploring what to do next. The Alexander Mackenzie Voyageur Association, in association with Parks Canada, is continuing in its efforts to secure a Federal proclamation for the route. Heritage Canada is exploring the concept of designating the route as a Heritage Region. At Trent University, I am completing a master's thesis in which, through a community based survey, I am examining how communities located along the route relate to their local waterway, both physically and culturally. There are also plans for the writing of an implementation strategy for the route during the winter of 1995.

The Alexander Mackenzie Voyageur Route is a truly unique heritage resource which requires careful planning for its evolution. It is essential to recognize the regional importance of the route while placing the overall route in a national context. The route is a tourism and recreation resource of international significance, but any future development considerations must continue to recognize the Alexander Mackenzie Voyageur Route's profound physical and cultural attributes.

Selected References

Gray, R. (1955, August). Across Canada by Mackenzie's track. *National Geographic.*

Labor, P. (1992, Spring). Canada: From sea-to-sea, by canoe; 1989-93. *Kanawa.*

Lamb, K. (Ed.) (1970). *The journals and letters of Sir Alexander Mackenzie.* London: Cambridge University Press.

Lavender, D. (1977). *Winner take all: a history of the trans-Canada canoe trail.* Moscow, Idaho: University of Idaho Press.

Morse, E.W. (1979). *Fur Trade Routes of Canada / then and now* (2nd ed.). Toronto: University of Toronto Press.

Smithers, J. (1994, February/March). The Mackenzie Expeditions; 1789/93, 1989/93 - a journey through history. *Explore.*

Woodworth, J. (1992, Spring). The Alexander Mackenzie Voyageur Route - 92/93; "Canada Sea-to-Sea". *Kanawa.*

Closing Address

Michael Valpy
Columnist for the Globe and Mail, Toronto
Michael is deputy managing editor of the Globe and Mail. He has been associate editor and national affairs columnist for the Vancouver Sun. For the Globe and Mail, he has been a member of the editorial board, national affairs columnist based in Ottawa, Africa correspondent and national columnist based in Toronto. He has won two National Newspaper Awards for foreign reporting, co-authored a book on the Constitution and produced numerous public affairs documentaries for CBC Radio. Michael owns a farm in Grey County and is at war with his local MPP over the future of the rural landscape.

MY DAUGHTER LESLIE, after graduating from high school, will be coming to Trent University in the fall. Those of you who went away from home for the first time to attend university will know her excitement and anticipation.

For Leslie, though, there is something else, something else exciting, that she will find in Peterborough. When I unfolded the conference conservancy poster a few weeks ago, I immediately saw the sketched facade of St. John the Evangelist Anglican Church, built in 1834, and my heart gave a happy leap. I was looking at my own history and at my daughter's history. Five generations ago, her great-great-grandfather was superintendent of the Sunday school at St. John's. She will see this church, and stand where her great-great-grandfather once stood. She also will see, a few blocks away, the house he built.

Nearly 30 years ago, I worked briefly in Peterborough as a young reporter. My grandmother, Kate, born in Peterborough in 1878, wrote to me from Vancouver with a detailed description of the house - a house she had not seen since she was a child of eight but could remember with precision clarity. Kate, more than anyone I've ever known, revelled in the experience of place.

And with her description and with help from the City of Peterborough's records, I found the house and photographed it, and called on its occupants, who were in love with it - and who boasted to me, the great-grandson of its builder, a carpenter, about the artistry of its construction. Such deep pleasure that gave me, this

preserving and conserving of my history. What pleasure it will give
Leslie. What a sense of belonging it will give to both of us, a feeling
of roots of responsibility - for it is true that we care most about what
we are a part of. But you people know this.

You know what Tony Hiss, in his wonderful book, *The Experience
of Place,* means when he writes: "Our relationship with the places we
know and meet up with... is a close bond, intricate in nature, and
not abstract, not remote at all. It is enveloping, almost a continuum
with all we are and think." As in my 19-year old daughter's thoughts
when she will stand where her great-great-grandfather stood more
than a century ago.

Tony Hiss, the son of Alger Hiss, if you want a piece of historic
trivia, has spent little time over the past two decades NOT thinking,
writing or teaching about place. "Until recently [he says] when people spoke about a vivid experience of a place, it would usually be a
wonderful memory. These days people often tell me that some of
their most unforgettable experiences of places are disturbingly
painful and have to do with unanticipated loss."

There is this church here which my daughter will soon experience
with all its personal history for her.

There was another church, in the tiny hamlet of Bognor, three
kilometres south of my farm in Grey County. My daughter was bap-
tised there. All that remains of it is the church bell atop a cairn. The
last five parishioners, farm families in my valley, tore it down rather
than have it sold to Toronto yuppies for a chic country place.
Whenever we drive past it, my daughter makes some sad comment
on its disappearance.

Hiss has wondered if we should not have some constitutional
rights to introduce our children to places we were introduced to as
children.

Indeed, we know that the preservation of childhood places sus-
tains us psychologically. We know that we all use long-lasting and
familiar buildings as a mnemonic device that can organize and
prompt our memories. That's where I went on my first date; that's
the place where my father worked.

We know that our cities, as Lewis Mumford has written, are places
where "the separate beams of life are brought together and issues of
civilization are brought into focus", places where ancient connections, origins and identities merge with overwhelming events that
suggest new opportunities, new dreams and new questions. And it
is the very fact that human beings are forever an unfinished species,
a succession of families, tribes and societies in transition to a new
awareness that necessitates the preservation of our built past as
markers for where we have been and where we are going.

"These places [says Hiss] have an impact on our sense of self, our sense of safety, the kind of work we get done, the ways we interact with other people, even our ability to function as citizens in a democracy. As places around us change, both the communities that shelter us and the larger regions that support them, we all undergo changes inside."

"The danger, as we are now beginning to see, is that whenever we make changes in our surroundings, we can all too easily short-change ourselves, by cutting ourselves off from some of the sights and sounds, the shapes or textures, or other information from places that have helped mould our understanding and are now necessary for us to thrive."

But you people know this.

And I am here today to celebrate you and your work. I am here to celebrate the past that is our present and our future. And I am here, I modestly hope, to send you forth from architect Ronald Thom's beautiful built-environment on the banks of the Otonabee River, to send you forth like Shelley's blithe spirits to scatter your thoughts across the universe. Or, at the very least, Ontario.

This is, indeed, a time for celebration, not of victory, because we will go on for a while yet destroying our architectural heritage, the gentle places of the past that partnered human beings, not domi-nated them, not numbed their sensitivies, not gave them the mes-sage of "Move on!". And we will go on for a while yet destroying the rural landscape that soothes our souls.

But what we can celebrate is the claimed beachhead of an idea and of a new attitude, a new moral value. What you can celebrate is the fact that you and your cause and your work will never again be at the margin of public policy debate in this province. You can never again be dismissed as tree-huggers or old-building huggers frivo-lously standing in the path of progress and development.

It is the advocates of limitless progress themselves who are being placed on the defensive. The progressive tradition of the past 250 years has rested on the denial of natural limits on human power and human freedom. That is against Nature. And, because it is against Nature, human beings are making the belated discovery that the Earth's ecology can no longer sustain an indefinite expansion of productive forces.

The notion of the disposable environment, both built and natur-al, the expectation of ever-increasing material desires and ever-increasing consumption, that notion and that expectation are on the road to being toast, George Bush notwithstanding. The Environmental Revolution has arrived. The environmental ethic will define the social agenda of the 1990s. It is surfacing everywhere.

The people, to date, are ahead of their governments. But that, too, is changing.

David Crombie, in his royal commission report on the Toronto Waterfront, a report wonderfully titled *Regeneration,* has written that environmental consciousness "has already begun to reorganize government policies, recast corporate strategies and redefine community and individual responsibility and behaviour. "And it is raising [he goes on] fundamental questions, spiritual questions, about the relationship of humankind of Nature and to God. It has become a force strong enough to change the face, form and function of places around the world."

Another royal commission, John Sewell's on planning in Ontario, has proposed in its draft report that considerations of heritage and the natural environment be integrated into all stages of the planning process.

Ontario's New Democratic Party government, while it may not march to the acclaimed applause of all the province's citizens, merits a great deal of praise for slamming the door shut on wholesale rural lot severances in beautiful Grey County.

The Niagara Escarpment Commission, undoubtedly to the profound distress of my member of the provincial Legislature, the crusading Bill Murdoch, has proposed, at the conclusion of its five-year review, strengthening developmental controls. The Rouge Valley has been saved, so far, from garbage dumps and condo jungles. People in southern Ontario now at least know the Oak Ridges Moraine exists.

And if nothing else, Canadian politicians are finding the right rhetoric. Let me quote to you from *A Liberal Vision of the Environment,* put out by federal Liberal environment critic, Paul Martin:

"We are in the midst of a profound shift in attitudes and values. In essence, Canadians have begun to adopt a different view of progress. Improvements in the quality of life, of things and of relationships are being regarded as a truer measure of progress than simple growth in economic terms."

"In the context [says Martin] of a growing preference for quality over quantity, protecting and improving the environment is not only an essential issue, it is the main principle upon which the quality of life depends. This may be the most significant change in public opinion in modern history."

In short, Mr. Martin has discovered that Canadians may perhaps not want to be the insatiable guests at the banquet of life.

It is in the United States, however, frequently such a useful social laboratory for Canadians, where innovative action to protect the built and natural environments has taken firm root.

The six-state New England governors' conference, in 1988, agreed to put together a list of all the unprotected open spaces and working landscapes within the region that New Englanders consider special places that help create the distinctiveness of their particular landscape. A number of states have passed legislation allowing for public bond-raising to buy up cherished open-spaces and cherished rural landscapes. Other states have put in place transfer-of-development-rights programmes that allow developers to buy the development rights off farms and transfer them, for extra-density bonuses, to places where development is deemed desirable, an idea that planners in the Niagara Region are interested in for saving the fruit belt. New Jersey has developed a state-wide plan that both contains new growth in already existing villages and small towns and puts a hard edge on their perimeters.

Still other states have schemes which commit farmers not to sell their farms for development for a set number of years in exchange for valuable free agricultural extension services. Moreover, there are increasing signs that northern U.S. farmers themselves, particularly in New England, confronted as Ontario farmers are confronted by both development pressures and the grim facts of traditional agriculture economics are standing firm and "renewing their vows to the Earth" [in Tony Hiss's lovely phrase] and are diversifying into a new array of boutique crops, specialty vegetables and herbs, prize-winning table wines, organic potato chips, fancy cheeses.

The Americans are ahead of us, and perhaps nowhere is this more visible than in the American public's rethinking of the human habitat. Americans are showing signs of becoming fed up with urban sprawl. They want to walk again. The reaction against growth is becoming a nation-wide phenomenon, a reaction which American town-planners Andres Duany and Elizabeth Plater-Zyberg, the gurus of the re-invented village, call unprecedented. "What is responsible for this bizarre antipathy," they write, "is not growth itself but the particular kind of growth we have in the United States. Suburban sprawl is cancerous growth rather than healthy growth, and it is destroying our civic life." They point out that Americans have shown over and over again that they will pay premium prices to live in the few traditional towns that remain along the Atlantic Seaboard. They will drive hundreds of miles to spend a weekend in places like Sonoma, California, just for the sake of experiencing the pleasures of small-town living. At Disneyland, they will spend more time wandering along the fabricated Main Street, U.S.A., than they do on the rides.

It is not hard to see why. In the suburban sprawl of Orlando, Florida, it has been estimated that each single-family household generates an average of 13 car trips a day. Another study has shown that the family second car costs $5,000 annually to operate, a sum large enough to supply the payments on a $54,000 mortgage at 10 per cent.

Every study done on suburban and exurban sprawl and rural strip development has shown that they negate healthy family and community life. They imprison the old and young alike who can't drive, but who, paradoxically, can walk. The old cannot go shopping, visit friends, get to a doctor's office, while children are kept in an unnaturally extended state of isolation and dependence because they live in places designed for cars rather than people.

The re-sale of rural strip-development houses far exceeds that of city and town houses, as their owners discover the aridness of life dependent upon the car. And as for bringing in more tax revenue to municipalities, what is rapidly becoming clear is that sprawled suburbs and rural ribbon development are turning out to cost more in expensive municipal services such as strung-out sewer lines and higher road maintenance expenditures.

Interestingly enough, New York City's environmental protection commissioner, Albert Appleton, has come up with a rough mathematical formula to measure rural landscape degradation. "The first five per cent of development in a countryside region [he says] generally does 50 per cent of the damage, in terms of altering people's mental geography of an area. And the second five per cent of development enlarges this damage by another 50 per cent." And while he allowed that the environmental damage caused by the first development in a region may vary tremendously from place to place, depending on the nature of the terrain and the kind of development involved, he said the disproportionate initial-impact formula seems to apply across the board. Frightening.

The good news, however, is that Americans are re-discovering the village, the village that was supposed to be dead but has turned out to be both too practical and too deeply embedded in the American imagination. All those Christmas cards of time-past hamlet scenes have kept it alive. Neo-traditionalism has become hot. It has even found its way into the thinking of York Region planners and politicians who have had Duany and Plater-Zyberk up to listen to their ideas.

Houses in a number of the new American developments are being built smaller, higher and closer together and in traditional cottage and townhouse styles. Streets are being made narrower to emphasize cosy village life. Shops, schools and even offices are being built within walking distance. The co-housing movement is attracting interest, where a number of homes are clustered around a large common house with shared facilities such as dining room, children's playroom, workshop and laundries, an idea that originated in Denmark in 1972. The list goes on.

I picked up Rachel Carson's *Silent Spring* the other day, that warning of ecological disaster that shocked the world 30 years ago when it was published. And I noticed for the first time that it was dedicated to Albert Schweitzer who said [Carson wrote] "Man has lost the capacity to foresee and to forestall. He will end by destroying the Earth."

The director of Toronto's Board of Education told me that the children she talks to in the Toronto school system are infused with bleakness about the environmental future of the world. At a dinner for Tony Hiss in Toronto a few weeks back, Richard Gilbert, the head of the Canadian Urban Foundation, spoke of the enormous difficulties being encountered in getting Metro Toronto's inner City residential intensification plans going. Frustration, bleakness, a doomsday prophecy.

It is said of journalists that their role in public policy debate is to come on the battlefield after the war is over and shoot the wounded. But let me repeat what I said a few minutes ago: I am here to celebrate.

The evidence is everywhere around us that we are beginning to show signs on this wasteful, wasteful continent of learning how to assert the goodness of life in the face of its limits, of learning how to weave limits and hope together, but a much more vigorous hope than one predicated on the expectation of ever-increasing material desires and ever-increasing consumption. I wish to celebrate that. There is a revolution in attitude.

The Niagara Escarpment will be here, in its beauty, long after my member at Queen's Park and the Grey Association for Development and Growth have passed from public life. I wish to celebrate that.

I wish to celebrate the continued existence of that church downtown where by great-grandfather once instructed the children of Peterborough on the state of their immortal souls.

And I wish to celebrate business executives like Jon Grant, the president of Quaker Oats Canada in Peterborough, who tirelessly works to debunk the lie that responsibility for the environment costs jobs. "Environmental investment [he has said], far from being an economic bogeyman, can be an incentive to efficiency and economic recovery... Until we adopt a waste-not, want-not mentality, Canada will not achieve competitiveness in the world."

Exactly. Recognizing the limits to growth and the limits to consumption means precisely returning to the values of thrift, of waste-not, want-not, that were embedded in the souls of the aboriginal peoples who first lived in Ontario and the petty bourgeois Scots and Irish settlers who came after them.

So I want to celebrate that. And I want to celebrate the local business people in Peterborough who understand those values of thrift and saving and conserving and who contributed generously to this conference in the middle of a recession.

I want to celebrate children who are becoming, as those of you will know who have them around, militant eco-terrorists, taking on McDonald's and their excessive packaging, taking on their parents, taking on governments.

I want to celebrate all the little things we are doing, such as giving taxbreaks to landowners who forfeit development rights in agreement with the Ontario Heritage Foundation, and urge that the little things become big things. We might, for example, try promoting the programme a little more strenuously. Few people have heard about it.

I want to celebrate people like Malcolm Kirk and the Collingwood Senior League who buy conservation land to preserve it.

Most of all, I want to celebrate how much we have learned in the past few years about our built and natural environments. For it is that knowledge which has enabled people like you to come in from the margins and wage your campaigns on a level playing-field.

It is the knowledge that certain buildings, and certain landscapes are more, far more, than mere economic chips, that they have intrinsic public value which must be preserved for the health of us all.

A UNESCO study, called *Growing Up in Cities,* found, from interviews with children in four countries - Australia, Argentina, Mexico and Poland - that no matter where they came from, inner city neighbourhoods or rural villages, "the hunger for trees is outspoken and seemingly universal".

A study by the Town and Country Planning Association of London, England concluded: "The rural needs of the urban child are not just the sights of the farm or the pleasures of running untrammelled through the woods or exploring the country park. They include vital personal experiences and discoveries like silence, solitude and the sensation of utter darkness."

Neglecting children's rural needs, says Roger Hart, director of the Children's Environment Research Group at the City University of New York, can impair their healthy development as adults. "Part of being a responsible adult is having a sense of responsibility for the environment. And you can only care for something you've grown to feel a part of."

This is the knowledge with which we can address the bleakness of our children who feel they will only know nature as an abstract concept.

And consider this knowledge, from a nine-year study of gallbladder patients in a hospital on the Isle of Wight. And you wonder sometimes who thinks up these research projects. In any event, those patients who could see a cluster of trees outside their hospital window were found to have shorter post-operative stays and take fewer moderate or strong painkillers.

I'd like to celebrate all that. I wish to celebrate the small towns in Grey County and elsewhere in Ontario that have escaped the blight of perimeter shopping malls and maintained the vibrancy of their Victorian and Edwardian central shops, and I'm sorry for Owen Sound, my county seat, which let the malls get built and now has a main street filling up with bingo halls and frumpy bargain bazaars and vacancy signs.

I'd like to celebrate how concern for the built and natural environment heritage of Ontario seeps through this multicultural society of ours.

I have no more direct connection with the Ulster farmers who came to my part of Grey County more than a century ago than my neighbour Di Tursi across the road. Their culture, if you like, their heritage, is not directly ours. Yet Di Tursi and I, he Italian me Anglo-Norman, we have made it ours, we both cherish the working landscapes they created and the simple, beautiful houses and barns they built.

I take my young son to the deciduous forest with its wealth of indigenous plant and animal life that's been created at the Royal Ontario Museum and I take him to Toronto's Black Creek Pioneer Village. And every time I go, I'm blown away by the racial and ethnic mix of children enjoying the experience to the fullest.

If you are wondering how the ethos of Ontario heritage awareness is faring in its transmission to children whose families have come here from every corner of the globe, you need question no further. They are making this Ontario heritage theirs. And I'm very glad to celebrate that.

Five years ago, Robert Bendick, the director of Rhode Island's Department of Environmental Management, called a press conference to announce that the suburbanization of the southern state, where all the beaches are, was now a fact and that the people of Rhode Island had only five years left to save all the lands in the state that were important to save. The result was, to say the least, dramatic. Within two years, the people of the state put together a coalition of environment groups and government officials which launched the largest per capital open-space financing program in the United States. Through referenda and local municipal initiatives, they raised $126-million to buy up undeveloped land and preserve it for the common good.

Mr. Bendick explained why. Most of the land in Rhode Island had always been privately owned but there was an unwritten code of the countryside that the owners of farms, forests and shoreline gave the public the use of these spaces. Thus private property had been functioning discreetly as public open space. In other words, there was a kind of state mythology at work. When that began to be eroded, and then truncated by the contemporary wave of development, the people reacted.

That's a very interesting story because we in Canada, we, too, have our mythologies. Ninety-two year old Bruce Hutchison is English Canada's greatest journalist-mythologer. I want to read to you a sample of Hutchison's mythology of our country. It is from the opening page of *The Unknown Country*, his first book, published exactly half a century ago. It is a little long, but I think you will find it worthwhile. And I apologise on Mr. Hutchison's behalf for its gender specificness, but it was composed in a different age.

"No one knows my country, neither the stranger nor its own sons. My country is hidden in the dark and teeming brain of youth upon the eve of its manhood. My country has not found itself nor felt its power not learned its true place. It is all visions and doubts and hopes and dreams. It is strength and weakness, despair and joy, and the wild confusions and restless strivings of a boy who has passed his boyhood but is not yet a man."

"A backward nation they call us beside our great neighbour, this though our eleven millions have produced more, earned more, subdued more, built more than any other eleven millions in the world. A timid race they have called us because we have been slow to change, because we have not mastered all the achievements nor all the vices of our neighbours."

"They have not known Canada. Who but us can feel our fears and hopes and passions? How can aliens or even blood brothers know our inner doubts, our secret strengths and weaknesses and loves and lusts and shames?"

And this is the part I like:

"Who can know our loneliness, on the immensity of prairie, in the dark forest and on the windy sea rock? A few lights, a faint glow is our largest city on the vast breast of the night, and all around blackness and emptiness and silence, where no man walks."

"We flee to little towns for a moment of fellowship and light and speech, we flee into cities or log cabins, out of the darkness and the loneliness and the creeping silence. All about us lies Canada, forever untouched, unknown, beyond our grasp, breathing deep in the darkness and we hear its breath and are afraid."

"No, they could not know us, the strangers, for we have not known ourselves."

That's pretty good stuff, pretty powerful stuff. Hardly the words of despair many of us feel about our Canada today. And, indeed, 50 years after it was written, it still says much to us. The good in it is that it touches the deepest and most powerful of all Canadian mythologies: the vast, powerful emptiness of the land, beyond our grasp and fearsome. It is this mythology that has been the well-spring theme of much of our literature, of the stories we tell ourselves about ourselves. That has been the essence of our huddling-together tribalness, our social solidarity, the source of our visions, our dreams, of so many of our great tasks: the railways, the CBC, our system of health care and other universal social services.

It is not a mythology of waste and despoliation, of a people who treat their land as no more than a bank account, now dirty and depleted. It is not a mythology of a people who are sprawling their habitat across the countryside, driving out other forms of life who have the same God-given right to existence as we do, and, indeed, whom we need.

"What is man without the beasts?" wrote Chief Seattle in 1855. "If all the beasts were gone, men would die from great loneliness of spirit, for whatever happens to the beasts also happens to man."

What have we done in 50 short years... my lifetime? If we have done no more than be insatiable guests at the banquet of life, and if we will do little more than that in the future, then we will, in this lovely land, in this lovely province, that is our home, make Albert Schweitzer's terrible prediction come true.

But I prefer to leave you on this beautiful afternoon with a more hopeful text. It is from Ecclesiastes, chapter one, verse four. Perhaps my great-grandfather once read it at the morning lesson in St. John's. It is this: "One generation passeth away and another generation cometh: but the Earth abideth forever."

You are special people, doing special work. I am delighted to have been given the opportunity to praise you for it and to thank you. Let me give you T.S. Eliot:

"We shall not cease from exploration

And the end of all our exploration

Will be to arrive where we started

And to know the place for the first time."

And because of you, the places where we started will continue to exist.

455 Hunter Street West

Rural Heritage

Heritage Awareness at the Country Roadside

Thomas F. McIlwraith
Professor, Department of Geography, University of Toronto.
Thomas, a Torontonian, has been exploring the countryside of Ontario since the 1950s, and this has led him into university study in historical geography. His MA thesis - a study of road transport in York County before 1867 - was completed at the University of Toronto in 1966, and he took his doctorate at the University of Wisconsin, Madison, in 1973. Thomas has taught cultural and historical geography on the Erindale campus of the University of Toronto since 1970, and has also taught at the University of British Columbia and McMaster University. He has published several articles on transportation and heritage matters and was a founding member of the Mississauga LACAC in 1976, serving as chairman between 1982 and 1985.

COUNTRY ROADSIDES TEND TO BE PLACES that even heritage-minded passers-by overlook en route to somewhere else, probably through lack of understanding. I invite interlopers to pause and become aware of the rural road, and particularly the context within which its individual elements lie. Such awareness will help assure preservation of the opportunity for future generations similarly to become acquainted with the rural road.

Roads present us with a paradox. On the one hand, the land survey of lots and road allowances - the cadastre - is indestructible, and will survive any force short of Armageddon. LACACs can add nothing. On the other hand, features demonstrating the survey are constantly modernized. Earth roads and rusty signs are obliterated as a matter of course, and again LACACs cannot expect to intervene with much success. The result is indifference, and potentially missed opportunities to celebrate two centuries of cultural change on the land.

Roadside features worthy of attention are so familiar as to be potentially contemptible and therefore not regarded seriously. The landscape of dispersed farmsteads will not change, but the function of the buildings and residents often does, and buildings disappear. Lilacs on a vacated site will sustain recollection of the basic freehold principle indefinitely into future generations. Likewise the woodlots that close the horizon view along concession roads circumscribe rural neighbourhoods, and impart a warp and weft to the landscape - all from the basic survey.

The contrast between land as a place to make a living and as a housing site does not change, but the emphasis has. Convenient access places farmsteads at the centre of the field operation, far from the roads. Farmhouse fronts may look out on the world, but that is just facade, and the real entrance is at the rear through the farmyard. Convenience has placed service hamlets at the centre of the road network, easily reached from the farms wherever roads intersect. And now, city-folk moving to the countryside for spacious affordable living buy road severances in corners of farms furthest from the farmstead.

Straight roads will remain straight, but sudden irregularities are smoothed for faster traffic. Human and technical failings caused jogs, and different surveying rules determine whether jogs occur at intersections, or between them. Residual wedges of land are yet another durable legacy of the survey, not to be forgotten. Nor will road allowance position change, even if its utility does. Celebrate those unused (plenty near Port Hope), those given (by popular demand, for special access), those too wide (deep ditch, interesting weeds, tree lines, and old fences, or lament the misuse of space), and those too narrow (enclosed ditch, no tree line, and a new fence). Appreciate that the Colonial Office had no idea what degree of access was needed, and how local residents have made pragmatic adjustments ever since.

Stress between survey and physiography or other cultural demand will not cease, but is never fully mitigated. A road defers to a stream in one place, while a stream defers to a road somewhere else. The road that defers to a railway embankment may resume its preferred course once the railway is torn up, leaving a residual ridge as legacy of the struggle. Finally, cadastral addresses do not change, but often become buried under non-rural naming decisions. Lot and concession addresses advertise a land-holding enterprise most Ontarians have never known - but are the richer for knowing - and the signs that announce them remind us of ephemeral roadside furnishings.

The roadside is a place for generic celebration of spaciousness. This differs from recognizing specific buildings, or even districts, but familiarity with it contributes inestimably to involvement in both. Generic celebration calls for taking pot luck with what one sees - all the big and little things close at hand, anywhere. Consider what the eye can behold from a fixed roadside vantage point. Better still, walk the five-mile circuit that constitutes a rectangle of survey roads in most parts of southern Ontario. Let the scene unfold, and be absorbed.

Further Reading

Fram, Mark. 1982 "The Customary Shores," in Mark Fram and John Weiler, eds., *Continuing with Change*. Toronto: Queen's Printer. pp. 33-103.

Jackson, John Brinckerhoff. 1980. "The Discovery of the Street," in J. B. Jackson, *The Necessity for Ruins*. Amherst, Massachusetts: University of Massachusetts Press. pp. 55-66.

McIlwraith, Thomas F. 1992. "The Fourth of Trafalgar: Continuity along the Ontario Road," in Donald Janelle, ed., *Geographical Snapshots of North America*. New York: The Guilford Press. pp. 333-36.

Meinig, Donald. 1978. *The Interpretation of Ordinary Landscapes*. New York: Oxford University Press.

Miller, Marilyn. 1978. *Straight Lines in Curved Space*. Toronto: Queen's Printer.

Rapoport, Amos. 1969. *House Form and Culture*. Englewood Cliffs, New Jersey: Prentice-Hall Publishers.

459 Hunter Street West

Rural Landscape Heritage Resources of the Peterborough Area

Alan Brunger
Professor of Geography, Trent University, Peterborough, Ontario.
Alan is currently a Professor of Geography at Trent University, spe-
cializing in the historical geography of land settlement in Upper
Canada. His publications pertain to such topics as the settlement
patterns and processes of early Ontario and ethnic and ancestral pat-
terns evident in the early censuses. Alan is currently researching cul-
tural and geographical patterns in the St. Lawrence "Entry" in the
19th century, and the cultural landscape of central Canada.

THE THESIS OF THIS PAPER IS THAT PROTECTION REQUIRES an inventory of the valued "thing", and protection becomes more difficult with diversity. Peterborough's rural landscape heritage is diverse, relatively poorly perceived and thus relatively unprotected.

Peterborough's diversity is linked to its marginal, or "edge" position in a regional sense. The diversity will be described through the results of the project Heritage Peterborough and subsequent local studies. The "edge" is a natural element of significance. In the first instance, the Peterborough area occupies the "edge" of the drift-covered part of southern Ontario, close to the granite Canadian Shield. The drift-covered area was developed as a "typical" Ontario agricultural landscape. The granite Shield was avoided by farmers and sparsely-settled. Owing to its coniferous pine forest, lumbering boomed and settlement, largely transitory, accompanied this industry.

The second "edge" condition is the water-land shore phenomenon. The extensive river and lake network was exploited early and permitted settlement penetration far in advance of the general frontier line in central Ontario. The waterside settlement was based on permanent agriculture and lumbering, and associated processing activities; later seasonal settlement involved resorts and cottages.

Rural Landscape Heritage Tours

In the project Heritage Peterborough, we devised five driving tours around the county. They were ranked with the premier tour including the "Seven Wonders". These were the widely-recognized sites of cultural and natural heritage in the area, only two of which were in the city - Hydraulic Lift-Locks and Hutchison House.

• The rural five are: 1) Lakefield, 2) Curve Lake Reserve, 3) Peterborough Petroglyphs, 4) Lang Century Village, 5) Serpent Mounds.

• Three are aboriginal sites, two archaeological and one contemporary artistic; (federal plaque - **Petroglyphs**, provincial plaque - **Serpent Mounds**).

• Lakefield is an authentic site, a rural town with cultural-literary association, as well as socio-economic significance; (three provincial plaques - **Strickland, Moodie and Traill**).

• Lang Century Village is a centennial project of the County of Peterborough, the authentic living outdoor museum and associated archives; a central collection of preserved buildings and artifacts mainly of the agricultural economy; (federal plaque - **Fife Wheat**).

Other Tours

The four secondary tours radiate from the city and encompass the geographical and cultural/natural diversity of the county.

• **Holy Land** - euphemistically named for the Township of Ennismore, once entirely Irish Roman Catholic in ancestry, the tour crosses the agricultural area south of the Kawartha Lakes and enters the edge of the granite at Buckhorn before returning to the city via the Curve Lake Reserve.

• **Cavan "Blazers"** - named after the local Orangemen of the last century, the route crosses Cavan Bog, before becoming scenic near the north shore of Rice Lake. Millbrook village has unspoiled 19th century buildings reflecting a service entre and rail junction. Return via provincial plaque site - **"Joseph Scriven"**.

• **Stoney Lake** - follows the waterside through the Otonabee River Valley via River Road, past provincial plaque **"T. and F. Stewart"**, along the Trent Canal route and seven locks dating from 1860 to 1904. Lakefield precedes Young's Point and its C.P. Traill plaque - one of six federally-recognized sites. The tour circumnavigates Clear and Stoney Lakes and includes the Petroglyphs on Shield Marble (both federal and provincial designation) and landscape of the early resort and cottage, 120 years old in this area. Southwards, the tour reaches the natural heritage area of the Warsaw Caves. Nearby Warsaw village has interesting buildings and associated 1830s immigrant heritage. The tour returns via Warsaw Road and Douro hamlet, with Irish Roman Catholic streetscape and the renowned P.G. Towns and Sons General Store.

• **"Mysterious East"** - tour proceeds to Belmont Township with its mining heritage, notably Blairton's iron mine of the 1860s, then to Havelock, an 1880s CPR town with notable railwaymen's residences and a recycled caboose. West to Norwood with notable early buildings. Sinuous esker-route to Westwood, Villiers and unique octagonal square-log silo, Serpent Mounds and Lang.

Conclusion

The Peterborough County area was marginal for most of its history, lying off the main "corridor" of the Great Lakes and on major natural resource boundaries, or "edges" such as the "drift-granite" boundary, and the lake-river shore of the Otonabee watershed. Its heritage includes natural diversity, aboriginal artifacts on both drift and Shield, and agricultural, lumbering, mining, transportation and recreational "industrial" activity.

The challenge of recording the diversity of this heritage is great and has only just begun. Protection is therefore minimal and losses occur as we speak.

529 Homewood Ave

Ontario's Landscape Legacies: A Model for A Province-Wide Inventory

Nancy Pollock-Ellwand
Assistant Professor, School of Landscape Architecture, University of Guelph

Nancy holds a Master of Architecture degree from the University of Manitoba. She is currently Assistant Professor in the School of Landscape Architecture at the University of Guelph, teaching design theory and the history of the cultural form as well as conducting research into inventory systems for heritage cultural resources. Nancy's professional services include: advising the federal government in its initiative to begin a national registry of heritage landscapes across Canada; acting as a liaison between UNESCO's cultural body, the ICOMOS History Gardens Committee, and Canada's landscape heritage efforts. Future research will include the creation of an interactive computerized archive that depicts the "story" of an historic landscape - Parliament Hill.

ONTARIO IS LOSING A CULTURAL RESOURCE in the rural environment at an alarming rate. The resource is the historic landscape. The loss is occurring because of encroaching urban development. These lands are usually given up easily because the importance of historic landscapes is not understood by land owners, developers, policy makers and the general citizenry. Urban cases in point are the recent losses of historic lands at: the Rockwood Academy, Rockwood, Ontario; Parkwood Estate, Oshawa, Ontario; and the Gibson House, Toronto, Ontario. These historic landscape losses are also happening in the countryside; however, these occurrences are not as well-known because these sites tend to have a lower profile.

Ontario's precedent-setting 1990 document on heritage policy, "A Strategy for Conserving Ontario's Heritage" has called for an increased profile for historic landscapes. Critical to this increased profile is the commencement of a province-wide inventory. The Province of Ontario recognized the need for such an inventory in the same policy review document.

"...Many submissions recommended that the Province develop a comprehensive inventory or register of provincially signifi-

cant heritage resources. Such an instrument is seen as critical
to the overall planning and management of important heritage
resources. A register would allow the Province to identify pri-
orities, apply protective measures, and offer incentives for the
conservation of key properties or sites...While much has been
done in the natural heritage area, there are no comprehensive,
easily accessible inventories of culture heritage..." (Ontario
Ministry of Culture and Communications, 1990, p.57).

However, an inventory has yet to be commenced. There are many
reasons for this resistance, yet one can probably cite two major factors for it: the immense scope of such as undertaking; and the
accompanying costs of data collection. These are powerful deter-
rents considering the severe economic restraints being placed on
governments today.

Despite these realities of spending cuts and the constraints on
governmental agencies, an inventory of historic landscapes is still
urgently needed. This paper discusses a model of inventorying historic landscapes which is well-suited to the times we live - cost-effec-
tive and community driven.

The discussion will cover the mechanics of community involvement in the data collection phase - how to involve, inform and activate interested members of a given area. As well, the utility and efficiency of a personal computer for data storage, organization and
output will be illustrated. The concluding section of the paper will
discuss how one community is now undertaking this task of inventorying an important element of the rural historic landscape: roadside trees. It is very interesting that the first community group to
commit to this important inventory work is a rural-based group: the
Puslinch Roadside Heritage Tree Society. The activities of this group
are indicative of the growing concern of rural residents with the
sanctity of their rural environments, of which historic landscapes
are an important component. Conservation of roadside trees is an
important step in the overall protection of rural heritage, which in
turn is an essential part of Ontario's rich legacy of historic landscapes.

The Legacy of Historic Landscapes: A Definition

When attention was first focused on historic landscapes the view of
this resource was rather narrow. A reflection of this was the definition given by the joint committee of the International Council On
Monuments and Sites (ICOMOS) and the International Federation
of Landscape Architects (FLA) in 1971 at the Historic Garden
Symposium, Fontainbleau: "...a historic garden is an architectural

and horticultural composition of interest to the public from the historic and artistic point of view." (Buggey and Stewart, 1975). This definition excludes the landscapes which are not associated with any structure; the working landscape deemed "vernacular" by the U.S. National Register (Keller, J.T. and G.P., 1989); and the environments that could be anything other than a garden. Ten years later, the *Florence Charter* of the ICOMOS/Historic Gardens Committee still defined the landscape in terms of "gardens" and as "architectural and vegetal compositions". (ICOMOS, 1981).

The tying of landscapes to a structure seems to have dogged the definitions that were adopted in Canada over the years. The Province of Quebec in its *Macroinventaire* of historic properties focused on architectural and historic landscapes that were recognized only in association with these structures (Buggey 1987). Other provincial inventories are dominated by architectural information, i.e. Manitoba (Manitoba Culture, Heritage and Recreation, 1985), Saskatchewan and Alberta.

Broader definitions were established in the work of Robert Melnick's *Cultural Landscapes - Rural Districts in the National Park System* (Melnick, 1984), in which he defined a "cultural or historic landscape" as one that "interacts, over time, with the medium, of the natural landscape to finally result in the landscape we see and experience. Another way to say this is that the cultural landscape is a tangible manifestation of human actions and beliefs set against and within the natural landscape". One understands that historic landscapes differ from natural ones through their relationship with humankind.

Of late there has been a more definitive statement produced from a joint meeting of the Alliance for Historic Landscape Preservation and the US/ICOMOS Committee on Historic Gardens and Sites (June 1990), describing what it terms "historic landscapes". These definitions were part of a three-part resolution that went forward to the 1990 meeting of the International Committee on Historic Gardens and Sites (ICOMOS), in Lausanne, Switzerland. It was an effort to expand the scope of the definitions regarding historic landscapes in the various charters (i.e. Venice, Florence, etc.) the Committee has produced over the years. A subcommittee was struck on this issue for the next meeting in Padua, 1991 (American Society of Landscape Architects, 1991). The resolution stated that an historic landscape has some of the following attributes: outstanding example of an acknowledged type of land use; having exerted influence on the arts and design; bearing testimony to past land use; associated with an idea or event;and being associated with an historic structure. This was an encouraging development and it helped to reinforce the decision to use the broader definitions adopted for this study.

In fact, the definitions given for historic landscape types in the U.S. Parks Service *Bulletin #18*, were most instructive in the composition of landscape categories for the inventory study. The award-wining work by Douglas Paterson and Lise Colby in British Columbia was also very useful in defining terms with a more common touch (since their document was geared to public consumption). They simply called a "landscape" any environment that has been influential in the lives of humans, stating "The word "landscape" can include but implies more than the garden with its trees and shrubbery. It refers to the larger world, the scene in which we move, work and play" (Paterson and Colby, 1989). The drawback of this work however is that a very long list (16) of heritage landscapes types was generated. It was a comprehensive listing. However, for the public's understanding, the list should have been organized thematically in broader landscape categories with a number of sub-categories.

After a review of the literature from across the United States, Europe and Canada it was decided to adopt a plainer terminology for defining "historic landscapes", the reason being that this inventory must be rooted in the community. Therefore the terms used must be clear so the community understands and will be more inclined to assist in the effort. To reiterate, the definition of a "historic landscape" is "any place made special by past association with humankind". The landscape categories developed for this inventory are also simply defined through the types of association the landscape had with humankind. There are six broad categories with numerous possible sub-categories:

1. **Historical Event** - military encounter, sporting event.

2. **Historical Activity** - transportation route, institutional.

3. **People** - native sites, association with famous people.

4. **Design** - examples of outstanding design, styles or designers.

5. **Plants** - horticultural or agricultural examples of note from collections to single species.

6. **Human Dimensions** - landscapes that have influenced or inspired a response because of memorable views, environmental conditions.

Inventory Structure

1. Form Structure

i) *Visualization* - The historic landscape inventory forms which were reviewed seemed to contain almost exclusively textural information. They were surprisingly un-visual for a discipline like landscape architecture, that relies so much on graphic information. However, the historic architectural inventories observed tried to incorporate a variety of simple graphics to explain terms used for features being recorded. These visualized inventories, in the case of architectural resources, are necessitated by the fact that much of the data collection is being done by lay people. A case in point is the successful Volunteer Survey Program of the highly-visual *Canadian Inventory of Historic Buildings* (Environment Canada, 1987). Presumably no diagrams are necessary to explain landscape features, if the individual completing the inventory is conversant with the specialized terminology of landscape architecture. However the premise of the inventory is that the bulk of the information will be collected by volunteers from the general population. An easy to follow, visualized form was therefore required (Figure 1).

ii) *Intangibles* - Another aspect which appeared to be almost totally ignored in all inventory examples was attention to the intangibles. Landscapes are more than that which can be measured and identified. There are the qualities of the site which are immensely more difficult to document but which give a soul to a place ... the "spirit of place". Descriptions should be included in the inventory of the intangibles of atmosphere, sensual perceptions, memories invoked, and so on. Perhaps this is not best done with words alone. The capability is now within some computers to hold video images. Perhaps this will be a better way to capture the essence of a place. Segments of oral histories will also be another effective method of understanding how individuals truly react to a particular landscape.

iii) *Indexing* - Indexes on the reviewed systems seemed to be largely limited to retrieving information by a site's location and some landscape features, e.g. the National Trust's survey of tree types in Great Britain (Marshall, 1983). Less work seems to have been done in terms of organizing information in a thematic manner (e.g. picturesque examples). This type of broad indexing is possible with the type of software chosen for this inventory since it is equipped with an archival programme that will allow the storing and presenting of information in any manner the author chooses. It provides the devices so the users can define and design their own indexing system: be it by name, location, date, feature or theme.

2. Community-Based Data Collection

i) *Grass Roots* - The data collection on these heritage sites is dependent to a large part on volunteer community organizations and individuals. This strategy grows out of a concern for the excessive costs that would be incurred by large-scaled bureaucratic data collection. In addition another major concern when data are collected by a centralized body, like the federal government, is that the community is alienated from the process. Therefore, the all-important measure of the public's perception of what is a heritage site in their own district, is lost. As Andre Fortier said at the **Heritage in the 1990's Conference**, "Data and analyses produced by federal organizations lead a government action without benefit of a great deal of consultation at the grass-roots level. The result has been a tendency to favour heritage mega-projects that are developed, directed and run solely by public servants" (Ministry of Communications/Ministry of the Environment, 1990). Culture is not collected from a disembodied centralized power. Culture is the reflection of the people and its exact nature is peculiar to each community. This has been the difficulty in the past with heritage inventories, they have not on the whole been well-founded in the community. A grass-roots approach is assumed for this inventory.

ii) Phased Collection of Data - Another observation which was made about a number of inventories reviewed was that they seemed to favour a two-phase approach to collecting information on a historic site, e.g. the National Capital Commission's landscape inventory in Ottawa (Tresch, 1980), the *City of Syracuse Landscape Resources Survey* (Walmsley, 1989), and the British Columbia Guide (Paterson and Colby, 1989). All seem to agree that at least two visits to a heritage landscape are essential to get sufficient information on a site. The first form is usually a simple questionnaire that is aptly called the windshield or walk-over survey by the U.S. National Parks Service (Department of the Interior, September 29, 1983). On this form general information about the site would be given: location, ownership and occupancy, size, condition, and statement regarding the importance of the site in the scheme of things (be it local, regional or national). This first walk-over would be completed on a number of sites across the inventory area. This would provide a context of action from which detailed reconnaissance (as per the U.S. NPS) of a selected number of sites would be determined. The second form would include: type of site (eg. institutional, native site, etc); size;address; legal description; ownership/occupant chronology; current uses; history of site and features; condition of site and features; "heritage value" (based on differing factors of historical integrity, adjacent context, development pressures, etc.); information and archival sources; and sketched site plan.

This concept of generic scan of a study area followed by a more intensive survey on a select group of sites, was adopted for the inventory. In addition, a third form (Figure 2) was instituted for the purposes of an initial sweep within an inventory area. This brief questionnaire is directed to individuals and groups who would be likely sources of information on heritage landscapes in a particular community or region, e.g. historical societies, garden clubs, environmental activists, and so on.

From this initial survey of interested community members, volunteers are sought to complete the windshield surveys of their communities. A listing of sites (compiled from the initial sweep) is given to these volunteers, along with a brief one-page form that could be easily completed driving around on a Sunday afternoon (Figure 3). In this deductive manner, i.e. from general sweep to selected walk over, a listing of potential heritage landscapes will be developed that is as complete as possible. As was stated this method also ensures that the foundation of the inventory is well-established in the knowledge of locals in their community.

At that point, a few sites are highlighted for further, more detailed survey. The individuals completing the third form are volunteers trained in the basics of heritage landscape characteristics assisted by inventory staff. All this information in turn is submitted to the Inventory Centre located at the University of Guelph. The computer at the School of Landscape Architecture is capable of receiving facsimiled information directly into its system. Finally information is held in a lay back position in the computer to allow Inventory staff to double check the data for accuracy and completeness.

iii) *Promotional Campaign* - Inherent in all this data collection is the mounting of a successful promotional campaign aimed at alerting the public about the nature of this work and the absolute need to have them involved. There are a number of examples in Canada of heritage landscape inventories that were commenced but did not succeed because the support of both the heritage community and the community at large was not there.

Therefore part of the strategy of the Inventory is actively to spread the news of this work through the community. Advertisements have been taken out in professional magazines and community newspapers alike, soliciting information on potential sites. In addition, a five-minute video was prepared, called **Landscape Legacy**, to explain what is meant by a "historic landscape" and why information is being collected on them. This video accompanies Inventory workers to public lectures (eg. the Puslinch Historical Society, the Kitchener/Waterloo Garden Club and the Staff Association of the Royal Botanical Gardens, Hamilton) to aid in the explanation of this project. After the video is shown the general sweep questionnaire is handed out to ask if any of the audience members knows of the existence of a "historical landscape" in their community. This video was also created to stand by itself when Inventory staff are not available to lecture in remoter areas. In that case the video is sent to the community along with the questionnaires.

Lecturing, writing articles, and doing interviews for TV, radio and local press has been the approach the Inventory has adopted. Only as a last option will direct mailing be used since the success rate with that has been less than satisfying. "In 1983, when the Royal Botanical Gardens in Hamilton undertook to create such a national inventory of pre-1920 gardens of historical integrity, they received only 37 responses to their 300 letters" (Buggey, 1985).

iv) *Data Input* - The NeXT computer system was selected for this inventory for its ability (among many other factors) to receive facsimiled information directly into the machine. It can also transmit facsimiled material to other sources; all this via an Ethernet connection to other machines via a facsimile modem. The NeXT computer has a high resolution image, but it must be remembered that the quality of the images facsimiled is as good as the machine receiving the transmission at the other end. Once in the machine the hand-written or typed survey information can be left as is or can be translated into a standardized format by an Inventory staff member.

Visual images (such as historic and contemporary photographs; context mapping; and original planning documents) can be scanned directly with the equipment available if they are within a 8 1/2 x 11" (legal) limit for hard copy prints. Larger pieces or material that can not be released to the Inventory team (eg. archival holdings) will be either photographed or videotaped, in situ. High resolution black and white photographs are preferred because a black and white monitor was selected for this work (it was felt that one tends to gather more nuances from these black and white images with their multiple tones of gray). The machine can also receive images scanned from slides; digitized from a copy stand; or lifted from a High 8 videotape of the material (Bruce, 1991). These images will then be transported to the machine via a network connection or they will be placed on optical discs and fed into the machine. These images are held within the machine in a standard format called TIFF (Tagged Image File Format).

The scanning of material occurs at a new facility established at the University of Guelph, The Visualization Centre. This Centre is connected to the University-wide network and will be equipped with copy stands for digitizing images, scanners for slides and hard copy documents and videotaped manipulation facilities.

As to the resolution or quality of the images that are scanned and placed on the NeXT, a few comparisons may help. The comparisons are based on the number of dots across the screen. The NeXT is 1120 x 832, comparable to a Macintosh 2. Whereas the top of the line IBM Personal Computer is quoted at only 1024 x 768. For comparison, a high end video image is still only 756 x 486. The scanning at the Visualization Centre can in fact far exceed the capabilities of the NeXT, having a resolution of 4000 x 3000 dots on the screen (Bruce, 1991).

As for capture of audio clips into the machine, the computer system selected is also equipped with stereo sound. All that is required to collect the audio clips is to connect a microphone into the machine and activate the sound recording software that comes bundled with the machine. The software package MediaStation is then used to place the sound bit into the appropriate file.

3. Multi-Media Data Storage
i) *The Technology* - Inventory tends to deal with the content of surveys rather than the technology. Some examples of computerized inventories however were analyzed from: the United States and its *National Park Service Register* (Keller, J.T. & G.P., 1989); the UK's *National Trust Survey* (Marshall, 1983); and the *Canadian Inventory of Historic Buildings* (Environment Canada, revised 1987). In all cases the information held on the computers was textural, no image files or audio clips were stored on the sites. This three-mode or multi-media presentation of information has

been the thrust of this phase of the Southwest Ontario Inventory. As previously stated, researchers on this project decided to select a computer system that can mount a multi-media presentation, along with an archival software package capable of manipulating these different types of data. Multi-media presentations of information however are not unprecedented, as witnessed by the work of the federal Department of Communications and their "Medialog" project. As well, there are other interactive experiments being mounted by the Museum Consortium of the United States.

Through the use of this Inventory's computer and software, the user can access conventional written descriptions on a site along with scanned images (eg. historic photographs, plans, period correspondence) and pre-recorded oral histories. A fuller understanding of the site will be gained immediately. An example of the computer screen that organizes all these types of information is illustrated in Figure 4.

ii) *Storage Capability* - All this high-tech wizardry does have its costs in terms of the space these images and audio clips consume. "For example, a typical computer aided design drawing is between 400 Kb and 1 Mb in size" (Law and Perrin, December 1990/January 1991). The research team was very cognoscent of the storage implications of this work when the computing system was selected for this Inventory. This is why the *MediaStation 1.52* software was selected. It is equipped with an item called JPEG which stands for the Joint Photographic Experts Group. JEPG allows for the compression of photographic images, (the most consumptive in terms of storage space) to a ratio of 30:1. This means an image file that consumes 30 Mb of information can be compressed to 1 Mb with a minimal loss of resolution. One can only expect these compression limits to be pushed upward with further technical advances.

In addition to the compression of information, the Inventory computer is equipped with a sizeable hard disk drive, 660 Mb. Beyond that capability the computer will be connected to the university-wide network, a CD-ROM system, thus making the reserve for the Inventory a virtually unlimited one.

4. Dissemination of Data

i) *Output* - The true test of this prototypical inventory system will be if the information is readily available to users. It is envisioned that the information can be accessed in a variety of ways, all the way from direct computer linkages and facsimile transmissions to hard-copy printouts and periodic publications of the system's holdings.

Obviously output timing will be dependent on the mode of transmission selected. Direct link into the computing system will be the most desirable. Systems created at an earlier time suffer long delays. For example, the *Canadian Inventory of Historic Buildings* has computerized their files (text only), however the system is not on-line. This IBM main-frame has a time-sharing arrangement that operates through a computer service bureau. A request for information does not receive a response for 48 hours (Environment Canada, revised 1987). A direct computer link with the appropriate applications would rectify such a situation.

As for direct computer links, the technology of each machine determines the quality of the images seen and the audio heard, as well as the amount of information one can access. There are a number of machines on the market that do have the capabilities of this Inventory's machine (eg. Macintosh and Sun Corporation). Yet all machines with or without all these functions (i.e. no sound and/or visual capabilities) will be able to link to the Inventory via an Internet system, if one is available. Thousands of institutions are now on this computer communication network. Machines other than NeXT will have to write special applications to access information, which will enable them to "interact" because almost all computing systems now available use a common language called ASCI (Bruce, 1991).

ii) *Organization of Data* - The Inventory terminal or those linked with it will be able to call up a screen such as shown in Figure 6. The Inventory entry shown is for the fifth category of the inventory: plants. In this case the historic resource is the heritage roadside trees in a township located south of Guelph, Puslinch Township.

The Inventory's General Screen provides basic site information regarding its overall description; historical context; and further sources of information. On-screen buttons may be activated by double clicking over the information desired (i.e. context mapping, site plans or historic and extant images). A button for the narrative will activate pre-recorded oral histories. Pressing the Detailed Information button will bring the user down to a more detailed level of data. Here further information can be accessed as to the actual historical elements and extant conditions.

Inventory Case Study: Puslinch Township's Roadside Heritage Trees

A struggle is taking place within a rural township in southwestern Ontario. The conflict is about trees - roadside trees that were planted over a century ago. The trees form a gridiron framework for a cultural landscape of agricultural origins with cultivated, fenced fields, grazing livestock and historic stone houses. The players in this rural conflict are those who have reason to cut down these roadside trees - Ontario Hydro, the provincial Ministry of Transport and the municipal government's road crews; and those who oppose their destruction - the Puslinch Roadside Heritage Tree Society. An essential part of the strategy to save the roadside trees is to inventory these trees. One must know the resource if you are to know what and how to save it.

1) Evolution of Puslinch Township's Roadscape

Puslinch Township's gridiron pattern is a product of the British land survey method which was instituted in southwestern Ontario in 1783. (Scott, 179). The squared land divisions lead to the squared road allowances surrounding the property owner's holdings. As clearing of the land proceeded and settlers' minds turned to matters beyond basic survival, the trees began to appear along the roadways. These are the trees in question today.

Organization of the landscape was fundamentally influenced by the straight line geometry of the British surveyors. This pre-occupation for the straight line was further reinforced by the planting of roadside trees, from 1860-1880, in the then denuded landscape. (ibid., p. 187). Farmers primarily chose Sugar Maple (Acer saccharum) for these plantings because of their hardiness; flexibility for different soil types; and the tree's penchant for broad branching, which was useful to provide shade in the summer and to collect and deposit snow in the winter for sledge-based travel. In addition, there was the added bonus of maple syrup production and the brilliant autumnal colours. (ibid., p. 189).

> "Farmers dug "Acer Saccharum" from their remaining woodlots and transferred these to the roadsides where they were planted 12-20' on the centre edge of the 66' road allowance...." (ibid., p. 190).

Now this geometry stands at the heart of a cultural landscape the Puslinch environmentalists are struggling to save. The straight line is an obvious expression of an anthropocentric view of the universe. Everything in the landscape is subordinate to the surveyor's line moving on relentlessly across the landscape regardless of topography, water bodies and vegetation.

> "The straight line in the landscape... ordered by Caesar Augustus.. was not merely a statement of power in the wilderness, but the enormity of its contradiction to the natural forms is in fact a statement of our own abilities..." (Dwyer, p.9).

The result of this human-centred view of the world has been the evolution of a distinctive cultural landscape with mixed farming, cedar-fenced acreages, and tree-lined roadways. The roadside trees themselves resulted from a government grant programme of the mid-1800's. (Scott, p. 190). "This programme was widespread in the province to the point where, until the nineteen-forties almost every rural road in Southwestern Ontario was lined on both sides with maples." (ibid., p, 191).

The ethic which resulted in these Euro-cultural landscapes has proven to have another influence. These tree-lined historic landscapes are now greatly coveted by many and are one of the factors contributing to the urban exodus to the countryside. It is a trend that began in the late 1950's with the great urban intensification of the Southwestern Ontario region. Ironically, as interest increased on the part of these exurbanites in the countryside, less of their idealized concept of countryside survived. Later populations in Puslinch Township have increased the demand for many services, including electricity. The result of this demand is the upping of voltages and therefore the need for wider clearances along the hydro easements. These easements frequently run parallel to the roadways. Therefore to accommodate these enlarged widths many trees planted in the mid to late-1800s are being felled. In addition trees are being removed by municipal road crews in the aid of upgrading more heavily travelled roads in the Township.

The crisis in the cultural landscape of rural Ontario is as pronounced as the crisis in the natural landscape. It is changing dramatically with factory-like architecture and larger land divisions of corporate farming; severances enabling residential strip development; and the loss of roadside character with the removal of trees. It is the roadside component of the rural landscape which concerns the Puslinch group. The crisis for roadside trees is multi-faceted and complex with many actors involved. "Roadside trees have been removed, roads widened and re-surfaced, and ditches deepened and culverts installed." (Scott, p. 199). Engineering concerns have held sway and roadside trees have suffered. The cultural roadscape has been dramatically altered by power line easements and by road widenings to enable higher traffic speeds. These cherished cathedral-like enclosures have also been lost as new standards for road widths have pushed the replacement plantings further apart. As well, the effectiveness of this enclosure has been diluted by the modern spacing standards of 12 to 18 m (40'- 50') centres instead of the original 4 m to 6 m (12' - 20') centres (ibid. p. 200). Added to this is the impact of Ontario Hydro and the Municipality's replantings that often use hybridized material such as Norway Maples - trees that have compact heads and grow slowly. These trees serve the purposes of maintenance crews charged with their care in the future, but the elegant spreading habit will not be realized with these tree types.

2. Strategies of the Puslinch Roadside Heritage Tree Society
The Roadside Heritage Tree Society is changing attitudes in that Township. The group is working towards what Nietzsche called the "transvaluation of values"; producing change in social, legal, political and economic values. (Blackstone, p. 17). Through advocacy of their cause they are gathering members of the Township and surrounding townships to aid in the work of the Society.

A phenomenal amount of work has been completed by the Society to save their roadside trees. They have written tree by-laws, pressured politicians, started tree nurseries, planted trees and most recently instituted an inventory system for the roadside trees (through the support of the Ministry of the Environment's Environmental Youth Corps Programme). The efforts of the Society also extend into the community's schools, where members have taught children about the importance of roadside trees. The school children began a tree nursery in their playground and have been involved in roadside planting with the assistance of the Society. The Puslinch group have also gone beyond the Township's boundaries reaching out to adjacent regions to encourage them in their struggle to save their roadside vegetation.

3. Puslinch Inventory Structure
The structure of the inventory for Puslinch's roadside trees has been tailored specifically for their resource, being valued equally for its historic and natural significance. The inventory was created in conjunction with the Society's vice-president, Gord Miller, a forester by profession. The form (see Figure 5) was tested over the summer of 1992 through the field work of four students hired by the funds provided by the Ontario Ministry of Environment. The Inventory's methodology is a precedent-setting effort which can easily be adopted by other rural townships facing the same demise of their roadside trees. Moving from a fixed point in the field (usually the centre-line intersection of two roads) the survey sets out in an identified direction, noting the location of individual heritage trees (over 35 cm

diameter); their species; their vigour; and the location of the all-important hydro easement in relationship to the trees. The information is then fixed to a global grid of the Universal Transverse Mercator (UTM) coordinates; and then logged into a computer database (in this case, MacII with a spreadsheet software). Now established, tested and refined the inventory will be taken over by volunteers from the Township. It is admittedly a huge undertaking, since there are over 140 miles of roadway through the Township that could potentially represent 40,000 trees. By the end of the summer of 1992 it is estimated that over 25% of the trees would have been recorded. Although not fully completed, a solid base is in place for the inventory of this historic landscape resource.

Conclusion
Puslinch Township is only one example of community-driven conservation of an important cultural resource - the historic landscape. What lies ahead for the Inventory is to realize development in three areas:

1. *Volunteer System* - to refine the process of involving volunteers in the inventory. The Inventory looks forward to instituting a more comprehensive volunteer system modelled after the Canadian Inventory of Historic Sites' Volunteer Survey Plan (Environment Canada, revised 1987) and the National Trust's volunteer programme, complete with training manuals and instructional videos.

2. *Technical Advances* - The nature of using computers is that the desire will be there to upgrade systems as technology advances. The areas that will likely develop for the Southwestern Ontario Inventory are threefold: computer interfacing, storage capabilities, and the institution of full-motion video. Work on the interfacing of different computer types with the computer system selected for the Inventory will be dependent on consultation with a programming expert, who will write applications specific to each machine. Storage capabilities will be advanced with higher compression limits being developed for both software and hardware running systems. As for full-motion video capture of sites, computer simulations and interactive systems, that is all imminent with new developments in computer technology.

3. *Definition of Significance* - Finally, the work to date on the Inventory has been an uncritical collection of data on heritage landscapes. The next step therefore lies in clarifying what is significant and what is not, at local, provincial and federal levels.

Again the literature will help in this determination of significance. Much work has been done to date in Canada with such work as Kalman's *The Evaluation of Historic Buildings* and in the United States with its *Standards and Guidelines* publications. "All landscapes that possess age are not significant, and what is significant must be determined from its connection to the historic theme(s) it represents and in relationship to a group of similarly associated properties" (Keller, T.J. and G.P., 1989).

The gathering of information for Puslinch Township is a demonstration of the process that could be employed for collection, storage and dissemination of data for historic landscapes. With a proven system in place it is hoped that both provincial and federal governments will be more inclined to commence this much needed work across this vast and culturally-rich and diverse landscape called Canada.

List of Figures:

FIGURE 1:

Example page from the detailed survey of heritage landscapes for the Inventory.

Owner/s-
Original:_____
Chronology of Owner/s:_____
_____
_____

5.SITE SIZE (dimensions or area):_____

6. SITE STATUS (please circle appropriate description):

  Access:

  Unrestricted -- Controlled -- No Access

  Alterations from Original- On-Site:

  Unaltered -- Altered -- Added To -- Loss or Removal of Features --
  Boundaries or Features Encroached Upon

  Alterations from Original- Off-Site:

  Unaltered -- Altered -- Added To -- Loss or Removal of Features --
  Boundaries or Features Encroached Upon

  Public Acquisition:

  Under Consideration -- In Process of Acquisition -- Not Under Consideration --
  Acquired

  Site Condition:

  Excellent -- Good -- Fair -- Deteriorated -- Severely Deteriorated

7. SITE DESCRIPTION (please circle appropriate descriptions):

  Land Forms

Level	Concave	Convex	Combination

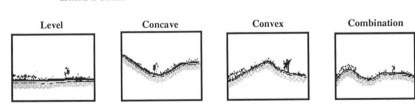

FIGURE 2:
Generalized questionnaire used by the Inventory for initial sweep of community.

Southwestern Ontario Cultural Heritage Landscape Inventory

The heritage found in the landscape around us is a valuable cultural resource that must be recognized. What constitutes a 'heritage landscape'? It is simply a landscape made special by past human associations. There will be a variety of landscapes considered for this Inventory, which can be broadly categorized as:

1. **Historical Event-** military encounter; sporting event.........

2. **Historical Activity-** transportation routes; institutional......

3. **People-** native sites; association with famous people.....

4. **Design-** examples of exemplary design, styles or designers.....

5. **Plants-** horticultural or agricultural examples of note from collections to single species....

6. **Human Dimensions-** landscapes that have influenced and inspired a response because of memorable views, environmental conditions.....

Please list any heritage landscapes you know about, giving their *location* and *historical associations* if possible. _____

_____

_____

_____

_____

_____

_____

Your name and contact number and address. _____

_____

Other people who may have information on heritage sites. _____

_____

_____

Please return this information to: S.W. Ontario Cultural Heritage Landscape Inventory

School of Landscape Architecture, University of Guelph
N1G 2W1   (519) 824-4120 Ext. 6577

FIGURE 3:
Brief survey to assist in windshield survey of heritage landscapes.

Public Acquisition:
Under Consideration -- In Process of Acquisition -- Not Under Consideration --
Acquired

Site Condition:
Excellent -- Good -- Fair -- Deteriorated -- Severely Deteriorated

6. LANDSCAPE RECORDED RELATED TO THE FOLLOWING:

Historic Event (please indicate time, place and story of the event):

_____

_____

Historic Activity (please indicate time, place and background of the
activity):_____

_____

Noted **Personality** or a group of **People** (please indicate any known
background):_____

_____

Exemplary **Design** (please indicate the designer, style or period site
may be associated):_____

_____

Outstanding **Plant** Collection (please indicate nature of the resource):

_____

Human Dimensions (please indicate any human interaction with the
landscape such as sacred or inspirational places):_____

_____

_____

                                              THANK YOU

FIGURE 4:

Example of computer screen for Inventory: General Screen - Plants: Puslinch Township heritage roadside trees.

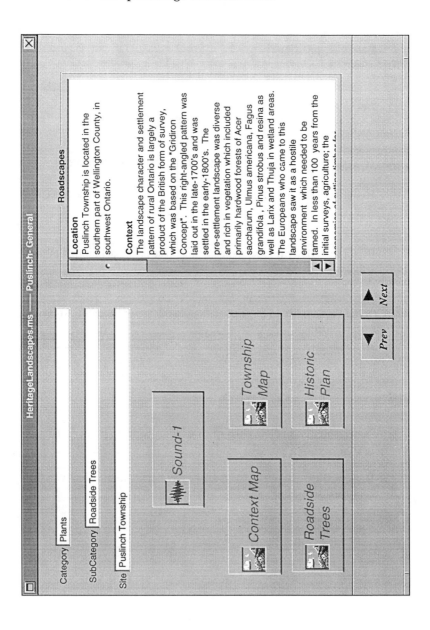

FIGURE 5:

Example of heritage roadside tree inventory field survey form.

SPECIMEN TREE INVENTORY   LOT and CONCESSION: DATE :

TREE NO	FIXED PT	DIST. (m)	UTM E. 565,	UTM N. 4,811,	SPECIES (CODE)	D.B.H. (cm)	CROWN (1-5)	PROBLEMS DIE.	PEEL	FUNGUS	SHAPE	ROOT	HRT ROT	INSECT	ADJACENT LAND USE	FENCE	NOTES:

Works Cited

American Society of Landscape Architects. "Historic Landscape Survey", National Survey Form.

____. Historic Preservation Open Committee. 1991. "Report on 1990 ICOMOS Meeting of the International Committee on Historic Gardens and Sites". Land and History. No.1 Vol.2, pp 2 & 5.

Barbour, Ian G. ed. 1973. "Western Man and Environmental Ethics: Attitudes Towards Nature and Technology". Addison-Wesley Publishing Co. Reading, Massachusetts.

Blackstone, William T. 1974. "Ethics and Ecology". Philosophy and Environmental Crisis. ed. Blackstone, William T. University of Georgia Press. Athens, Georgia, pp. 16-42.

Bruce, D. 1991. Conversations with Mr. Bruce, Senior Systems Analyst, Computing Services, University of Guelph.

Buggey, S. 8/9June, 1987. Report on the proceedings of the Canada/ICOMOS: Historic Landscapes Committee held in Montreal, Canada, p.1.

____ July, 1985. "Protection, Restoration and Interpretation of the Land". Paper presented to the Canadian Society of Landscape Architects, Saskatoon, Canada, p.8.

____ and Stewart, J. 1975. "Canada's Living Past: Historic Landscapes and Gardens", quoting from the proceedings of the joint meeting of the International Council on Monuments and Sites and the International Federation of Landscape Architects. 1971. Fontainebleau, France: ICOMOS. Historic Garden Symposium-Recommendations, p.1.

Canadian Environmental Advisory Council. 1987. "Canada and Sustainable Development." Minister of Supply and Services. Ottawa.

(The) Daily Mercury. July 19, 1990. "Going Out On A Limb, Group Aims To Save Roadside Trees." Guelph, Ontario.

____. July 20, 1990. "Saving Country Trees Lauded." Guelph, Ontario.

Dalibard, Jacques. 1991. "Our Environment is our Heritage." Momentum 1991: Heritage and Environment. ICOMOS-Canada. Ottawa, pp.6-7.

Dwyer, Gary. Summer 1984. "Honest Contextualism: A Discourse in Cowardice, Symbiosis and Humility." CELA Forum. Vol.1, No. 4. pp. 40-43.

Environment Canada, Parks. revised 1987. "Canadian Inventory of Historic Buildings: Guide." Architectural History Branch.

____. 1991. "Canadian Parks Service Proposed Policy." Environment Canada. Ottawa.

Frawley, Kevin. 1990. "Rural Cultural Landscapes; Some Unresolved Issues." Landscape Australia. Australian Institute of Landscape Architects. No. 1. Mont Albert, Australia, pp. 93-95.

Goodchild, P.H. May 1990. "Some Principles for the Conservation of Historic Landscapes"' Draft paper prepared for the UK/ICO-MOS: Historic Gardens & Landscape Committee.

Government of Canada.Minister of Supply and Services. 1990. "Canada's Green Plan." Ottawa.

____. Ministry of Communications/Ministry of the Environment. 1990. "Heritage in the 1990's - Towards a Government of Canada Strategy", Summary Report, Proceedings from a conference held in Edmonton, Canada, pp.3,4 & 11.

____. Ministry of Environment. 1979."Exterior Recording Training Manual". Canadian Inventory of Historic Buildings. Parks Canada.

Guelph Tribune. March 13, 1991. Editorial. Vol. 6, No. 11. Guelph, Ontario. pp.1.

Gunter, Pete A.Y. 1974. "The Big Thicket: A Case Study in Attitudes towards Environment". Philosophy and Environmental Crisis. ed. Blackstone, William T. Athens, University of Georgia Press, pp. 117-137.

Hiss, Tony. 1990. "The Experience of Place." Knopf Inc. New York, N.Y.

Historic Sites and Monuments Board of Canada. 1988. "Catalogue of Extant Buildings and Gardens with a Positive Recommendation by the HSMBC from 1919 to 1987". C.I.H.B. Section, Architectural History Branch. Volume 3. Ontario.

(The) Institute of Advanced Architectural Studies. February 1984. "Documenting a Garden's History". Centre for the Conservation of Historic Parks and Gardens. United Kingdom.

____. "Form 1: Site Recommendations" and "Form 2 : Site Report". Centre for the Conservation of Historic Parks and Gardens. United Kingdom.

ICOMOS/Historic Gardens Committee. 1981. "Florence Charter".
Hough, Michael. 1989. "City Form and Natural Process."
Routledge, New York.

Keller, J.T. and G.P. 1989. "How to Evaluate and Nominate
Designed Historic Landscapes". National Register Bulletin #18.
US. Department of the Interior, National Park Service,
Interagency Resources Division, pp.2 & 5.

Kitchener-Waterloo Record. July 23, 1990. Editorial. Kitchener,
Ontario.

Law, C.S. and Perrin, L.E. December 1990/January 1991. "Optical
Disk Technology: A New Natural Resource for Landscape
Architects". CD-ROM End User, pp.38 & 39.

Manitoba Culture, Heritage and Recreation. 1985. "Heritage
Building Inventory Form".

Marshall, J.M. 1983. "Computerization of Landscape Surveys". APT
Bulletin, Vol. XV, No. 4.

McHarg, Ian. 1973. "The Place of Nature In The City of Man."
Western Man and Environmental Ethics; Attitudes Towards
Nature and Technology. Addison-Wesley Publishing Co.
Reading, Massachuetts, pp. 171-186.

Melnick, R.Z. 1984. "Cultural Landscapes - Rural Historic Districts
in the National Park System". Washington: US National Park
Service, p.2.

(The) Municipality of the Township of Puslinch. Version January
29, 1992. "Draft Roadside Heritage Trees Model By-Law."

Norton, William. 1989. "Explorations in the Understanding of
Landscape: A Cultural Geography." Greenwood Press. New York,
N.Y.

Ontario Association of Landscape Architects. October, 1991. "Final
Report of the Tree By-Laws Advisory Committee." OALA News. p.5.

Ontario Hydro. "Keeping The Trees". Publication of the Agency.
Ontario Ministry of Culture and Communications. 1990. "A
Vision of Heritage: Heritage Goals for Ontario". Toronto:
Queen's Printer for Ontario, p.5.

____. 1990. "A Strategy for Conserving Ontario's Heritage: The
Report of the Ontario Heritage Policy Review". Toronto: Queen's
Printer for Ontario, pp.1 & 57.

Paterson, D.D. and Colby, L.J. 1989. "Heritage Landscapes in British Columbia: A Guide to Their Identification, Documentation, and Preservation". The Landscape Architect Program, The University of British Columbia, Canada.

(The) Puslinch Pioneer. 1990-Present. ed. Linda Craig. Puslinch, Ontario.

Puslinch Roadside Heritage Tree Society. 1990. Membership Form. September, 1991. "First Annual Report of the Roadside Heritage Trees Society." Newsletter No. 3.

St. John's Municipal Council. April, 1991. "The St. John's Tree Regulation." Municipal Council. St. John's, Newfoundland.

Scott, Owen R. 1979. "Utilizing History to Establish Cultural and Physical Identity in the Landscape". Landscape Planning. Elsvier Scientific Publishing Company. No.6. Amsterdam, pp. 179-203.

Steatfield, D. April 1969. "Standards for Historic Garden Preservation". Landscape Architecture, p.198.

Taylor, Ken. 1989. "Rural Cultural Landscapes: A Case for Heritage Interpretation, Conservation and Management". Landscape Australia. Australian Institute of Landscape Architects. No. 1. Mont Albert, Australia, pp.28-35.

Tresch, P.S. 1980. "Inventory of Period Landscapes and Features:. ASLA-OC Newsletter. Vol. 4, No.3, pp.12-15.

Toronto Star. June 29, 1990. "Citizens Demanding Protection of Private Trees." pp.2

University of Guelph, Winter 1990. "The 5000 Days: Environmental Prospectives and Human Choices". 58-20568, Course Manual, Guelph Distance Education. Guelph.

U.S. Department of the Interior, September 29, 1983. "Archaeology and Historic Preservation; Secretary of the Interior's Standards and Guidelines". Federal Register: Part IV. US National Park Service. pp.44724-25

____. 1990. "Guidelines for Evaluating and Documenting Rural Historic Landscapes." National Register Bulletin #30.

Walmsley and Co. Inc. April 1989. "Syracuse Historic Landscapes Resources Survey". Syracuse, New York. p.7.

(The) Wellington Advertiser. Monday, August 20, 19990. Guelph, Ontario.

White, Jr., Lynn. 1973. "The Historical Roots of Our Ecological Crisis". Western Man and Environmental Ethics; Attitudes Towards Nature and Technology. Reading, Massachuetts: Addison-Wesley Publishing Co. pp.18-30. (reprinted from, Science, March 10, 1967.Vol. 155. pp. 1203-1207. Copyrighted by the American Association for the Advancement of Science).

The Heritage Inventory of Uxbridge Township

Ian K. Woods
I.K. Woods & Partners Inc., Chartered Surveyors
A Fellow of the Royal Institution of Chartered Surveyors, Ian is the senior partner of I.K. Woods & Partners, Inc., Chartered Surveyors. Ian's project experience spans 32 years in 26 countries. His involvement with numerous heritage related projects covers a wide range and includes a Heritage Inventory of Uxbridge Township, forensic work for the 1892 Officer's Quarters in Penetanguishene, a preservation study of Gooderham and Worts Distillery, and over 1,700 Heritage Building Surveys across Ontario.

THE INVENTORY STARTED OUT AS JUST AN IDEA, following the reality of seeing years of destruction of the built heritage of the Province. Experience has shown that the attention given to a building or location is often frustrated by the lack of documented data, or has to be researched quickly on a panic basis to provide the decision makers with creditable, not fabricated information.

We have always considered that Built Heritage is only one factor of a Heritage Inventory or Register. Using some of the basic methodologies of the famous English Domesday Books, which were assembled by early Surveyors in the years around 1085, we created a detailed format which included everything except genealogy and archaeology. This inventory is very detailed and covers both past and present, Industrial, Commercial, Residential buildings and sites; as well as Natural, Engineering, Farming and Ecclesiastical sites and locations.

Our practice was commissioned in 1990 by the Township of Uxbridge to prepare a comprehensive Heritage Inventory of the Township, Town and Villages covering the time span from the First Nations to 1910. This is the first time this kind of in-depth inventory has ever been made in Canada, and represents the team effort of the Uxbridge Council, Uxbridge LACAC, the Scott Uxbridge Museum and ourselves. Uxbridge originally thought that there were around 300 locations, but it is likely that the number will exceed 2200! Carried out over a period of 21 months, the end result will be about a 16 to 20 volume set of books.

The four key elements of this large undertaking were:

1. Exhaustive Research:
Every available source was researched to establish the magnitude of the task, but information was still uncovered in the field work process.

2. Master Plan:
Dividing up the Township in manageable geographical areas and locations, as the Township is a modern combination of the old Uxbridge and Scott Townships both covering about 102,000 acres in land area.

3. The Field Work:
The physical site investigations and recording of found information. This frequently tested or expanded on the original research.

4. The Inventory Records:
It was decided after more research to confine each location to one double sided page. Side one would be data, with side two showing two coloured photographs each depicting two elevations of the Building. Some locations show copied old photographs of map layouts so the reader can compare these with modern photographs. Side two also shows final data, such as life expectancy, map/layout orientation and designation recommendations. Side one incorporates our own grading system which identifies the importance of the location.

The inventory uses a complex coding system, but is very simple to modify. It also combines a wealth of historical information within its pages. It has however, revealed the many usual gaps in the information available for heritage purposes, yet allows and encourages the citizens and Heritage Uxbridge to see their enormous heritage wealth, and add to the information already found.

We believe that we have established a wide ranging Inventory foundation which both the present and future generations can use and enlarge upon.

While the Inventory sets a very high standard for this type of record, it has been the result of combined enthusiasm and efforts of the Uxbridge Heritage "Team" which has made it work.

Rural Heritage Conservation Districts - A Case Study of Rainham Township

David McClung

HERITAGE HALDIMAND STUDIED A PART of Rainham Township for designation as a Heritage Conservation District under Part V of the Ontario Heritage Act in 1990-91. This was the first study of its kind for a rural area in Ontario. The district selected for study included nine Mennonite farmsteads, a tannery, a Mennonite church, a cemetery, the site of a one-room school house, and a native archaeological site, along with 1,200 acres of cleared farmland, 500 acres of forest, and a section of undeveloped Lake Erie shoreline.

The basic settlement pattern within the district has remained unchanged since it matured in 1860. It is of great interest for several reasons. First, the unusual shape and size of the parcels result from a major error in the original township survey. Lots intended to contain 100 acres in fact contained as many as 330 acres. In addition, farmsteads and other facilities were located in response to cues in the natural environment rather than in response to the survey: farmhouses were built over springs to provide indoor running water; church and school were located in forest clearings to shelter them from powerful Lake Erie winds. Finally, the settlement pattern illustrates patterns of contacts between the Mennonite settlers, Americans from across the lake, and the local native population.

The oldest house in the district was built in 1823, the newest in 1917. The houses were built in a variety of local materials - plank, timber frame, brick, balloon framing and brick veneer, and poured concrete - and all are of types clearly derived from German and Pennsylvanian antecedents: the continental log house, the Pennsylvania four-over-four, and the Rainham-South Cayuga two-door house. The oldest and newest barns date from the 1840s and the 1930s, respectively.

Despite its historic and architectural importance, the area studied was found to be in a state of serious decay. Several of the houses were vacant; others were only partially occupied; and the heritage value of another had been severely compromised by recent alterations. More than half of the barns had fallen totally out of use. Soil and water degradation and forest depletion were also all evident.

The total population had fallen far below historical levels and was made up mostly of elderly people with modest levels of income and education. In fact, this state of decline was one of the main reasons for pursuing the designation of the district in the first place. It was hoped that designation would generate interest in the area, that architectural conservation grants might encourage rehabilitation, and that a relaxing of the strict agricultural zoning would allow farm families to increase and diversify their incomes through small, farm-based tourism initiatives.

While the majority of landowners favoured designation, several objected on three main grounds. First, there was the question of the effect designation would have on residential severances, a major source of income for cash-strapped farmers. One non-resident speculator also feared designation would hinder his plans for a lakeshore estate residential development. The second objection came from active farmers who feared they would be saddled with a collection of obsolete farm buildings they could not afford to keep up and would not be allowed to modernize or tear down. Finally, there was the predictable and not entirely unjustified concern about unnecessary government interference with private property.

In addition to the objections of some landowners, the effort to have the district designated was hampered by the inherent limitations of Part V of the Ontario Heritage Act. Although the area was 99% open space, and the open space was essential to the character of the district, Part V deals only with buildings. Therefore, it presumably could not be used to deal with rural landscape resources such as lanes, fencerows, orchards, and forests, all elements crucial to the character of the district.

Moreover, Part V deals only with the exteriors of buildings. In this case, all of the buildings are just as important for their interiors as for their exteriors, for the interiors communicate much more about the early inhabitants' way of life. Finally, the administrative structure that the designation and management of the area as a Heritage Conservation District would necessitate might prove quite onerous to a small rural municipality and frustrating for harried farmers to deal with.

Therefore Heritage Haldimand is not at this time pursuing the designation of the district under Part V of the Ontario Heritage Act. Rather, it is seeking a different type of protection through the application of a new type of zoning known as "Environmental Protection". It is hoped this new type of zoning will effectively protect some of the district's more important heritage features while at the same time removing some of the restrictions the current "Agricultural" zoning places on the establishment of viable economic enterprises that are complementary to, but different from, agriculture.

Although neither the designation nor the new zoning is yet in place, the attention focused on the area through the study has already resulted in repairs to two houses and one barn whose owners had previously become discouraged by the burden of maintaining essentially empty buildings. It has also resulted in the sale of one badly neglected property to enthusiastic new owners who have already invested in a number of heritage-friendly improvements with the guidance and advice of Heritage Haldimand. With continued attention and effort, this interesting rural Ontario landscape may yet be preserved.

525 Homewood Ave.

Recreation
and Tourism
Heritage

The Bigwin Inn

Douglas McTaggart
Author
> *Douglas was born in Toronto and grew up in the valley known as Hogg's Hollow. Continuing a tradition established in the 1930s by his great grandmother, his family made weekly excursions to the Lake of Bays during the summer months. In later years, Douglas studied history and economics at the University of Cambridge, England, and subsequently graduated from the Florida Atlantic University at Boca Raton with a Bachelor of Arts degree in Political Science. Today, he is a federal public servant with the Canadian government.*

IT IS A PLEASURE TO HAVE THE OPPORTUNITY to discuss the protection of historic recreation buildings and landscapes. In the following pages, I will introduce you to a colourful story, a microcosm of Canada's environmental, archaeological and architectural heritage. We will tour Bigwin Island and the now defunct Bigwin Inn - once the largest summer resort in the British Commonwealth. After inspecting the site and noting its present condition, I will be mentioning some recent proposals which advocate both redevelopment and new development on Bigwin Island. To begin with, I would like to discuss very briefly a few aspects of the island's historical background as they pertain to the original development of this grand old resort.

Historical Background
Located approximately 180 miles north of Toronto, amid the scenic beauty of Muskoka, is the beautiful Lake of Bays. Largest island on the lake, 500 acre Bigwin Island is named after Ojibway Chief Joseph Big Wind. It was here that he and his people established a summer settlement and several native burial grounds.

By the late 1800s, a tourism industry had been established on the Lake of Bays. To capitalize on the increasing popularity of the wilderness vacation, a gentleman by the name of C. O. Shaw conceived of building an island resort. In 1911, he acquired Bigwin Island and shortly thereafter retained Simcoe county architect John Wilson to design his new hotel.

Site and Layout
Reassessing the plans of traditional summer resorts, Wilson concluded that the wide variety of activities of a large cosmopolitan

summer hotel should not be all under one roof and that the layout of the buildings should be spacious in every respect.

At first glance, the layout of the hotel complex may appear to be relatively simple, almost random. To the contrary, Wilson's conceptualization went through many revisions in its deliberate attempt to surpass mere functionality.

Occupying various sites along the natural curve of the shoreline and in the wooded forest immediately behind, Wilson positioned each building to form a series of aesthetic relationships with one another. Instead of forming structural barriers against the environment, Wilson embraced the natural surroundings of Bigwin Island integrating them with the layout of the buildings. Accordingly, the layout tied itself to a fundamental part of the Canadian identity, the natural landscape. Bigwin Inn was a hotel at one with nature, in perfect harmony with its site.

To that end, Wilson advocated a close relationship between landscape, layout, design and the materials used in construction. His extensive use of natural materials, particularly wood and stone, symbolically linked the art of architecture with the surroundings of Bigwin Island. The hotel took on organic qualities.

At the same time, paradoxically, Wilson attempted to master nature. To overcome the risk of fire, a fate which had consumed many of the frame hotels of the day, Wilson used reinforced concrete as his primary building material. Billed as fireproof, Bigwin Inn was the perfect embodiment of an era of self-assured security.

Soon after the designs were completed, construction of the colossal project began. With delays resulting from World War I, it was almost a decade before Wilson's elaborate drawings materialized into structures of plumb and level lines. Within those years, however, glass, wood, stone, steel and concrete were transformed into the eclectic architecture of the Bigwin Inn, a powerful masterpiece compounded out of numerous parts into one harmonious whole, form following function.

Offering its patrons an unsurpassed array of entertainment and recreational facilities, Bigwin Inn opened its doors on June 26, 1920.

Norway Point and the Steamer Bigwin

For guests, holidays often began at Bigwin Inn's mainland docking facility, Norway Point. Here, automobiles were parked on the lot and steamer tickets purchased from a purser's office for the ten-minute cruise over to the island. Other structures surviving at Norway Point include Bigwin's mainland riding stable and a frame baggage room.

These buildings are in relatively good condition today requiring glass panes, new shingles, wood fascia and fresh paint to stabilize their present condition.

Built by the Polson Iron Works of Toronto, the 66-foot steam screw yacht Bigwin ferried guests from the dock at Norway Point to the Bigwin Island steamer wharf. Although denuded of many of her original appointments, the 83 year old oaken-hulled vessel is in a rare state of preservation. Encrusted with a rich patina, the boat survives as an important part of the country's nautical heritage.

The Covered Walks

Constructed by German P.O.W.s of the Great War, a network of covered walkways linked the steamer wharf on Bigwin Island to the formal entrances of the resort's main buildings.

Although some need realignment, most of the walkways are in fair condition today requiring some roof repairs and weather proofing of their cedar components.

The Rotunda

Upon arrival, guests were escorted beneath the covered walks to the main reception building, the Rotunda.

Broad verandas surround the Rotunda's main floor on three sides and were designed by the architect to eliminate visual and psychological barriers between indoors and out, thus uniting the two in harmony.

From various points on the verandah, richly furnished wood doors open to reveal massive stone hearths. Offering a visual symphony of natural forms, some have stone armchairs, built into them on the hearth side with benches, pedestals or urns built on the exterior.

A building of baronial proportion, the interior space of the Rotunda was one of John Wilson's master strokes. Below a heavily beamed and raftered ceiling, the edifice features a gallery and an expansive hall known as the Great Lounge. Here, room partitions were dissolved into one great flowing space. Among those registering at the Rotunda's front desk were Gordon Sinclair, Clark Gable, Carol Lombard and Prime Minister John Diefenbaker.

Considering its age and the fact that virtually no maintenance has occurred for over twenty years, the Rotunda is in relatively good condition today and exhibits no apparent differential settlement. However, there are some leaks in the roof and most floor joists are damp. If left unchecked, they may soon fall victim to decay.

The East and West Lodges

Guest sleeping accommodation at Bigwin Inn consisted of two lodges, one to the east and one to the west of the Rotunda. Inside, each of the three storey lodges measured over 55,000 square feet and contained 142 private rooms.

Today, the East Lodge is set aside as a separate property from the resort property and is occupied by condominium owners. As a result of a virtually fruitless renovation project twenty years ago, the West Lodge has been abandoned, its interior stripped of plumbing, electrical and decorative carpentry work. For the time being, the building is in good structural condition, the concrete foundation and walls sound.

The Juliana Cottages

Sited on a flat plateau, the stone bungalows of the Bigwin Inn Cottage Colony were designed by John Wilson in a Prairie style, typified by long horizontal lines, low proportions and quiet skylines.

Once the summer retreat of Crown Princess Juliana of the Netherlands, the cottages are in excellent condition today, each privately owned and maintained.

The Tea House

Built in 1929, a 4,000 square foot dodecagon tea house boasts an interior finished with a ceramic floor, two fireplaces and vaulted ceiling.

The concrete foundation, masonry walls and roof are in excellent condition today requiring only reshingling and replacement of wood fascia to preserve its structural integrity.

The Dining Room Complex

The concrete dining room complex contains three main parts: a two-storey dodecagon containing the main dining room, a smaller one containing the marine dining room, and behind, a multi-level service wing.

Equally important to the design of the building, and a great part of its substance, is the space that the walls of the building define.

To complement the interiors, Wilson manipulated the use of natural light with placement of fireplaces, doors and windows. Embodying various qualities of organic architecture, gallery windows, french doors and a clerestory around the perimeter of the room amplify the interior space, visually bringing in the outside environment. Visitors dining amid the elegance of the room included Joseph Atkinson, President of the Toronto Star, film star Franchot Tone, writers Greg Clark and Ernest Hemingway.

With Roman archways and lattice balconies framing beautiful views of the island forest and Lake of Bays, an arcade serves as an intermediary between the interior space and outside environment.

Adjoining the main dining room, the marine room was designed in a similarly grand fashion. Below, a large room known as the Casino functioned as both a cinema and lounge.

Today, the dining complex is in varying states of condition. The stucco veneer on the exterior walls has deteriorated but the concrete walls themselves show minimal cracking and no apparent differential settlement. While the concrete floors of the kitchen and lounge are in excellent condition, moisture has caused deterioration in the wooden boards and joists of the dining room floors. The steel reinforced roofs of the dining rooms are sound but the flat roof of the terrace suffers from considerable deterioration. With failure in some of its wooden components, areas of the ceiling have collapsed and the floor below is now subject to water shed from the pitched roof.

Boat Livery

Located further along the shoreline, a two-storey gabled building housed storage facilities for the resort's boat livery.

The concrete foundation and walls of the livery are apparently sound and exhibit no apparent differential settlement. The roof requires replacement of some of its shingles, eaves and fascia.

Pavilion

Located next to the Livery is the Pavilion. Massive in size, it provides a sense of architectural drama in keeping with the dining complex. Cantilevered over the water, the structure provides sheltered slips below. Above, the Pavilion's fir walls feature detailed woodwork, including ornamental railings which incorporate the design of the Union Jack.

Inside, the room was used for various functions including the fourth Commonwealth Conference held in 1949. The Pavilion also hosted many great international entertaining talents including Herbert L. Clark, Count Basie, Duke Ellington, Art Hallman, Ellis McLintock, Gisele Lafleche Mackenzie, Guy Lombardo and Mohawk bass-baritone Os-Ke-Non-Ton.

Subjected to years of wave and ice action, the concrete piers on which the building rests require repairs and in some areas resetting. The frame structure itself demands some adjustments to compensate for settlement. To prevent further structural deterioration, the roof shingles, fascia and some eaves should be replaced and all wooden surfaces of the structure weatherproofed.

The Tower

On the highest point of the island, a concrete observation tower rises from the forest floor. From the observation deck, spectators could enjoy breathtaking views of the Inn and its setting, a vast wilderness of primeval forests and wind-swept waters. It was this view of the Canadian landscape that Group of Seven member Franklin Carmichael captured on canvas in 1927.

With some spalding around its base, the tower is showing signs of age. The concrete structure appears to be sound with minimal repair work being required in order to arrest deterioration.

The Golfcourse and Golf Clubhouse

Built under the supervision of Stanley Thompson, a noted landscape architect, the hotel's golfcourse opened in 1922. By 1930, a clubhouse had been erected and 18 holes were in play. Recognizing man's ability to radically alter the landscape, the course was carefully designed to preserve the environmental heritage of the island and the archaeological heritage of its First Nation burial grounds.

Today, twenty two years after the course closed, the facilities only remotely resemble their former stature. The golfcourse is in a state of natural regeneration. While the roof and second storey of the clubhouse have been removed, the first storey walls and foundation are sound and could conceivably serve as the foundation for a restoration project.

Other structures located in close proximity to the golfcourse include a log shanty, stone stables, a 3,000 foot concrete airstrip and staff dormitories.

The men's staff camp was deserted in 1960, ten years prior to the abandonment of most of the Inn's other structures. Having drifted into oblivion, deterioration in the wood components has led to structural failure of the roof. Of similar vintage as the resort's other concrete buildings, the staff quarters are a graphic demonstration of what the future may hold for other structures on the island.

The Future

The future of Muskoka itself is in question. Over the last few years, the Muskoka area has been subjected to a relentless revision of the natural landscape and built environment. Sprawling across the countryside, massive development projects have all too often compromised the integrity of environmental and architectural heritage sites. Collectively, such projects are rapidly transforming vast areas of the region into harsh, urban settings overwhelming in scale.

In 1990, local publications raised the profile of Bigwin, suggesting the possibility of new residential development around the perimeter of the island, residential development on the island's interior lots, as well as potential rehabilitation of a golf course, Tea House and Rotunda. They noted that development was temporarily restricted to existing uses by an interim bylaw and that only limited expansion of these uses was permitted until various assessments (including engineering, biophysical, limnological, landscape, visual, land use and financial studies) were completed by Bigwin Resort and Development Corporation and R.A.P. Trading Corporation who control the majority of the old resort property, the Township of Lake of Bays and other stakeholders.

In conclusion, Bigwin Island is a rare microcosm of Canada's environmental, archaeological and architectural heritage. The ultimate destiny of this landmark is yet to be determined. If the great legacy of Bigwin is to survive as testimony to an important part of the Canadian identity, the landmark demands immediate protection against the implications of an ill-defined future.

494 Gilmour Street

The "Chateau" at Wanapitei on Lake Temagami

Bruce and Carol Hodgins
The parents of Bruce Hodgins acquired Camp Wanapitei and the Wanapetei Chateau in 1956. Carol Hodgins, a physiotherapist and an author of material on wilderness cooking and trip equipment, is currently the Manager of the Wanapetei chateau. Bruce Hodgins joined the Trent University faculty in 1965 and is Professor of History. Between 1986 and 1992, he was the Director of Trent's Frost Centre for Canadian Heritage and Development Studies. Since 1971, he has also been President of Camp Wanapitei Coed Camps Ltd. He is co-author (with Jamie Benidickson) The Temagami Experience: Recreations, Resources, and the Aboriginal Rights with Northern Ontario Wilderness (Toronto, 1989).

IN 1991, AFTER A FAIRLY LENGTHY STRUGGLE, we secured for the Wanapitei Chateau, constructed of logs in 1933, official Building Designation under the Ontario Heritage Act. Following this, in 1992, we secured a Rehabilitation Grant from the Ministry of Culture and Communication. Much restoration and reclamation work had already begun in 1989; now we will speed things up, over the next few years, as the building continues to be used as a small wilderness recreational and conference lodge in association with the Wanapitei Wilderness Centre and Youth Camp.

Captain Ed Archibald, in 1931, established Camp Wanapitei by the remote northern inlet (Red Squirrel River) of Lake Temagami. The core log buildings for the camp were constructed by the Maki family, recent immigrants from Finland who lived on the site over several winters. In 1933-34, the Makis constructed the Chateau for adult lodge accommodation. It has been in (non-winter) use ever since. In its middle decades, it served primarily as accommodation for fishing and hunting groups. In 1956, it was acquired by Stanley and Laura Belle Hodgins. In the seventies and early eighties, its condition deteriorated severely. We acquired control in 1988. Recently, it has been used as accommodation for parents visiting the youth camp, for family groups, small conferences, and university seminar retreats, and for adult canoe trippers before and after their voyages.

The building was constructed in the Finnish, chinkless style with each log being scribed and coped so that it exactly fits on the one beneath it; the principal tool used for this was a two-handed draw knife. Except for the heavy-planked pine floor in the downstairs main lounge and for the two massive white pine beams which support the upper floor, the building was erected entirely from local poplar. The plan of the Chateau follows the shape of a cross with the primary but shorter axis being formed by a grand entrance veranda facing west, with a balcony above, and a central lounge area anchored by a magnificent stone hearth. The secondary axis is created by flanking pairs of bedrooms, on both floors, all of which open onto full width porches or balconies.

A rather unique feature of this Designation is that the Wanapitei Chateau is north of the counties and outside of any municipality, a fact which many believed would bar it from consideration. The Act requires official local endorsement. Wanapitei exists without road access, without Ontario Hydro, and with only a radio phone (since 1977) as communication with the outside. There is, of course, no LACAC.

Success required persistent effort and the enthusiastic support of Mary Lou Evans, the provincial LACAC Advisor, Fred Cane, Conservation Officer with the Heritage Branch of the Ministry of Culture and Communication, who visited the site, and Tamara Anson-Cartwright also of the Ministry. We used the joint Temagami Planning Board as our local authority. This Board bridges the organized Township of Temagami and the unorganized Islands of Lake Temagami and its three mainland patented holdings including Wanapitei. The Board ultimately approved the Designation and passed the enabling bylaw. The required detailed inspection and report by a professional heritage architect, while costly, was both legally necessary and extremely useful to us; Andre Scheinman's overnight visit was thus essential for the future of the project. Although in late 1991, we were told by the Ontario Heritage Foundation that despite our successful Designation, the cupboard was bare, we learned in February 1992 that an equal Rehabilitation Grant from the Ministry was indeed available.

The broader significance of this victory is that relatively remote recreational properties in northern Shield country, that are of architectural significance, but only modestly over the 50-year minimum age limit, can be designated. Presumably, in our case, this was because the Chateau is a distinguished poplar log building that is one of the oldest continually-used summer lodges in Northern Ontario and because of the multicultural element involved in the Finnish construction and style.

The Chippewa Park Carousel, Thunder Bay, Ontario

Michele Proulx
Thunder Bay Community, Recreational and Parks Division
  Michele worked for a number of years as a contract researcher in the Planning and Policy section of the Thunder Bay Parks and Recreation Department. Michele is at present a graduate student in the Frost Centre for Canadian Heritage and Development Studies at Trent University and is writing her thesis on the cultural landscapes of older urban parks.

Background Information

The Chippewa Park Carousel has brought joy and excitement to countless numbers of children and adults since it was purchased from Mrs. Maude King of Fort Erie, Ontario, on June 21, 1934. The Fort William Parks Board bought the carousel for $583.33 when Mrs. King's travelling carnival went into bankruptcy while operating at Chippewa Park.

The Chippewa Park Carousel represents a living fragment of simpler times gone by; it is one of fewer than two hundred intact hand carved wooden carousels still functioning out of an estimated eight thousand produced during the golden age of carousels.

The Chippewa Park Carousel is a two-abreast 'County Fair' model, designed to be dismantled frequently and transported by train or horse-drawn wagon from town to town. No one can know where the carousel travelled between the time of its construction (some time between 1918 and 1920) and its purchase by the City of Fort William in the mid-thirties.

The knowledge of the historic and artistic significance of the carousel had been evolving for some time. It was during a visit of representatives from the Royal Ontario Museum in November of 1987 that the awareness of the intrinsic and economic value of the carousel became heightened. Although visiting for other reasons, the comments of the ROM representatives spurred Department staff on to evaluate the situation. This led to the preliminary consideration of a display of Chippewa Park's carousel animals by the Thunder Bay Art Gallery. The gallery's director, while expressing interest in a carousel exhibit, also acknowledged concern for the carousel's security and conservation as well as the pressing need to authenticate the carousel.

Further carousel research involved contacting the Director of Parks for the City of St. Catharines who overviewed that community's restoration efforts with their three-abreast Dentzel carousel. A contact for the American Carousel Association was thus obtained.

The American Carousel Association's Conservation Chairman, Charles Walker, was contacted by phone in early January 1988. Subsequent correspondence with Mr Walker established the Chippewa Park carousel's identity as a C.W. Parker carousel and one of only three similar carousels known to exist. Mr. Walker also referred the Department to Mr. Frederick Fried, the foremost authority on American three-dimensional folk art, in order to arrange for authentification of the Chippewa park carousel.

Frederick Fried visited Thunder Bay in June of 1988. He spoke about carousels with the Parks and Recreation Department staff and with interested members of the community. Mr. Fried's assessment and valuation of the Chippewa Park carousel represents the basis of the city's commitment to the better protection and continued operation of our carousel. In the words of Frederick Fried, carousels are "the original form of the mobile, containing all of its elements; painting on the rims, wooden sculpture, motion and music" (Fried, 1988).

General History of the Carousel
The Carousel, as we know it today, boasts a long and illustrious history. Its oldest and simplest form comes to us by way of a Byzantine bas-relief circa 500 A.D., where carousel riders, clinging to the end of ropes, were spun around a turning centre pole (Fraley & Sinick, 1987, 7). The Italian 'carosello' or 'carosella' or 'garosello' translates as 'little war' and refers to an Arabian game adopted by the Spanish crusaders and carried throughout Europe in the 17th century. This was a contest between skilled horsemen with the objective of catching small clay balls containing scented oil; unsuccessful contestants were "enveloped in the 'smell of defeat'" (Manns & Shank, 1986, 9).

By mid-seventeenth century, the French Royal Court was holding an event called the 'carrousel'; these pageants involved skilled horsemanship wherein knights contested their skills with the scented clay balls as well as in attempts to spear a gold ring with a lance while riding at full gallop (Manns & Shank, 9). The most famous and enduring of these events was 'Le Grand Carrousel' of June 5 and 6, 1662 held by Louis XIV to impress his teenaged mistress Louise de la Valliere (Fried, 1964, 18). Le Grand Carrousel was held in a square between the Tuilleries and the Louvre, still referred to as the 'Place du Carrousel': "saddle makers, tailors, wigmakers and jewellers concocted extravagant creations for both horse and rider participating in an event that resembled a midday gala rather than a 'little war'" (Manns & Shank, 9). This day time fancy-dress ball, which involved a circular parade upon ornately decorated horses, most certainly influenced the fancifully carved trappings of carousel horses two hundred years later (Fried, 1988).

By 1680, the French had developed a mechanical carousel that was used as a training device for the ring spearing tournament. Carved horses and chariots were suspended from beams that radiated from a central pole; a horse, a mule or a man supplied the locomotion (Fried, 1964, 19). Riders sat on the horses and tried to spear a ring that hung just outside the perimeter; this soon became generally popular and spread throughout Europe (Fraley & Sinick, 8).

In 1832, a crank drive carousel was developed both in France and in England; a handle was attached to a set of gears connected to the centre pole. The faster the crank was turned, the more swiftly the carousel rotated. In the words of Frederick Fried: "The French had provided the name, developed the carousels introduced by the Turks, and added the brass rings to the mechanical ride. They then brought it to the highest stage in which it could be driven by man or beast. It was the English who provided the tremendous stimulus which advanced the carousel into a new epoch" (30).

In 1870, an Englishman by the name of Frederick Savage mounted a small steam engine on wheels, fitted a series of wheels into a 'cheese wheel' into which were fitted radiating beams called 'sweeps' (Fried, 31). This rotating frame supported various types of seats for riders and allowed for both an increase in the weight a carousel could hold and an increase in its size (Fried, 31-33). Savage also designed and patented the overhead cranking device that produced the up and down motion for the carousel horses - the 'jumpers' or the 'gallopers' (Fried, 31).

Historical records attest to the presence of the carousel on North American soil as early as 1825, but these crude 'Flying Horses' were constructed by wheelwrights and farmers in their spare time (Fried, 51-52). The first person to successfully establish the manufacture and distribution of the carousel was Gustav Dentzel, the son of a German cabinetmaker and carousel builder, who arrived, alone, in Philadelphia in 1860. Gustav built his first simple bench-seat, horse-powered carousel in the late 1860s. With its positive reception he established his factory and began to produce and operate carousels (Fried, 52). Thus began what is known as the golden age of the carousel.

Contemporary North American Styles of Carousels

There were three general styles of carousel constructed in the United States of America between 1870 and 1930. The Philadelphia Style was established in the 1870s by Gustav Dentzel. It is characterized by realistic but colourful horses and menagerie animals (giraffes, zebras, rosters, lions, tigers, bears, ostriches, camels, rabbits, cats, dogs, frogs, goats, elk, elephants and hippocampi) that graced the large, lavish, three and four-abreast stationary carousels built for amusement parks, seaside resorts and other countries (Fried, 58; Manns & Shank, 19).

The Coney Island style was pioneered by Charles I.D. Looff of Brooklyn, New York, who built his first carousel for the Coney Island seaside resort in 1876. The style is characterized by flamboyance; very flashy and highly stylized horses and menagerie animals with wild gilt manes and ornate trappings were mounted on large stationary carousels, constructed for resorts and amusements parks. (Fried, 62; Manns & Shank, 19).

The County Fair style was founded by Charles W.F. Dare of Green Point, Brooklyn, in the late 1800s. It is characterized by simplicity and greater mobility. The C.W. Parker Company and the North Tonawanda Company both constructed carousels for the North American County Fair circuit (Manns & Shank, 19). Their contrast to the stationary carousels is best illustrated by these statements from Painted Ponies: "In the sleeked-down style of the County Fair Carousels, form and function were as closely united as the wooden horses and their built in saddles... The County Fair breed was developed to gallop across the country side in a whirlwind of one night stands" (Manns & Shank, 175).

The C.W. Parker Carousel

The builder of the Chippewa Park carousel, Charles Wallace Parker, was born in April of 1864 in Griggsville, Illinois. In 1869 his family moved by 'prairie schooner' to Abilene, Kansas. Parker, who had worked as a farmer and a janitor, began his career in the entertainment business with the purchase of a shooting gallery. Upon the realization of his investment he bought into a second hand carousel with two partners. After a successful tour with the carousel, Parker bought out his partners; his persistent tinkering with the carousel inspired him to construct his first carousel in 1892. Within three years the C.W. Parker Carnival Supply Company was in production (Fried, 84; Manns & Shank, 181).

The self-titled 'Amusement King' referred to his carousels as 'Carry-Us-Alls' stating that he had heard some Negro riders calling it that (Fried, 85). By 1902 Parker had established his first travelling carnival and by 1906 his company was supplying his own and other carnivals with carved wagon showfronts, shooting galleries, concessions, banners, ferris wheels, monkey speedways using live monkeys as drivers on fixed courses, band organs, railroad cars, portable electric lighting plants and his portable 'Jumping Horse Carry-Us-Alls' (Manns & Shank, 181; Fried, 86). In the years of its operation, (until the middle of the 1920s), the C.W. Parker Company constructed approximately eight hundred Carry-Us-Alls with numbered identification plates on the center pole (Manns & Shank, 194).

C.W. Parker produced three 'design periods' of Carry-Us-Alls; the Chippewa Park carousel is from his best period (Walker, 1988). Unlike other carousel manufacturers, Parker produced horses exclusively. In the words of Frederick Fried (129), his early horses were "in a class by themselves, long and sinewy with thin sensitive heads and manes rolled back in gentle 'S' curves...". These early horses 'pranced' in an upright position. After the Parker factory moved to Leavenworth, Kansas in 1911, the horse design changed to the outstretched position. This new design produced dramatically posed horses with their forelegs curled for a lunge and their hind legs kicked out. The identical leg position made the erection and dismantling of the carousels easier. The horses were stacked on wooden frames for transport by rail or horse-drawn cart. These horses were designed "to take a minimum of space and a maximum of abuse" (Manns & Shank, 183). They had hollow heads and necks, laminated bodies, solid tails and legs; ears were close to the head, tails were short and embellishments had few protruding edges (Fried, 130; Manns & Shank, 183).

Parker used the Kansas countryside and midwestern culture for inspiration in the designs of the horses' trappings. Horses were carved with fish dangling from the cantle, dogs' head cantles and Parker's favourite - a cob of corn on the back of the saddle (Fraley & Sinick, 20). The Chippewa Park carousel horses sport both dogs' heads and cobs of corn carved on their cantles. As well, many horses produced in the Leavenworth factory were shod with real metal shoes that were inscribed with "11 Worth" (Manns & Shank, 188). The Chippewa Park carousel has many horses who still wear their original factory shoes.

In 1917, Parker secured the copyright for the designs of a new set of horses for his carousels; although smaller than previous designs, the horses hold stiff, exaggerated poses; Frederick Fried (87) refers to them as "horses of great character and distinction". Fried (130) refers to Parker's mention that he 'imported' carvers during this period. Manns and Shank (194) refer directly to a group of World War I German prisoners of war who were allowed to work for Parker. These talented woodworkers gave Parker's horses a distinctive identification characterized by "wild wind blown manes, pompadour forelocks, bobbed tails and lavish saddle decorations". Horses with their head stretched up in the 'stargazer pose' also became popular figures on Parker's carousels. The Chippewa Park carousel hails from this design period.

Design and Construction

In general, it took approximately forty hours of labour to produce the typical carousel horse. The basic contour patterns were designed by the master carver; general shapes were cut out by hand or by machine and fastened using wooden dowels and rabbit hide glue. Poplar, pine and basswood were used by these craftsmen. The body was assembled like a box; strong, light and transportable. The head and legs were glued and carved separately and attached to the roughed out body whereupon the final carving took place (Fraley & Sinick, 13). The head and mane were reserved for the most talented carver and from this evolved the phrase "head man" to designate the person in charge (Manns & Shank, 21). The side of the horse that faced the audience, the 'Romance' side, was more ornately carved than the side of the horse facing inward.

Chariots with bench seats were included on all types of carousels. Their style and decoration varied, yet they all served to carry "the faint of heart, small children and women too modest to straddle a horse" (Manns & Shank, 14). The Chippewa Park carousel has two rather plain chariots. Although Parker included chariots on his carousels, these chariots have been modified by persons unknown since the construction of this carousel.

'Crestings' or 'rounding boards' refer to the upper decorative outside parts of the carousel. Some, like the Chippewa Park carousel, have carved frames surrounding mirrors. On other carousels, these frames contained painted panels "whose subjects varied from the sublime to the ridiculous" (Fried, 163). The Chippewa Park carousel's rounding boards also sport carved dragons and flowers all contained within a simply-carved frame. These rounding boards have been modified in the years since the carousel's construction.

The drive mechanism of the carousel was contained behind decorated wood panels at the centre of the entire unit. Once again, the degree of decoration of these panels varied between styles of carousels; but they all served to provide further visual stimulation for the carousel riders. The Chippewa Park carousel's centre panels are simple boards framing stylized medieval lions, which may or may not represent the original factory design.

Motive power for the carousel evolved from man or horse to steam to electricity. The Chippewa Park carousel was purchased with an Eli Motor Drive steam engine, which although not operable, still resides at the Park. The carousel's mechanism is presently powered by electricity.

The carousel ride would not be complete without music. Early carousels were often accompanied by live musicians. As the industry evolved, military band organs with decorated facades became closely associated with the carousels; often they were provided with power from a small engine drawn by a belt from the main drive mechanism (Fried, 178). The Chippewa Park carousel was purchased with a Wurlitzer band organ, which although pleasing to the eye with its original painted panels and wooden cabinet, is no longer in operation.

The builder of this device, Franz Rudolph Wurlitzer, emigrated to Cincinnati, Ohio from Germany in 1853. While working as a bank cashier, he sold handcrafted wooden musical instruments in his spare time. In 1861 he established his own factory; opened his first retail store in 1865, and in 1909 began to manufacture band organs with his patented self-winding roll mechanism. By 1920 the Wurlitzer Company dominated the band organ market (Fried, 198).

The End of the "Golden Age of Carousels"

The end of the golden age of carousels was brought about by a series of developments. The 'age of mechanization' introduced the carving machine, whereby many identical horses could be produced from a stock of preset patterns of horse heads and bodies. World War I caused a shortage of supplies, and the Great Depression caused a significant decline in the demand for carousels. Both of these economic developments made carousel production less profitable; survivors switched to simpler machines and/or mass production. The final development occurred in the 1940s with the widespread use of aluminum and associated improvements in the casting process (Manns & Shank, 14; Fraley & Sinick, 124). Wooden carousel horse construction was rapidly replaced by the far more expedient production of aluminum carousel horses.

In the years since their 'golden age', wooden carousels have had to withstand many threats to their existence. Frederick Fried, in the course of research for his 1964 book, *A Pictoral History of the Carousel* (215), surveyed amusement ride insurers and discovered that "fire and other forces of nature destroy at least two large park-type carousels each year". Neglect and lack of awareness over the decades have also taken their toll.

Since the publication of Frederick Fried's ground breaking work on the carousel, there has been a resurgence of interest in the wooden carousel with associated benefits and threats to the continued survival of remaining intact carousels. At present, these antique wooden carousel animals are prized collectibles, much sought after by folk art collectors who will pay tens of thousands of dollars for a single carousel animal. This has resulted in the dismantling of many old carousels estimated at five to seven per year (Walker, 1988) Their sale, piece by piece at auction, can net the seller and the auctioneer vast sums of money.

This threatening situation has resulted in the formation of organizations committed to the preservation of intact wooden carousels. Groups such as the American National Carousel Association have undertaken to census still intact carousels and to lobby actively for their preservation. Journals and newsletters dispense information about carousels, preservation efforts, maintenance and restoration techniques. These organizations encourage the establishment of local advocacy groups in cities with carousels and through projects such as Adopt-a-Carousel, they foster a wider base of support.

Appraisal

In June of 1988 Frederick Fried came to Thunder Bay to undertake an assessment and valuation of our Chippewa Park Carousel. He described the carousel as:

"A complete operating two-row carousel with two chariots, each seating four passengers, and mounted by twenty-eight hand-carved and decorated jumping horses, fourteen in each row, all mounted on a 42 foot diameter platform. Overhead is a rim of sectional panels, each identically adorned with rustic carvings. All suspended from a centerpole supported and surrounded by an A-frame, the sectional gear, the drive mechanisms, and the upper illustrated panels hiding part of the equipment, all covered by a circular canopied covering of brightly-coloured fabric.",

and declared it to be in good, safe, stable, operating condition. Mr. Fried deduced a market estimation of value of the carousel, in "consideration of the increasing rarity of Parker carousels especially in excellent condition with unusual folk art carvings of the horses and decorations" [sic] and emphasized the need for attention to security and conservation.

The Wurlitzer 146B band organ and the Eli Motor Drive were also assessed and valued by Mr. Fried. The band organ dates from the second decade of this century and is described as a 'duplex type playing rolls of music by compressed air from a chest of bellows'. The organ is contained in a wooden cabinet and two rolls of music remain, although not in usable condition. The Eli motor drive was also made by the Wurlitzer Company of North Tonawanda in the second decade of this century. The Eli motor drive is inoperative and although it is repairable, the cost estimate of repairs would require a part-by-part examination.

Issues and Challenges

The Chippewa Park, C.W. Parker Carry-Us-Alls, is one of only three remaining examples of its kind. Adding to this rarity are its size - a two-abreast model; and its western origin - carousels made further away from New York are more rare (Walker, 1988). Furthermore, this carousel is in excellent condition. The cold and relatively dry Thunder Bay climate has prevented the damage caused by wood boring insects, a problem that plagues wooden carousels in more southerly locations. The wooden horses have also been protected by the many layers of paint they have accumulated over the decades. The closest similar carousel is in Crossroads Village, Michigan (Walker, 1988). West Vancouver also possesses a larger Parker carousel and other Canadian cities who can lay claim to carousels of other makes are Toronto at Centre Island, Canada's Wonderland and St. Catharines, Ontario.

Some municipalities, for example West Vancouver, are engaged in attempts to raise enough money to purchase the carousels residing within their city limits. Thunder Bay is very fortunate in this regard, having purchased the carousel, in full, for $583.33 in 1934. This advantage of ownership includes associated responsibilities. Although the City of Thunder Bay is not pressed to raise purchase funds, responsible ownership of our carousel entails the allocation of funds for secure and proper storage, restoration to original factory condition, and public relations to raise community awareness.

Appropriate storage involves attention to security from fire, vandalism and theft as well as conservative temperature and humidity control. Most stationary carousels of the past and the present are contained within pavilions that allow protection from the elements as well as year-round access to the ride. The carousel should be contained; optimally within a modern building whose design is based upon period carousel pavilions.

In order to preserve the integrity of the Chippewa Park carousel, acknowledgement of its unique status as a working piece of art is in order. It is important to keep the carousel in operation while having it restored to its original beauty, using the most up-to-date curatorial and conservation techniques available.

Finally, the community should be made aware of this unique heritage. The Chippewa Park carousel is irreplaceable and thus deserving of recognition for its value as a piece of art and of appreciation of its status as an example of three-dimensional folk art. City residents and tourists should have the opportunity to enjoy a ride on our carousel while appreciating it as a source of civic pride and as a source of nostalgia for our childhood and for times gone by.

Issues and Challenges Update
In early 1990, the relocation of the Chippewa Park carousel was discussed within the context of planning for the development of the new Kaministiqua River Heritage Park located adjacent to the downtown core of the former city of Fort William. Development of this park has proceeded in stages as capital funds have become available, precluding the immediate development of an area large enough to contain a carousel pavilion.

In 1993, a master planning process for Chippewa Park was initiated. In the course of this ongoing process, it has become evident that the carousel should remain in its appropriate context. In fact, the carousel represents a unique opportunity to focus the revitalization of Chippewa Park on the theme of the carousel within the context of the old style, "seaside" park. And finally, the Thunder Bay Art Gallery is planning to undertake a winter display of the carousel horses within the next year or two.

The future of the carousel remains ultimately the responsibility of both the citizens of Thunder Bay and the members of City Council. As awareness of the heritage value of the carousel is heightened, it is hoped that both the political will and the resources are found to restore and to preserve the carousel in its most fitting context, that is at Chippewa Park, where the carousel has resided for sixty years.

References
Fraley, Tobin and Sinick, Gary. *The Carousel Animal*. San Francisco, CA.: Chronicle Books, 1987.

Fried, Frederick. *A Pictorial History of the Carousel*. Vestal, N.Y.: The Vestal Press Ltd., 1964.

Fried, Frederick. Lecture at Chippewa Park, June 14, 1988.

Manns, William and Shank, Peggy. *Painted Ponies: American Carousel Art*. Millwood, N.Y.: Zon International Publishing, 1986.

Walker, Charles. Personal Communication, January 20, 1988.

Cultural
Tourism

Tourism: Niagara-on-the-Lake

Jim Alexander

NIAGARA-ON-THE-LAKE IS SITUATED at the estuary of the Niagara River and Lake Ontario. Because of its strategic position in regard to transportation and agriculture, it was settled by Natives, long before the white man. Historically, control of the mouth of the Niagara River was vital to the fur trade and later to the expanding development of the Upper Lakes. Here, the French in the early 18th century built Fort Niagara which passed to the British then to the Americans. In the later 18th century, the British built the Navy Hall complex and Fort George on the opposite shore.

In 1792, Lieutenant Governor John Graves Simcoe arrived and established the first capital of Upper Canada in Newark until 1797 when the capital was moved to York, now Toronto. Newark became the legal, administrative and cultural centre for Upper Canada. The town grew prosperous with the influx of United Empire Loyalists and civil servants.

During the War of 1812, the retreating Americans burned Newark to the ground. After the war, Newark was re-constructed to an even finer scale. In the late 19th century, the county seat was moved to St. Catharines and Niagara-on-the-Lake drifted into one of the recurring cycles of "boom and bust".

By the turn of this century, Niagara-on-the-Lake became the preferred location for summer homes of rich Americans. Large estates were established on the prime locations in town not controlled by the federal government.

From the very beginning, there has been a large military presence in the Town - Fort George, Fort Mississauga, Butler's Barracks, Camp Niagara and the Commons. In fact, the former military reserve, which is under the control of the Canadian Parks Service, represents 28% of the total area of the Old Town.[1]

The army continued to provide much needed revenue through Camp Niagara up to 1967. When the properties were transferred to Parks Canada and this revenue ceased, another basis was emphasized - agriculture. Many canning factories were built and the fresh fruit from Niagara was shipped by steamer to the St. Lawrence market in Toronto from the docks at the end of King Street. By the mid-1950s, even this activity stopped. Niagara-on-the-Lake became a backwater town, with tourism in the summer providing some employment.

In 1962, the Shaw Festival was launched with an amateur project housed in the old Court House. It quickly took on a life of its own. The ever-increasing clientele, mostly from Toronto and the Buffalo area, brought new life to Queen Street - the town's commercial district. At the same time, more and more of the historic homes were being purchased and restored by outsiders and Niagara-on-the-Lake became a preferred address. The "Old Town" became a media darling and as a result pressure for new housing and infilling started and put a great strain on the existing town services.

In 1972, the Old Town of Niagara was merged with the Township of Niagara to become the Town of Niagara-on-the-Lake, causing much acrimony among the residents. The votes in the old township eventually gave the rural areas control. A growing number of residents in the Old Town became concerned over the lack of protection of the built heritage. The ever-increasing pressure of tourism brought on by the Shaw Festival and the natural and historic beauty of the Town, changed Niagara dramatically. The stores on Queen Street rapidly changed from general public service to simply tourist service, while the rest of the Old Town became a bedroom community.

The Shaw Festival outgrew the old Court House and they proposed building a new theatre on a piece of the Commons - the battle lines were drawn. The rural-controlled Council allowed the new theatre in 1972. The success of the theatre brought increasing pressure not only on the tourist facilities, but also on development - both commercial and residential. A large number of the affected residents were initially introduced to Niagara by the Shaw.

In 1974, George Doxey, Professor of Economics at York University, was commissioned to produce an extensive study on the future of tourism in Niagara-on-the-Lake. One of his conclusions was that there was a substantial cost to the taxpayer. The residents of the Old Town now had the ammunition to try to curb the commercial development.

In 1977, Proctor & Redfern Limited was commissioned by Parks Canada to prepare a report on the economic impact of tourism development proposals in Niagara-on-the-Lake. The estimated 1977 visitation was 874,536 with an increase to 1,394,000 by 1986.[2] Parks Canada developed a proposal to spend $5 million on their facilities in Niagara-on-the-Lake. Residents in the Old Town organized to oppose this development and when the Director General of the Ontario Region of Parks Canada arrived to announce the project, he was greeted by a well-orchestrated demonstration in front of television news cameras from Buffalo and Toronto. The project was cancelled and Fort George became a non-entity with visitation remaining static for the last 15 years at approximately 85,000 per season.

The town's charm and reputation has attracted many visitors, not only to the theatre but to enjoy the parks, history, natural beauty, shops, architecture and lifestyle. In the past ten years, tourism has taken on a life of its own and the town has accommodated its ever-increasing numbers with development. We are now at the saturation point and parking and congestion must be addressed.

In 1991, Niagara-on-the-Lake elected its new Council with the majority of the members from the rural areas. They faced some seemingly insurmountable problems - the agricultural tax base has dried up because of free trade; a very high unemployment rate exists in the Peninsula; the cost of government and the increased demand on the town's infrastructure guarantee a hefty increase to an already overtaxed constituency. The only light at the end of this tunnel is to increase the revenues generated by tourism while trying to maintain the heritage aspect. The Council has, in the past year, considered a number of developments which were strongly opposed by LACAC and the previous Council, such as parking meters on the main street of the Heritage District, the paving of backyards for parking, the opening of side streets for commercial operations and the rezoning of residential to commercial use - all within the Heritage District. These are just a few of the problems.

I believe that tourism is a double-edged sword - there is a positive aspect to it as well. It is only through public appreciation that our heritage is going to be preserved and it is the responsibility of LACAC to monitor development proposals to ensure that the integrity of this community is maintained. What gives LACAC the power is this public awareness. The tourist comes to Niagara-on-the-Lake to experience the ambience of a quaint little town steeped in history, to eat at one of the fine restaurants and to take in a play at the Shaw. If the Council-of-the-day turns the Town into just another commercial strip, we lose the major draw for the tourist and we will slip into the cycle of "boom and bust" again. Because of the political system in place, where Councils shift between the Old Town and the rural area, the only protection that the residents have is this public awareness shaped by tourism.

There is a growing sense of community in Niagara-on-the Lake. Many of the new residents have become involved in such organizations as the Visitor and Convention Bureau, the Friends of Fort George National Historic Parks, etc. Over the past five years the Canada Day celebrations were resurrected, the New Year's Levee, Christmas Stroll, candlelight dinners in historic Navy Hall, peach festivals, strawberry festivals, etc. The success of these activities relies to some extent on the participation of tourists; but the reason for their organization is to profile our community concern about the preservation of our cultural and built heritage. This summer marks the 200th anniversary of the landing of Simcoe, organized by a citizens' committee with representation from a variety of community organizations joining together to celebrate our culture.

This concern and involvement of local residents has to have a profound effect on those who would endanger our heritage for short-term gain. "Related to the Old Town of Niagara, the question becomes simply, do you wish to become a service centre for tourists or remain a living community which by its very reality draws the admiring visitor?"[3]

Notes

1. *Tourism in Niagara-on-the-Lake.* G.V. Doxey & Associates, 1974, p.2.

2. *The Economic Impact of Tourism Development Proposals in Niagara-on-the-Lake*, Proctor & Redfern, 1977.

3. The Future of Tourism in Niagara-on-the-Lake, G. V. Doxey, November 20, 1974.

References and Further Readings:

Tourism in Niagara-on-the-Lake, G. V. Doxey & Associates, 1974.

The Future of Tourism in Niagara-on-the-Lake, G. V. Doxey & Associates, 1974. (Talk given to the annual meeting of the Chamber of Commerce.)

The Economic Impact of Tourism Development Proposals in Niagara-on-the-Lake, Proctor & Redfern, 1977.

Tourism Management, Georgian College of Applied Arts and Technology (Year 3 student marketing project).

The Economic Impact on Niagara Region, Region Niagara Tourist Council, October, 1987.

Queen & Picton Streets Heritage Conservation District Plan, Nicholas Hill, June 1986.

1991 Fort George N.H.S. Visitor Survey, The Coopers & Lybrand Consulting Group, January 31, 1992.

Cultural Tourism: Port Hope

A. K. Skulthorpe

Port Hope attracts three types of tourists. Those who are interested in architecture and history, antique hunters and those who are fishermen.

Port Hope has an unusually fine commercial streetscape and a remarkably large stock of well-preserved buildings, both large and small. The Architectural Conservancy of Ontario Inc., Port Hope Branch, offers a service of guides. If buses come to Port Hope, an A.C.O. member will give a tour from one to three hours with emphasis on either history-architecture or just a general tour. The A.C.O. also runs a house tour every fall. The tour is limited to 1500 people and has been sold out for many years. The revenue from this is between $17,000 and $18,000 which means that the A.C.O. has enough money to make an impact on town preservation. It also brings many people to the town and these people tend to return.

Attractive to the person interested in history and architecture is the large number of antique shops in the town. Sunday is a really busy day in Port Hope. Instead of the town being deserted, there are people on the street going from one antique store to the next. Trinity College School parents also tend to browse around the town. Twenty years ago, most parents were hardly aware of the town. They would come off Highway 401 and go directly to the school and never get into the downtown itself. This is no longer true. The antique stores are very conscious of their patronage.

Our other type of tourist comes to the town for the fish. The Ganaraska River which runs through the town is one of the best cold water streams on the north shore of Lake Ontario. Rainbow trout and Chinook salmon swim up stream to spawn and there is a fish ladder to allow these fish to go above Corbett's Dam. Interestingly enough, when the first dam was built across the Ganaraska in 1797, there was a fish ladder to one side of the dam as the founders of Port Hope were just as interested in allowing the fish to spawn upstream as we are today.

Literally, at certain times of the year, we have hoards of people standing cheek to jowl along the river bank; in fact it is so crowded that it is hard to see how they can avoid hooking each other. A few years ago there were no tourist amenities at all. In recent years, we have more and better restaurants and there has been an effort made to accommodate the fishermen. The Chamber of Commerce has placed Johnnies-on-the-spot for the fishermen and there is a small restaurant at the end of Mill St. plus two chip wagons on the west side of the stream. It is difficult to gauge how much the tourists affect the commerce of the town. In the case of the fishermen, their interests are focused and they patronize food stores, restaurants and bait and fishing tackle shops.

It is also difficult to know just how important those interested in the architecture of the town are to the local businessman. There are always strangers on our streets and wherever tourists go, they will always leave some money behind them in the town.

The question is how much more tourism does Port Hope want? There is a fine line between enough tourists to have an economic impact on the town, and too many tourists so that the town loses the atmosphere which drew the tourists here in the beginning. It is not really so much the people themselves, but more the out-of-town entrepreneurs who follow the tourists hoping to make a dollar from the situation and who have no feeling about the town itself that are a concern. These people would gladly tear down an old structure and put in an unsuitable highrise and call it progress.

If an area becomes really magnetic, the Councils are often so busy providing tourist facilities and being pleased at the revenue that is being brought into town that they do not preserve aspects of the town's heritage as they should. This in turn can so easily damage the ambience of the town which is the main attraction.

Port Hope has never catered to tourists as some towns do. We have very few good restaurants and some tend to close before the out-of-town tourists wish to dine. However, we are beginning to have more good ones and now have several bed and breakfasts, in interesting older houses.

As our harbour is contaminated by Eldorado's waste, we have lost most of our sailing tourists. The town has been working on a harbour redevelopment scheme which, when finished, will again attract the sailors to Port Hope. There are members on the Harbour Implementation Committee who wish to see this development but not at the expense of Port Hopers. We have no wish to see high-rise hotels at the waterfront.

There are many people in town who see the danger of too much tourism, but it is such a fine line that we are uncertain when or how to control tourist development.

Urban
Heritage

The Peterborough Armoury:

Notes for Remarks at the Ceremony for the Unveiling of a Historic Sites and Monuments Board of Canada Plaque Commemorating the National Historical and Architectural Significance of the Peterborough Armoury

Thomas H. B. Symons
Chairman, National Historic Sites and Monuments Board

REVEREND SIR, MINISTER, Warden, Your Worship, Ladies and Gentlemen, Mesdames, Messieurs:

Je vous souhaite la bienvenue aujourd'hui à cette occasion si riche d'histoire.

I am very happy, ladies and gentlemen, to welcome you, on behalf of the Historic Sites and Monuments Board of Canada, to this special ceremony, commemorating the Peterborough Armoury.

It is the responsibility of the Historic Sites and Monuments Board to advise the Minister of the Environment and the Government of Canada upon the identification and commemoration of buildings, sites, and monuments, and of persons, events, and movements that are of national significance because of their historical or architectural importance.

By these means, and in such gatherings, we recognize and affirm the central importance of heritage and of conservation in our lives and to our identity. It is a particularly happy and appropriate thing that the participants in the Ontario 1992 LACAC Conference are able to be with us as special guests for this occasion.

From time to time, the Historic Sites and Monuments Board initiates reviews of specific topics or national themes - such as, Native history, heritage railway stations, the court houses of Canada, cultural pluralism, or city halls, to name but a few current examples - to see whether a balanced attention and appropriate recognition is being given to the subject, on a trans-Canada basis, in the country's programmes of conservation and recognition. Such surveys also make it possible to establish criteria and benchmarks upon which to base the selection process.

In 1987, in response to various inquiries, the Board decided to initiate such a review of the historic armouries and drill halls of

Canada. As the result of this study, the Board has recommended the commemoration of seven such buildings, located across Canada, as outstanding examples of their period and region. The Peterborough Armoury is now the first of these to be commemorated.

This Armoury is, indeed, one of the finest surviving examples of Canadian Drill Hall architecture. Built at the height of the Edwardian era, it recalls a Romanesque fortress, with its splendid turrets, crenellated roof line, and arched troop door. It is one of the largest and best designed military base structures dating from this period in Canada.

For nearly a century, the Armoury has been a landmark in Peterborough's cityscape, meeting the needs of famous local regiments and reserve military units, and, also, playing an important wider role in the life of this city and of the Valley of the Trent. From here four generations of Canadians have offered their service to our Country. It is truly a part of the heritage of all Canadians.

The Board had no difficulty, therefore, under the terms of its mandate, in recommending to the Minister and to the Government of Canada that the Peterborough Armoury is of national historical and architectural significance and in directing the preparation of the plaque in its commemoration, which will be unveiled here this day.

London's Talbot Block - What Did We Learn?

Nancy Tausky,
University of Western Ontario

Nancy Tausky has been involved with the London LACAC for four years and has been the Vice-Chair for the past two years. She teaches English at the University of Western Ontario and is the co-author of Victorian Architecture in London and Southwestern Ontario. Nancy is currently working with Peterborough graphic artist, Louis Taylor, on Historical Sketches of London, which will be published soon. Nancy chaired the ad-hoc sub-committee which dealt with the designation of the Talbot Block in London.

The Talbot Streetscape

Under the guise of various numbered companies, Cambridge Leaseholds Ltd. purchased during the early 1980s most of the properties in what was arguably London's most historic commercial block, bounded by Dundas, Ridout, King, and Talbot Streets, and situated directly across from the courthouse at the forks of the Thames, where the city of London began. Though preservationists acquainted both Cambridge and the City Council with the importance of the area as soon as the buyer was publicly identified in 1983, the buildings around three sides of the block were demolished by 1986, and the fight for the remaining streetscape, on Talbot Street, became a cause celebre for the next five years. The preservationists, under the umbrella of the Talbot Streetscape Coalition, won many significant battles: Council passed the "Patton Bylaw", giving Cambridge the concessions necessary for proceeding with development on the vacant parts of the block, but retaining the buildings of the Streetscape; Council later designated the buildings under the Ontario Heritage Act; and, as time was running out on the 270 days of protection from demolition under the Act, the City cooperated with the Coalition in supporting a private member's bill, introduced in the Provincial Legislature by MPP David Winnigerr, giving London the right to refuse demolition permits on designated properties until a building permit has been approved. That Cambridge won the final victory was therefore the more disillusioning: the buildings were torn down last fall, after Council voted to give Cambridge all zoning concessions it needed for a promised gargantuan development, to be erected at an unspecified date in the future, and agreed to the immediate demolition of most of the Streetscape in return for a well landscaped parking lot. The landscaping has not yet materialized, and the Talbot Inn, which still remains because part of its facade is to be preserved, is untenanted and unmaintained.

It would perhaps be comforting if one could point to a major error or oversight in tactics and feel that at least a positive lesson emerged from the many years of intensive effort and the massive public support for saving the Streetscape. But my own feeling is that we could have done little more than we did towards furthering our cause. In fact, the odds were always against those fighting for preservation: Cambridge was constantly incalcitrant in its opposition to saving the buildings,and standing up to a major developer went strongly against the grain for London's traditionally pro-development city council. It could be argued that the Talbot Coalition achieved a remarkable feat, if ultimately a useless one, simply staving off demolition for as long as it did.

It seems to me that the Coalition evidenced two broad and significant strengths. The first was in its extremely casual organization. The Coalition never had formal memberships, rules, or bylaws, officers, or even regular meeting times. It depended on a couple of strong leaders who took the responsibility for keeping abreast of developments and organizing efforts when particular goals needed to be met, and a core of very dedicated and creative people who could be relied on for continual advice and help. The main advantage of this informality was the openness and responsiveness of the organization: anyone willing to help was welcomed; few needed to feel imprisoned by long-term obligations. The main disadvantage was such an "organization" could have no official status; as a result, the London Branch of the Architectural Conservancy of Ontario played a crucial role within the Coalition, in that it could receive charitable donations, apply for grants, and otherwise take responsibilities for those actions requiring some form of official status. LACAC's role in the battle was relatively limited. When LACAC joined forces with other groups, in June of 1988, to commission a feasibility report from Toronto architect, George Baird, Council insisted that no LACAC funds could be spent on the study. In subsequent dialogues, it became increasingly clear that LACAC could be most effective in its arguments with Council if it adopted the role of the disinterested expert. LACAC consistently advised in favour of retaining the Streetscape, and it prepared extraordinarily comprehensive Reasons for Designation in an effort to make them as persuasive as possible. But LACAC, by both mandate and policy, was precluded from many of the activities of the coalition: hiring consultants, rasing money, demonstrating, lobbying, and openly campaigning.

The greatest virtue of the Coalition's campaign was undoubtedly the variety of fronts on which it operated. The initial defense of Streetscape, in the Stokes Report, was on the grounds of its architectural and historical importance, and these concerns were presented, in various forms, throughout the campaign: architectural and historical considerations were necessarily paramount in the Reasons for Designation, and Cambridge's final "compromise", to provide two new Victorian streetscapes, again made the issues of style and history prominent. But we discovered that planning and economic issues were more likely to interest Council members, and less likely to be cubbyholed as the concerns of an elitist fringe group. Our greatest advances were made on professional grounds, using the services of a lawyer and of various professional consultants. Particularly influential were the Planning Study carried out by Dr. William Code, an urban geographer who teaches at the University of Western Ontario, and the report compiled by the Toronto firm of Baird/Simpson, showing 1) how the Talbot Streetscape buildings could be practically and economically integrated into the Cambridge scheme, and 2) offering a viable alternate plan for the block. The Coalition sponsored a number of projects designed to raise money for this professional help: it printed and sold posters, buttons, and T-shirts; held a large "heritage auction"; and solicited money directly through telephone calls and letters. The Coalition also worked hard to increase public awareness about the importance of the Streetscape. For example, it sponsored two large demonstrations, "Hands Around the Block" in May 1987 and "The Talbot Street Relay" in August 1988; two art exhibits; and a soapbox day involving various speakers on the downtown mall. It also maintained a constant lobbying effort towards Council members, made efforts to win greater support from the downtown business community, and sought out sympathetic developers interested in purchasing the Streetscape from Cambridge. With the help of lawyer Alan Patton, the Coalition was responsible for soliciting the support that pushed Bill 18 through the Legislature.

In the numerous postmortems following the final debacle, various suggestions have been made about conditions or further activities that might have worked to the preservationists' advantage, and I've selected seven of these suggestions as particularly noteworthy. But I present them with the caution that not all of these suggestions could have been effected, and possibly only one would have significantly altered the final outcome.

1. A controlled negotiation
The sudden turnabout on the part of City Council, in the spring of 1991, was instigated at a private meeting between a Council

negotiating committee and Cambridge. Two influential Streetscape supporters, the Mayor and the Deputy Mayor, returned from Toronto wholeheartedly committed to Cambridge's compromise offer of two new Victorian streetscapes, along Dundas Street and Talbot Street respectively. In fact, the new offer was essentially no different from the old: the historic buildings were to be demolished, except for the partial facade of the Talbot Inn, and the mall was still to have controlled entrances. Moreover, Cambridge was not committing itself to a particular building date, and still had no tenants lined up. Thus the reason for the councillors' changes of heart was far from evident, and the presence of a disinterested facilitator, such as one provided through the Centre for Livable Places, might have diminished the effects of either naivete or corruption. Just how LACAC or the Coalition could have introduced such a negotiator is not clear, since neither group was itself allowed to be involved with the negotiations.

2. More extensive soliciting of support from the commercial sector.
Despite considerable effort, we never did get the majority of the downtown merchants on our side. And, while we did find developers willing to purchase the block from Cambridge, we did not attempt to get a group of London developers together, bringing pressure of their own.

3. More extensive campaigning for pro-heritage candidates in city elections.
Our best hope for the future is in introducing new faces in Council rather than in attempting to change deeply implanted positions.

4. A stronger Heritage Act.
For a couple of years we were actually in the curious position of trying to keep the buildings from being designated while the developer was pushing for designation, and our whole object, of course, was to keep from starting on the 270-day countdown, while Cambridge wanted to get it out of the way. A stronger Heritage Act could prevent such a situation.

5. A Standing Assessment Policy.
The final tragedy of the entire denouement to this drama came when, during demolition, it was discovered that London's first town hall was in fact still remarkably intact underneath the brick veneer of the southernmost building - and Cambridge refused to

stall demolition long enough for the structure to be removed. The bylaw requiring Cambridge to allow documentation of the property, introduced in Council at the last minute, was too vague to ensure a proper documentation or to force delays in Cambridge's expeditious destruction of the old buildings. As a result, LACAC is now working on describing a set of conditions which will automatically be included in a development agreement, carefully delineating a developer's responsibilities in the event that a historic structure is demolished on his site, or in the event that his property is thought significant in relation to its archaeological potential.

6. Promote a broader concept of heritage, applicable to immigrants and suburbanites.
Despite a large number of very committed people involved in the fight for the Talbot Streetscape, the campaign ultimately suffered because some Wards made it clear to their aldermen that the heritage issue was only a core area concern.

7. Proactive measures
Mark Gladysz discusses this in the next paper.

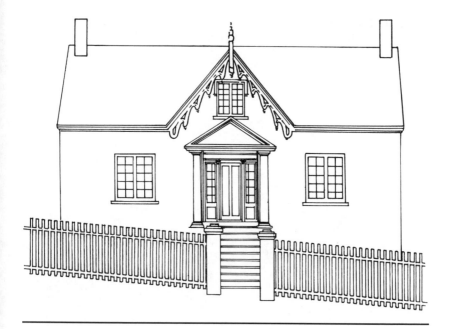

Hutchison House
Brock Street

London's Talbot Block - What Did We Learn?

Mark Gladysz
Heritage planner, City of London
Mark is a graduate of the University of Winnipeg with a B.A.
Honours in Urban Studies. He also attended York University where
he graduated with a Master's degree in Environmental Studies, spe-
cializing in Historical Preservation. In a program co-sponsored by
the Universite de Montreal and McGill, Mark received specialized
training in conservation. Mark also hopes to pursue a Ph.D. in the
field of tourism development. Over the past three years, Mark has
been a Heritage Planner for the City of London. Previous work expe-
rience includes three years as a Parks Planner, the position of
Heritage Consultant to the Town of East Gwillimbury, and
Conservation Officer with the Ministry of Culture and
Communications. Mark enjoys collecting and refinishing antique
furniture and is currently renovating a 90 year old house.

I WOULD LIKE TO PREFACE MY COMMENTS today with something I heard on the radio which perhaps represents our inability to fully understand the implications of our actions. Recently a journalist asked a top official of the Peoples Republic of China what he felt was the impact of the French Revolution 200 years later. The official responded that it was too early to tell.

Similarly, it is perhaps premature to determine what we learned or did not learn from the Talbot Block demolition. I do feel the most instructive aspect of this whole matter has been the role of the citizen groups and the Non-Government Organizations, which is what Nancy Tausky covered in her paper.

First, I would begin by saying that very little can be learned from the decision-making process which led to the Talbot Block being demolished. My sense, from having spoken to many of the people involved, is that nothing positive resulted from the process, particularly that no guarantees or regulatory conditions were negotiated between the developer or the City to guide development on the site. No commitment to build anything but a surface parking lot was extracted in the negotiations, even though the City had been given the authority through Bill 18 to deny a demolition request until a building permit had been approved.

I have a few comments on how Cambridge handled the situation and the response of the City. First, I would suggest that Cambridge Leaseholds pursued a course of action which did not secure favourable public relations, though eventually they got everything they wanted. Second, turnover on City Council reflected the growing public disaffection with Cambridge's inaction and resulting deadlock. However, prevailing community values were not supportive of the Block's preservation, despite the activities of a small, but surprisingly influential heritage lobby. Third, it was Council's unwillingness to commit serious public monies to preserve and integrate the block into a new development which undermined their negotiating ability.

So my first comments focus on Cambridge's handling of the City Council and public. It would appear Cambridge chose a poor development strategy. In the first stage, between 1981 and June 1987, Cambridge was complacent. They had no plan for dealing with City Council and made no attempt to develop support for the project. In the next stage, Cambridge tried to convince Council with financial agreements. By making extensive modifications to their plans, they tried to convince City Council to delay a decision on another downtown mall in favour of their's. Until the end of 1987, Cambridge made limited attempts to raise public support. When efforts to delay the Campeau mall failed, Cambridge approached downtown businesses with their plans and attempted to enlist them as allies to help influence Council. From 1988 until the end Cambridge increasingly began to make threats to Council; this was particularly noticeable in the last few months before the demolition occurred.

There was increasing escalation beyond the municipal level which culminated in December 1990 with the passage of Bill 18 and a need to manage sustained citizen resistance. Council's capitulation in September 1991 can be ascribed more to expediency than to anything else. With an election looming and the deadlock ongoing, anything seemed better than the status quo. Perhaps the Councillors felt the fallout from the demolition would be less problematic than the ongoing stalemates, and they were right. No member of Council suffered fallout from the demolition.

My last point is that City Council made it very clear that the public was not going to play a role in the preservation of the streetscape when it moved that no public money was to be used to save the block or to expropriate it. This position perhaps more than anything ultimately sealed the fate of the buildings. London has traditionally not favoured using public funds for anything other than basic services. A public/private sector partnership just was not there. The Council, like the community, was polarized between those who wanted to save the block and those who did not. And without a serious negotiating position, it was only a matter of time before the block was demolished.

The destruction of the Talbot Block should not be a surprise in the context of what I have outlined. What was a surprise was the sustained, well-funded, and sophisticated public resistance and its impact. The maneuvers to delay the demolition through zoning, securing special legislation from the province and the designation of the buildings under Part IV of the Ontario Heritage Act would have been meaningful in the context of a serious negotiating environment and inclusive as opposed to exclusive decision-making. But this was not the case and it leaves the observer to ask what was it all for?

588 Stewart Street

A Restoration Project By Heritage Sault Ste. Marie Inc.

Wilhelm Eisenbichler
Associate Director of the Sault Ste. Marie Public Library.
Wilhelm holds a Master of Arts degree from McMaster University, specializing in Renaissance and Reformation Studies and a Master of Library Science degree from the University of Western Ontario. Actively involved in local heritage issues, Wilhelm is the Chairman of the Sault Ste. Marie LACAC, a member of the Sault Ste. Marie Historic Sites Board and was the Chairman of the 1988 LACAC Conference. Wilhelm has also taught history at Algoma University College and plays trombone with the Sault Ste. Marie Swing Band.

IN THE FALL OF 1984 THE SAULT STE. MARIE Local Architectural Conservation Advisory Committee (LACAC) resolved to participate in the Community Heritage Fund Program administered by the Ontario Ministry of Citizenship and Culture. This grant program, which was followed by the Preserving Ontario's Heritage grant program in 1987, permitted municipalities to establish Non-Profit Community Heritage Corporations to manage a revolving fund. The Community Heritage Fund, as this fund was called, could be used for local heritage restoration and conservation purposes. The Ministry of Citizenship and Culture encouraged municipalities to participate by providing seed money which matched, according to a formula, the amount of money that the municipality put into the fund.

In November of 1984, following a presentation by the Sault Ste. Marie LACAC, the Sault Ste. Marie Municipal Council agreed to participate in this program. The municipality made three contributions of $25,000 to the Community Heritage Fund, for a total municipal contribution of $75,000. These contributions were spread out over three fiscal years: 1985, 1986, and 1987. Matching provincial funds amounted to $130,000, for a total Community Heritage Fund of $205,000.

Heritage Sault Ste. Marie Inc. was established in September 1986 as a non-profit corporation to administer the Community Heritage Fund. The corporation could receive grants and donations to promote community heritage, acquire and dispose of property, make grants, loans and loan guarantees for heritage purposes, and enter into contracts and easements for heritage purposes.

Management of the Corporation was by a twelve-member Board of Directors, six of whom were LACAC members. Members brought a wide range of expertise from many professional areas, including architecture, construction, heritage conservation, land surveying, law, real estate and appraisal, banking, municipal planning and development, and local politics.

From the beginning Heritage Sault Ste. Marie planned to use the Community Heritage Fund for a restoration project. It was not interested in using the fund to make grants or loans. By February 1987 a specific building had been identified as a potential project and preliminary contact had been made with the owner. "Upton", as the residence was known, was built in 1865 as the home of Wemyss Simpson, the last factor of the Hudson's Bay Company in Sault Ste. Marie and the first member of Parliament for Algoma. This was one of the premier heritage buildings in Sault Ste. Marie, having both architectural and historical merit. The municipality had designated this property under the Ontario Heritage Act in 1983. Unfortunately, the residence had been progressively deteriorating from neglect and abuse. For a number of years it was being used as a boarding house. In many ways this had become a problem building for the neighbourhood.

In July 1987 Heritage Sault Ste. Marie purchased 10 Kensington Place with the intent of restoring it and then re-selling it. Using photographic documentation, Heritage Sault Ste. Marie sought to restore the exterior facade of Upton to its original 1865 look and to update the interior to a modern functional use that would ensure the building a viable future. After exploring a number of possibilities, it was decided to convert the interior to three, two-bedroom, luxury condominiums.

Work commenced in March 1988. By December of that year the renovations and construction phases were basically complete.

The most visible and impressive element of the exterior restoration was the rebuilding of a large verandah that had been completely removed. For this portion of the work, Heritage Sault Ste. Marie received a $58,000 grant from the Ontario Heritage Foundation in return for a heritage easement on the building.

The major difficulties encountered in this project were delays in the construction timetable, delays in the legal registration of the condominiums, and difficulty in arranging bridge-financing for the project.

By October 1990, Heritage Sault Ste. Marie's involvement with the project was over. Each condominium had been sold, and Algoma Condominium No. 6 had been legally registered and turned over to its own Board of Directors. Heritage Sault Ste. Marie, using the Community Heritage Fund, had been successful in saving a heritage building that was on the brink of being lost through neglect. With the completion of this project the Community Heritage Fund, which had been $205,050 at the start of the project, showed a remaining balance of approximately $88,000.

While the Community Heritage Fund was not able to make a financial profit from this project, the community had benefitted from the investment made by Heritage Sault Ste. Marie. The neighbourhood around 10 Kensington Place had received a renewed and up-dated heritage building that has a functional and secure future, and the city has gained an enriched residence that is generating increased assessment for the municipality each and every year.

607 Stewart Street

Relocation of Threatened Heritage Structures To A Municipally-Owned Subdivision: Markham Heritage Estates

Regan Hutcheson
Heritage Co-ordinator in the Strategic Policy Division of
Markham's Planning and Development Department
  Regan functions as the principal planner in the heritage planning
  area and assists in fulfilling the heritage policies of the Official Plan.
  He also provides technical and administrative assistance to Heritage
  Markham (LACAC). Prior to his association with the Town of
  Markham, Regan was a Senior Planner in the Heritage Resources
  Planning Section of Marshall Macklin Monaghan Limited, a nation-
  al consulting firm.

Introduction

The Town of Markham, located to the north of Metropolitan Toronto, is home to more than 150,000 individuals. Since 1976, when the population stood at 56,000, growth has been substantial. The opening of a major highway from Toronto in the mid-1970s further accelerated the urban development of the Town. However, amidst rapid change and growth, Markham has been successful in retaining much of its early character and charm through the introduction of various heritage conservation strategies.

These strategies include the individual designation of structures under Part IV of the Ontario Heritage Act; the establishment of heritage conservation districts under Part V of the same Act; the use of municipal controls such as zoning and special sign area by-laws, site plan control and other planning tools; and the creation of special policy initiatives such as the recent approval of Private Bill 38 in the Ontario Legislature which provides the Town with greater control over demolition of designated heritage properties. Another special policy initiative of the Town was the development of Markham Heritage Estates which is the subject of this paper.

Background

Since 1981, over forty structures which were listed in the Markham Inventory of Heritage Buildings have been demolished. After examination, the majority of these structures were deemed not to be of sufficient architectural or historical merit to warrant retention and demolition was granted. However, there were at least seven cases in the past decade where structures of significant heritage merit could not be retained on site due to incompatible development such as road widening or new highways. While some interest was shown in relocating these structures for continued use as residences, the associated costs of acquiring a lot in Markham and relocating the structure were considered prohibitive.

Although the Town requires that every effort be made to preserve heritage buildings on the sites where they were originally constructed, the Town has recognized that situations may arise from time to time where the objective of on-site conservation cannot be achieved. To retain significant residential heritage buildings which are under serious threat of loss, the Town has created an innovative heritage conservation measure of last resort called Markham Heritage Estates.

The "Heritage Subdivision" Concept

Markham Heritage Estates is a "heritage subdivision" specially designed to accommodate relocated heritage structures in a residential setting. A 7 hectare parcel of land adjoining the Markham Museum lands was acquired by the Town for this undertaking. This unique community can accommodate up to thirty-eight heritage structures in a residential environment capable of providing contemporary living within a framework of established heritage conservation principles and practice.

Markham Heritage Estates features a paved, fully serviced residential subdivision characterized by a number of interior roads and an arrangement of lots that has no historical allusions or pretensions. The residential setting is one of contemporary planning, engineering and design standards. A Landscape Master Plan has been developed for the subdivision to introduce historic landscape treatment to the public areas.

The lots in Markham Heritage Estates are originally owned by the Town and are sold below market value to individuals in possession of an eligible heritage structure. The amount saved on the price of a lot helps provide the incentive for a purchaser to relocate and restore the structure. As the structures are often donated or can be obtained for a nominal fee, the cost of relocating and restoring a threatened heritage structure can compete with the cost of a modern home. The town is committed to recoup its development expenses from the sale of the thirty-eight lots.

Building Eligibility

All candidate buildings for Markham Heritage Estates must be located within the present boundaries of the Town of Markham and should be listed in the Markham Inventory of Heritage Buildings. Buildings located in a heritage conservation district or study area will generally not be considered for Markham Heritage Estates. After a detailed evaluation, those structures found to be of architectural and/or historical significance are considered for the subdivision.

Once a building has met the above criteria, it also must satisfy the Town's policy for the relocation of heritage structures. It is a principle of the Town and the Ontario Heritage Foundation that all significant heritage buildings should be retained on their original site to maintain historical and contextual integrity. Before a building can be approved for relocation, it must be ascertained that all options for on-site retention have been exhausted. As such, relocation to Markham Heritage Estates must be a proven last resort for these structures. Once a structure has met all of the eligibility requirements, the Town places it on a list that is available at the Town offices. The Town assumes no responsibility for contacting persons interested in eligible buildings.

Lot Allocation

Once an approved building has been secured by an interested person, that person must demonstrate to the Town that they have the financial capacity to undertake successfully the entire project. This procedure requires the applicant to prepare a budget proposal which addresses factors such as lot cost, relocation expenses, insurance, restoration costs, a landscaping allowance and professional fees.

When both the building and the applicant are approved, the applicant submits a lot allocation application providing the applicant's lot preference and scale drawings of the subject building and any proposed additions or accessory buildings. Although there are many planning and design factors considered in the lot allocation process, the impact on the overall streetscape is the prime consideration. Therefore, the Town has final approval on which lot is selected for the building.

Once a lot is approved by the town, the applicant enters into an Agreement of Purchase and Sale with the Town. This legal agreement commits the applicant to various terms and conditions such as:
• to own and reside in the house for a period of at least
• five years;
• to relocate the building to the approved lot, complete the exterior restorations and first phase of historic lot landscaping within a period of one year;

- to submit all proposed works to the Town for approval prior to construction and carry out plans as approved;
- to participate in special programs including plaquing and exterior photography.

A Site Plan Agreement between the applicant and the Town is also required prior to the building relocation. The Site Plan Approval process provides the various Town Departments with an opportunity to review the site plan and building elevations. As part of this process, a detailed restoration plan based on a thorough examination of historical, physical, pictorial, oral and documentary evidence is required to guide the preservation of the heritage building. A historic landscape plan is also required as part of the Agreement.

Relocation, Restoration and Landscaping
The relocation of the building to Markham Heritage Estates is the responsibility of the applicant. However, the Town does require that the building be moved as a complete unit and will not consider the dismantling of heritage buildings for reconstruction.

As previously indicated, all restoration plans must be approved by the Town and the exterior work must comply with the Markham Heritage Estates Restoration Guidelines and the approved Site Plan Agreement. The original exterior should be restored to as close to the documented original as possible.

As many heritage buildings are considered small by modern standards, lot sizes were designed to allow additions and accessory building. The design treatment of new additions and accessory buildings are subject to established heritage conservation principles and practice as outlined in the Town guidelines.

Landscape development and enhancement is a crucial aspect of the site planning for each residential lot. Attempts may be made to re-establish significant, documented landscape features around each building or establish typical landscape features which are judged to be appropriate to the building's style and period within the Town. Guidelines have been prepared to assist in the front yard historic landscape treatment of individual lots. The Town has also prepared an overall landscape plan for the perimeter of the development on the road allowances.

Concerns
Although the concept has received widespread support from the general public, the Ontario Ministry of Culture and Communications (M.C.C.) expressed initial concern. The Ministry felt the motives behind the concept were commendable, but that the formation of a

heritage subdivision was conceptually unsound and administratively problematic.

The main concern of M.C.C. was that much of the heritage value of any building relates to its context, environment and associated features and that once a building is moved, much of its heritage value is destroyed. The fear that Markham would end up with a random collection of old buildings with minimum heritage value on their new sites was expressed. There is no argument from the Town that a heritage building loses its contextual and environmental value once it is relocated. However, given that the current Ontario heritage legislation provides limited demolition control powers; that only threatened buildings of significant architectural or historical merit outside of a heritage conservation district or study area are eligible; and that the alternative in most cases is demolition, the Town believes a heritage subdivision is a viable option of last resort. Further, one could argue that the past integration of many heritage buildings into new commercial and residential developments has proven to be equally ill-fated when it comes to retaining contextual and environmental integrity.

In response to allegations that developers will have little incentive to preserve buildings on their original sites or to incorporate them sensitively into new development, the Town has incorporated policies into its Official Plan requiring that all retention options be exhausted prior to relocation consideration. In addition the Town is one of three Ontario communities to have obtained special legislation from the Ontario Legislature to provide additional demolition control on designated structures. This special legislation helps strengthen the Town's negotiating position especially in the rural areas in Markham where designated heritage buildings, under no development pressures, are often initially abandoned, allowed to deteriorate and then threatened with demolition.

The Town has gone to great lengths to ensure that Markham Heritage Estates does not become a "dumping ground" for unwanted buildings of architectural and/or historical significance. It is hoped that the Subdivision will further increase public awareness and modify negative attitudes towards the conservation and re-use of built heritage resources.

Conclusion

The Town is proud of this unique conservation initiative and has invested a significant amount of time, staff resources and financial commitment in this project. Given that no other project of this type could be found in Canada, the administrative procedures, policies and guidelines had to be developed by the Town. Based on the experience encountered with the first few applicants, various procedures and policies have been and continue to be reviewed and revised to clarify and improve the process.

To date, seven buildings have been approved for Markham Heritage Estates. There is no overall timeframe to complete the project as a lot is only allocated when an eligible building is truly threatened. When completed, the restored buildings assembled at Markham Heritage Estates will comprise a rich, built legacy of once threatened, predominantly rural heritage residences indigenous to the Town of Markham, which will continue to serve a residential use for many years in the future.

Facadism or Partial Retention

William N. Greer
Heritage Consultant, Toronto
William is a registered architect with expertise in all aspects of the
heritage preservation process which was effectively practised in his
15 years association as Chief Architect with the Toronto Historical
Board. He is currently working in private practice as a Heritage
Consultant. William holds a Master of Science degree from Illinois
Institute of Technology and a Bachelor of Architecture from the
University of Toronto. He is currently affiliated with numerous her-
itage organizations including the Society for the Study of
Architecture in Canada, Heritage Canada, and the Ontario
Historical Society.

FACADES FORM THE BUILDING ENVELOPE which encloses areas of functional use. However, facades have greater meaning than mere
physical presence. The influence of an owner's concept of architectural style and local history as well as craftsmanship and use of
industrial materials are generally reflected in facade design.

An increase in public interest in architectural heritage preservation has been demonstrated in contemporary urban redevelopment.
Resulting solutions have produced questionable and commendable
results in the treatment of buildings and facades.

The term "facadism" has been a mocking and derogatory term often
applied by preservationists to specific examples of architectural preservation that do not meet the perfection of doctrinaire standards for the
conservation of entire buildings. A symposium in Montreal three years
ago was held on the theme of facadism. Dinu Bumbaru, of Heritage
Montreal, reported that facadism (or partial retention) was defined as
"an attitude relating preservation to the transmission of cultural values
to future generations". This attitude links preservation to the reality of
the issues involved -property development, urban planning, legislation, degree of professional competence and a fragmentary vision of
heritage. These issues affect how we should initially deal with the identification of our built heritage, who should be involved and what
process should be followed in the management of change to it.

In the management of standards for preservation of the built
environment, decisions must be made about what is important and
what is not. Such decisions can be affected by local, social and eco-

nomic conditions, by legislation at various levels and by the principles established in the various international charters for the preservation of the built environment, as advocated by organizations like the A.C.O. and interpreted by the LACACs.

When a heritage property is seriously threatened with change or demolition, one approach is to be dogmatic ("authoritative assertion of opinion") and demand that the entire building be preserved - plan, interior detail, building form and facades - or abandon it for demolition. This implies that nothing less than perfect preservation and full retention can possibly be tolerated.

The alternative approach is to be pragmatic ("systematic testing of the truth and value of ideas by their practical consequences"), analyze the issues, establish the most appropriate extent of preservation and see that quality is achieved in all architectural designs for the project. This process must be carefully managed to include participation of the public representatives, professional advisors and municipal planning and heritage staff.

Implementing this second approach to include retention of the most important facade or section of a building in a development would be undertaken with the full understanding that heritage significance could be thereby diminished. The Toronto Historical Board adopted a policy and guidelines for considering options when full retention was found to be unattainable under specific circumstances.

The fact that projects in Toronto and in Montreal have ended in partial retention has been due to pressure exerted by the types of issues faced by development in downtown cores where many heritage buildings are located and where high density development is generally permitted in the zoning bylaws. Some of these examples are architecturally unsatisfactory. Nevertheless, public response to facadism or partial retention has been positive in many projects. They feel that retention of familiar facades is a meaningful representation of continuity when treated with architectural sensitivity. On the other hand, they are concerned about the incongruous placement of heritage fragments in contemporary architectural designs.

Partial retention is a failure when there is a lack of attention to the fundamental principles of architectural design. Scale, form, materials and compatibility in the context of the site and building plan have been neglected. Criteria and guidelines for accepting partial retention must be clear to all concerned at the start of negotiation and strictly implemented when acceptance of the "last resort" preservation is inevitable.

The environmental waste of demolition without regard to the inherent future usefulness of whole buildings, significant facades or construction materials must now be assessed and accounted for regardless of principles to the contrary.

Salvaging Heritage: The Non-Profit Way

Matthew F. Schultz
Philadelphia Architectural Salvage Ltd.

As a teenager, when several historic buildings were threatened in his hometown of Lansdowne, Pennslyvania, Matthew began his involvement in the historic preservation movement. He participated in the creation of the Greater Lansdowne Civic Association, which forced the local officials to create a more progressive local planning code. While pursuing an Urban Studies degree at Temple University, Matt created a house painting company that addressed the special needs of older structures. After graduating in 1986, he was hired by the Philadelphia Historic Preservation Corporation to create a program now known as Philadelphia Architectural Salvage Ltd. Matt has also authored articles for publications including the Old House Journal concerning the reuse of salvaged building materials. Along with his wife, Judie, he is currently restoring a 1896 Queen Anne Style home located in Lansdowne. Their efforts have been chronicled in the Old House Journal and the Philadelphia Inquirer.

THE PRACTICE OF SALVAGING MATERIALS from buildings is not a new phenomenon. The Romans helped themselves to the stone from the Coliseum to build their homes or add on to them. Societies have always reused building materials for a variety of reasons such as lack of raw material, high costs, or because of their value as art.

Non-profit salvage yards have been created because preservationists have come to understand that buildings are demolished for a variety of reasons, some valid, some not. The preservation community has come to realize that it does not have the ability to save every historic resource and that salvaging materials from doomed buildings makes economic and environmental sense. Well-made and aesthetically pleasing materials are made available to restorers with the hope that they will be used in an appropriate manner and lead to structures being rehabilitated with their architectural integrity intact.

Raw materials once common and popular have been overused to the point of extinction. The most well known, long leaf yellow pine has been eradicated and is available only from buildings which have been demolished. The pine trees which grew along the eastern coast were noted for their straight grain and density. These two attributes made such pine a perfect wood for ship masts, and for structural members in buildings. Today, it is sought for these same reasons but it is extremely difficult to locate and very expensive.

The direct environmental effect of salvaging reusable building materials is obvious. Anything which is reused saves space in the landfill. The indirect effect of salvaging and providing historic materials is to encourage the rehabilitation of existing housing stock, which takes less energy and materials than the alternative, to build new housing. The existing housing is most often located in urban areas which are accessible to the environmentally friendly mass transportation system. Also, if these structures are rehabilitated there is one less building that must be built on an undeveloped piece of land in the surrounding suburbs, thus preserving open space.

Salvaging materials from historic buildings is not universally accepted in the historic preservation and museum communities. Some insist that the practice encourages demolition. When urban homesteading became popular during the early 1970s in Baltimore, Maryland many people sought reusable building materials in historic buildings which were structurally unsafe. After several accidents, the City's Commission for Historical and Architectural Preservation created a program known as the Baltimore Salvage Depot. The program involved city workers stripping dangerous buildings of their elements, therefore taking away the incentive to enter the unsafe buildings. The Depot then sold the materials to the residents of Baltimore at a price which encouraged their reuse. This effort made great strides in legitimizing the salvaging of materials from historic buildings.

In 1987, the Philadelphia Historic Preservation Corporation (PHPC) recognized that in excess of 100 buildings were to be demolished to make room for a new convention centre in centre city Philadelphia. Commercial, residential, and industrial buildings were to be razed to make room for the structure which is being counted on to draw large numbers of conventioneers to the historic city. The City was unable to spend the money necessary to document the doomed structures and it was realized that this group of buildings contained a great amount of reusable historic building materials. With these two issues in mind, the Pew Charitable Trusts provided seed money for the creation of a new organization, Philadelphia Architectural Salvage Ltd. (PASL). PASL is dedicated to (1) the salvaging and resale of reusable historic building materials, (2) photographically documenting structures slated for demolition, and (3) conducting home rehabilitation/maintenance workshops for low and moderate income homeowners.

A private non-profit organization like PASL has several advantages that a for-profit business has not. Not only can it accept grant money from foundations, but it can enter into contracts to accept publicly-owned assets, such as individual building materials or salvage rights. PASL entered into contracts with local, state, and federal agencies. The largest contract is with the City of Philadelphia's Department of Licenses and Inspection which is charged with demolishing over 1000 dilapidated structures per year. PASL has official permission to enter the doomed structures to salvage materials. Also, PASL with grant money, provides services free to the public that a for-profit business would be unwilling to undertake; namely, documenting buildings for archival purposes and providing home rehabilitation/maintenance workshops for owners of older buildings at no cost.

In five years, PASL has received approximately $650,000 donations-in-kind. The materials salvaged include doors, hardware, claw foot bathtubs, lighting fixtures, signage, bars, fencing, flooring, and various decorative items.

The customer base for the business is varied. Homesteaders, artists, antique collectors, contractors, and homeowners from every income level take advantage of this resource. Initially, there was a ban on antique dealers. This was done because the items were priced artificially low to meet the needs of the end users. PASL did not want to act as a wholesaler for antique dealers. Out of financial necessity, that policy was changed and prices were increased to deter antique dealers from taking advantage of PASL.

The recession has taken its toll on PASL. Costs have been dramatically reduced due to lack of sales. PASL also faces an odd dilemma. With the downturn in the real estate market, there is less pressure to demolish buildings to make way for others, hence there are fewer materials available to sell. In addition, the City of Philadelphia is having its own financial crisis. It is unable to raze buildings at the same rate as in previous years. Without supply and demand, a business will obviously experience some pretty serious problems. Hopefully, the organization will be able to survive the current financial climate in the United States and continue to serve the preservation community in the Philadelphia region.

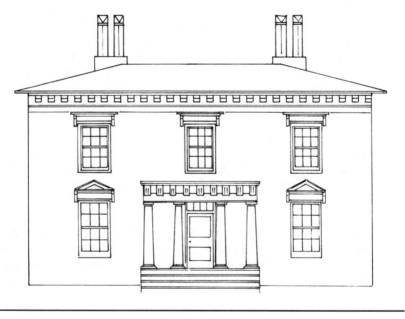

Engleburn
206 Engleburn Avenue

Construction Management: The Team Approach to Restoration

J.D. Strachan
J.D. Strachan Construction
James has twenty years of experience in the construction industry in a variety of projects such as the restoration of University College and the building of Canada's Wonderland. Prior to forming J.D.Strachan Construction, he was Chief Estimate and Special Projects Manager for Fairwin Construction Limited. James is the Chairman of the Township of King LACAC.

I AGREED TO DISCUSS CONSTRUCTION MANAGEMENT and the Team Approach to Restoration and I will. But what I really want to focus on is money and how to control it effectively during the construction process.

There should be nothing mysterious about restoring older buildings. Sure there are a few tricky areas like the Morgan Philips method of re-attaching plaster, matching the compressive strength, colour and texture of the mortar to the existing brick and checking the absorption and flexural strength of replacement slate tiles. But mainly the challenge in restoration is doing it within a limited budget. First the Owners then the Contractors. Given the expertise available through the Owner, the Architect, the Engineers, the LACAC, the Ministry, the Contractor and the Sub-Trades, with an unlimited budget, and careful selection of the players, it should be relatively easy to produce excellent results. The fact is that at some point in the project each of the players is forced to start making decisions not in terms of what is best for the building but what they can afford to include.

Before I discuss the management process, I will look at the contractual differences between working on a Construction Management Contract and a Stipulated Price Contract. The Canadian Construction Association publishes standard forms of contract for each type of arrangement. CCDC 2 is the Stipulated Price Contract and CCDC 5 is used for Construction Management. I think it is important to note that these papers are very much a layman's interpretation of the construction documents. Interpretation of either of these forms of contract is a very complex issue and interpretation of these documents is an ongoing activity of the Courts. The main differences between the two contracts are as follows:

1. The stipulated price contract establishes one contract between the General Contractor and the Owner with the Architect named as the Owner's Consultant. Ironically, although the Architect has many functions within the stipulated price contract, he is not actually a party to the contract. Similarly, all responsibility for the work, reporting, etc. from sub-trades is through the General Contractor. There is not direct relationship between sub-trades and the owner. Therefore, their initial contract or any changes to their scope of work must be dealt with through the General Contract.

   With the Construction Management Contract the Construction Manager assumes a role similar to the Architect in that he becomes the Owner's agent and in fact in most cases the Owner will sign contracts directly with the sub-trades and make payments to them as their work progresses. All negotiations for changes to the scope of work can be conducted directly between the Owner and the sub-trade with the Architect and the Construction Manager acting as advisors.

2. With the Construction Management Contract there need not be an upset cost established for the total project. The fee for the Construction Management services, which can range anywhere from 3 to 15%, is usually based on an outline scope of work and approximate budget. The final costs of the sub-trade work are a net cost to the Owner without additional mark-up.

3. The Stipulated Price Contract requires a precise definition of the final scope of work before the Contractor can be engaged. This means that the Contractor's involvement usually begins after all design and budget decisions have been made and requires a firm commitment by both parties as to what the actual work will entail. With the Construction Management approach, the Contractor can be engaged even in the pre-design stage and his expertise used to review budgets, methods of construction, materials, etc. With restoration work, more so than new construction, the General Contractor's input, during this stage, is key to the success of the project. Rather than speculating on items such as scheduling, phasing, staffing, availability of equipment and expertise, the Architect and the Owner can plan early very specific details regarding these issues with the Contractor's resources in mind.

4. Significantly, the stipulated price contract has no requirement for the General Contractor to provide overall budget control either before or during construction nor does the Owner, unless specific arrangements are stipulated in the tender documents have control over when a sub-contract is let or the terms of the sub-contract. Conversely, the Construction Manager is required to prepare an update budget and schedules as the project progresses from pre-design to post construction.

5. What if it doesn't work out or the chemistry is wrong? What if the grants don't come through? Or if early in the project conditions are uncovered that significantly change the scope of the work and require re-thinking of the practicality of proceeding at that time or at all?

The Stipulated Price Contract has provisions for cancelling the contract due to lack of performance on the part of the General Contractor or failure to pay on the Owner's part. However, there are no specific provisions made for quantifying the costs to cancel the contract. The documents committee should realize that once the contract is let, and without any provision for detailed reporting of the costs, or purchasing and sub-trade commitments by the General Contractor it is impossible to determine an accurate formula for cancelling the work and compensating the Contractor. If this becomes an issue, the Owner is in a very precarious position. He must deal through the Contractor to negotiate a final settlement and besides direct costs, can be liable for things such as lost anticipated profits, overheads and profits for the entire project from both the General Contractor and his sub-trades. By contrast the Construction Management Contract establishes a fee breakdown for different stages of the work and the costs to cancel.

Assembling the Team
Throughout this paper I have interchanged the terms construction management and contractors. They are two separate entities and on many new projects it is preferable to have a firm that provides management services only. Restoration is a specialized field and my recommendation would be to engage a manager with "in-house-trained forces" to complete portions of the work.

Article A-2 of the agreement sets the tone for the relationship by defining the Owner, Consultant and Construction Manager as the "Construction Management Team". In effect what you are doing is agreeing with the Contractor on a reasonable fee for his involvement at the start and bringing him on side with yourself and the other consultants. This changes the Contractor's relationship with the sub-trades as well. With the Stipulated Price Contract the Contractor is ultimately responsible for the performance of the sub-trades. Should disputes arise regarding cost, quality of work, schedule, etc., the contractor cannot be expected to act as an impartial advisor. As Construction Manager his first responsibility is to the Owner.

I am often reminded of the comparison of the astronaut hurtling out into oblivion and looking around him and knowing that every component of his space craft has been assembled by the lowest bidder. Each step of assembling a team in a restoration contract should have an accountability element in terms of overall costs. However, the two key players (besides the Owner), the Architect and the Contractor, should be selected with performance rather than price as the first criterion. Construction Management affords the Owner much greater flexibility in this regard since the amount to be negotiated for this fee may only represent 1 or 2% of the total construction costs. This represents a tangible commodity that should be relatively easy to negotiate a satisfactory deal for all parties. The common misconception is that by opting for the Stipulated Price Contract, the Owner gains some measure of security. Although this can be true, when we look at the tendering process you will see that most times the initial bid does not reflect a good value and by the time the project is finished any security has long been relinquished. Construction Management, on the other hand, allows the Owner and Architect full participation in the tendering process and the ability to take measured, timely steps in the commitment to the various parts of the work and their execution. The belief is, that for better or worse, with the stipulated price method of contracting "at least we know at the beginning how much we are going to pay for the project".

I have several problems with this. First because of the tendering process which I will explain in more detail later, it is not always clear whether you are getting good value in the original base bid. You might start out getting a lot less than what you actually paid for. This might not be apparent to anyone, including the Contractor until well into the project. The second problem is that the scope of work for a restoration project grows and changes as the work proceeds. Probably 20-30% of the cost of any restoration project goes towards stripping away old finishes or treating visible structural faults. It is unrealistic to expect that before this process is complete anyone can determine exactly what work will be required to finish the project.

Tendering Process - Pricing the Work

There are many misconceptions among Owners and even some Architects of exactly what happens during the tendering process and how the final price is arrived at. Some of the more popular theories include:

- That we weigh the drawings and the price is arrived at by a formula: dollars per pound.
- The mythical contractor's dart board with a series of prices on it.
- The coin toss to decide whether an outrageously high or low bid will be submitted.
- The most popular misconception that we actually know the exact price of the work and the only variation is in our mark-up.

Like all myths, each of these theories has some basis in truth. However, the more established method is much more complex and uncertain.

Each general contractor invited to bid the work represents a network of in-house staff, suppliers and sub-trades. If we stopped right here it would be simple. Contractor picks up the drawings, consults his network, receives prices, assembles the final price and submits his bid. However, when you introduce 3, or 5 general contractors, each with their own network, elements of which are common to some of the contractors and completely unknown to others; add to this the fact that the input from competing general contractors subs or suppliers is often not available until the closing minutes of a tender, if at all, and the fact that each general develops his own strategy with his trades to price the work, that is the scope of work that they are to include, the scheduling of the work, access, etc. you begin to get a very complicated scenario.

Finally, I should mention the most "erroneous" conception of all: given a three week period to prepare a bid that the contractor actually spends the full three weeks preparing his bid. Tendering projects can be a weekly or even daily exercise in a busy general contractor's office. The 3 week period allows for site tours, take-offs by sub-trades and estimating. However, the actual time spent on the estimate is probably no more than 2-4 days and the time available to do the final analysis before submitting a bid with all critical information from subs and suppliers available is seldom more than the last hour (and usually the last 10 to 15 minutes) before the bid closes. I once had an Architect sit on a tendering closing for one of our projects. The flurry of activity in the dying moments before a tender is completed can be a hair-raising experience. After the tender was completed and we were reviewing the events of the last hour, he commented he was positive I must have been a gun slinger in a previous life.

I think you can begin to see how the dart board and the scales start to offer a viable alternative. But this isn't all, consider the following:

1. Not all trades give the same price to each general contractor. Depending on their past experience with the contractor or their alliance with one general.
2. Not all subs bid on the same scope of work. There can be any number of combinations offered like painting; painting and plastering; painting, plastering and drywall; painting and drywall; or any of the above with or without restoring existing surfaces.
3. Despite a sincere effort to obtain prices for all elements of the work it may turn out that the general doesn't receive prices for one or more of the trades for a variety of reasons.
4. With some of the generals a particular tender date may coincide with other activities in the office and your bid may receive less than a full effort.
5. There may be sections in the document which fail to properly define the scope of work and artificially influence the pricing by sub-trades.
6. For some of the generals, the "chemistry" could seem all wrong. This is a very elusive element and obviously almost impossible to quantify, but for the majority of the contractors, the brief one or two hour site tour is the only opportunity they have to access how the Owner, Architect, Contractor team will function during the job. For some, this brief encounter may not be a positive experience and this could drastically affect the final price.
7. If tendering were an exact science, why wouldn't everyone put in the same price?
8. Quite often sub-trades from competing general contractors will deliberately submit inflated quotations to confuse the other generals.
9. It is not unusual to get a 20-25% spread in the prices received from 6 or 7 sub-trades. However, it is equally common to only receive the lowest and the highest bid. Then it must be decided in a matter of minutes if the spread in prices represents the lowest and highest bids you would have normally received (for any or all of the reasons given above) or if the low bidder actually understands the true scope of work.
10. Some restoration contractors can be decidedly weak in some areas of their network. This could be of particular concern when considering building for conversion to museums. Many restoration contractors, while perfectly capable of completing the work, lack the network of sub-trades required to obtain competitive prices on the sophisticated mechanical electrical systems in the short period of time given.

This is only a brief overview of the tendering process but I think it gives enough of an insight that we can compare it to the construction management method.

1. The Construction Manager can and should be appointed long before the actual work is to be sent out for tender to allow him adequate time to gain an indepth understanding of the proposed scope of work.
2. When the documents are issued to the sub-trades, all information flows through one source. There is a consistent approach to the project.
3. The tenders can be staged to allow sequential tendering of the work giving all parties the opportunity to review site conditions, scheduling, etc. on a trade-by-trade basis rather than the whole project at once.
4. It has been our experience that sub-trades are much more receptive and quote you better prices if they know you have the work rather than being just one of several bidders.
5. The list of proposed sub-trades can be screened with the Owner and Architect before the tender rather than after.
6. The final team is selected on a trade by trade basis rather than selecting one contractor with his chosen network.

By choosing the construction management approach you ensure competitive bidding but as importantly, you ensure a workable team where all the players have a clearer understanding of what is required.

Tips on Working with Your Construction Manager

First of all, use the standard CCDC Document No. 4 with as few revisions as possible as the basis of your contract. Although not fool-proof, this document has been revised many times and tested in the Courts. It provides a good basis for your agreement. Having said that, the Appendix-Reimburseable Expenses allows all off-site overhead costs such as management salaries, travel, bookkeeping, etc. to be charged on an hourly rate. I personally find this a bit too open-ended and prefer that these items be grouped in the fee and the final costs known by everyone before the work proceeds.

Wherever possible, portion the work into concise well-defined packages and obtain competitive bids from anyone but the Construction Manager. One of the advantages of engaging a Contractor as Construction Manager is the flexibility offered by access to his labour force. However, just as with the stipulated sum method, the ultimate objective should be to limit your exposure to cost over-runs.

It is important to remember that not all General Contractors bring the same resources and strengths to a project. There is a wide variation from those who provide a Management or Broker Service to firms who have in-house capabilities to complete carpentry, masonry, plaster repair, etc.

Engage the Construction Manager as early as possible in the process. You want to take advantage of his expertise in construction methods and budgeting doing the design phases as well as construction. The sooner he is involved, the more help he can be. Be specific in your requirements in terms of the number and timing of budget updates, personnel to be assigned, frequency of meetings. Perform some detailed research into the Construction Manager's previous projects to ensure they match yours. A list of well-known successful restorations is a good starting point, but does the firm have experience in the specialty elements that you will be completing, such as, slate roofing, window restoration, complex mechanical systems, masonry repointing, etc.

Expect to pay 5 to 15% depending on the size and complexity of the project. Part of what you are doing in engaging a Construction Manager is ensuring the Contractor payment for adequate management by senior personnel of your project. Don't be fooled by unrealistic fee proposals. Part of the objective is to ensure adequate management and the cost of this should be reflected in the fee.

If someone were to ask me what is the role of the Contractor during the construction process, the expected answer would be that he determines the method of construction and provides the labour force to complete the work. However, the overriding task for the Contractor is to take risks. Where the work is not that clearly defined or the methods of completing it unknown, the Contractor assigns a value to the work and risks that his assumptions are correct.

So at the end of the day, as they say, what's the difference? The difference is that with Construction Management you are assured of a team where all the players have been screened and coached before submitting their bids. Everyone starts the project with a much better understanding of what is required of them and an established realistic price for each element of the work. At each level it is absolutely essential to ensure that all the participants start the project not only with a competitive price but one which, assuming the work is performed correctly, gives them the opportunity to realize at least a marginal profit. To do otherwise is only courting disaster.

Architectural
Integrity
and
Human Needs

Architectural Integrity vs Human Needs

Lois Harte-Maxwell
Councillor, City of Peterborough

Fulfilling a life-long interest in politics, Lois has served on many Committees and Boards for the City of Peterborough and the Province of Ontario. Of particular interest are Human Rights Issues, which have kept her extremely active in the area of access for the physically challenged. Past positions include: Provincial Coordinator for the Youth Job Corps Program; Coordinator of Special Transit for the Physically Disabled for the City of Peterborough; District Campaign Secretary, Ontario March of Dimes. Lois is currently involved with the City of Peterborough Buildings Committee, among other things, to oversee implementation of a Barrier Free Access program for all City owned buildings.

Accessibility

In this article on Architectural Integrity vs. Human Needs, I will be providing the perspective of one who has had a disability since childhood. Dealing with architectural barriers has been, therefore, an integral part of daily living - not something viewed from afar. I will elaborate on the following aspects:

- Isolation of disabled people
- Historical background of the struggle for access
- Current access
- Looking forward to the future

In the September 28, 1991 issue of the Globe and Mail, Adele Freedman was particularly incensed by what she described as "The latest and potentially most brutalizing of a series of additions and subtractions that are being allowed to undermine the architecture of Champlain College". This, of course, was the proposed 13.7 metre ramp to provide access to this building here at Trent University.

I submit that the concern expressed over the **potential** brutalization of Champlain College ignores the real and actual brutalization of generations of disabled people - people who were not so much shut-ins, but shut out of this and other public facilities! To be fair, Adele acknowledged that, "no right-minded person would argue buildings should not be adapted to satisfy special needs". The question is though, how to adapt and by what criteria, both practically and with respect to architecturally significant buildings.

Isolation of Disabled People

I have an accessibility guide book. It's a guide for disabled people to help take the uncertainty out of visiting new locations and to alert them to barriers to access. Imagine needing such a guide to one's own community. But these barriers are a reality not simply an inconvenience! How would you feel if you were effectively barred from participation in your community because of architectural barriers? In 1976, as Coordinator for a similar guide, I was not surprised that about 95% of our churches were inaccessible. Were they architecturally significant buildings? Yes, many were, but if one didn't know better it almost seemed that churches had many steps and were elevated in order to get closer to God! As a result because of architectural barriers disabled people were denied the opportunity to be a part of the worshipping community. Churches, museums, hotels, municipal buildings, educational facilities, in fact most public facilities were inaccessible. And those most basic of all facilities, public washrooms were almost a rarity!

Put yourself in the shoes of disabled people. Pretend you are among the 14% of the population who have a disability. It can't happen to me you might say. Well, it's only a matter of time - some of you will develop a disability, there is no doubt about it! The matter of inaccessibility will be real and very pervasive.

Am I being too blunt? Do I lack sensitivity toward our architectural heritage? I say unequivocally, "No!" I am saying, that as a person who represents disabled people, I have an obligation to tell our story about the need for access to public buildings. We are the public too. And today to say that disabled people have been hurt by being shut out is an understatement.

We want people to know that we have a right to celebrate our heritage too. We care about our roots and those who came before us. We care deeply about those fine buildings which were their homes and meeting places. We respect the need to preserve and protect our heritage.

Historical Background of the Struggle for Access

For centuries, people with disabilities have struggled to cope in an inaccessible environment. For the most part, they struggled in quiet resignation. But that changed particularly in the early 1970s. People with disabilities began seriously to question their lack of access to the services and facilities they were contributing to as taxpayers. The inaccessibility of public facilities fuelled a fire of discontent that was not destined to go away.

In those days, there were no legislated requirements regarding accessibility in Ontario. I recall in fact, preparing a brief for a Peterborough organization of disabled people calling for changes to the Building Code to reflect the need for access. We were one of many organizations across the province calling for change. In 1974, the Ontario Building Code was amended to recognize the need for access in many classes of buildings - it was not retroactive. Consequently, those buildings erected prior to that time were not affected. I recall that when the Code was amended, the private sector raised a hue and cry that the economic sky would surely fall in. Well, that was not the case.

In the latter part of the 1970s, organizations of disabled people continued to lobby for access. It was recognized that discrimination based upon disability continued to occur. The apartment to rent suddenly was NOT AVAILABLE TO A BLIND PERSON! The woman in a wheelchair was ASKED TO LEAVE A RESTAURANT because when she came in from the rain, her wheelchair left water marks on the floor! Astounding - but true! Disabled people lobbied for an amendment to the Ontario Human Rights Code to prevent blatant discrimination.

The government of the day unleashed one of the largest cries of outrage ever witnessed in this province when it proposed protecting the rights of disabled people with legislation - separate from and not a part of the Ontario Human Rights Code. I can assure you that disabled people were united in totally rejecting the notion that separate meant equal! After months, under considerable pressure, the government had no option but to withdraw the travesty they proposed. As one who was in the midst of this controversy, I can recall these events as vividly as if they were yesterday. In 1981, I was present at a gala dinner in Toronto as a guest of the government to help celebrate the inclusion of disabled people as a protected group under the Ontario Human Rights Code.

Current Access

While I have only briefly touched upon some of the historical realities regarding inaccessibility, you will appreciate how disabled people have struggled to become active participants rather than passive observers. Today we have many more accessible public buildings. Lifts and ramps are being installed. Most new buildings with the exception of private homes are being properly constructed. Why? Because it's the right thing to do? Because of amendments to the Ontario Building Code and the Ontario Human Rights Code? Because the advocacy continues? Basically, it's for all of these reasons.

The Peck Stone House
183 Mark Street

Architectural Integrity vs Human Needs

John Ota
Education/Technical Advisor, Ministry of Culture & Communications.
John is a graduate architect and has worked in architectural offices in
Toronto and New York, including the Barrier Free Design Centre in
Toronto. He has taught in the Barrier Free Design Course at Ryerson
Polytechnical Institute and is a past member of the Toronto Historical
Board. John holds a Master of Science Degree in Architecture and
Historic Preservation from Columbia University.

Guidelines for Accessibility

The current standard for disabled access in all buildings including historic structures is outlined in the *"Guidelines for Assessing Accommodation Requirements for Persons with Disabilities"* published by the Ontario Human Rights Commission in 1988. In the debate to deal with architectural integrity vs. human needs, the Ontario Human Rights Commission has clearly sided with meeting human needs first and architectural integrity second.

In this presentation I will outline:
- the historical context of the architectural conservation movement and the historical context of the Human Rights Commission Guidelines.
- the meaning of the Guidelines for historic structures.
- examples of access into historic buildings; and
- some suggestions on working with the Guidelines.

Context of Heritage in Ontario

Following the Second World War, the face of North American cities and towns changed dramatically as historic buildings from the 19th century were demolished and replaced by modern buildings or shopping malls. Interest in historic architecture was minimal.

However, by the late 1960s and early 1970s a new movement developed which encouraged the preservation of historic structures. Central to this movement was a renewed appreciation of the beauty, detail and craftsmanship of historic architecture.

Within this context, the government of Ontario came under intense pressure from the public to enact legislation which would protect historic buildings. In response, the province passed the

Ontario Heritage Act in 1974. The Act gives municipalities the power to designate historic structures and sets out the functions and procedures to be followed in the implementation of a heritage program. By the 1990s the movement to preserve historic buildings has become so established that it is now a crucial social and economic factor in the development of cities and towns around the world.

History of the Ontario Human Rights Commission Guidelines
During this same period of the late 1970s and 1980s, the movement to promote the rights of people with disabilities made important gains. However, a major disappointment was that there were no explicit legislative measures taken to assist in removing barriers for disabled people. Two factors led to amendments to the Human Rights Code and the development of accessibility guidelines in the 1980s.

One factor was the passing of the Canadian Charter of Rights in 1985. Section 15 of the Charter guarantees equality under the law, free of discrimination based on grounds such as sex, race and mental and physical disabilities.

A second factor was the landmark Huck legal case in Saskatchewan in 1984. Mr. Huck, a disabled person, was able to enter an Odeon movie theatre in his wheelchair, but the only available seating to him was in the front row of the theatre. The Court ruled that Odeon Theatres must offer their services to the general public equitably regardless of physical disabilities.

What Are the Guidelines?
The Guidelines are not law. The Guidelines provide guidance from the Human Rights Commission for the public concerning accessibility issues.

The Guidelines have not been tested in the courts. If a case came to court challenging the Guidelines it is possible that the court might not wholly uphold them. An important reason that the Guidelines have not been tested in court is that the Human Rights Commission can mediate complaints and so far most complaints of this sort have been settled through mediation.

What Do the Guidelines Mean for Historic Buildings?
The Guidelines mean that workplaces, services and facilities must be adapted in such a way that persons with disabilities can participate in society in much the same way as persons without disabilities. This includes people who have visual and hearing impairments.

In the case of historic buildings the Guidelines are saying the dignity of the disabled person comes first, the historic appearance of the building is a secondary concern.

Examples

Working with the Guidelines requires great creativity and sensitivity on the part of restoration designers. The following are three historic buildings which have been made accessible and have also maintained their historic integrity. Each example has required a separate design and as in the case of all historic buildings, every situation is different.

1. George Brown House, Toronto

The first example is the George Brown House in Toronto which was beautifully restored by the Ontario Heritage Foundation. The traditional entrance to the George Brown House is located at the front of the building and is inaccessible for people with disabilities due to the high stairs. During the restoration, the main entrance was relocated to the side of the building.

The positive feature of relocating the main entrance is that all visitors to the house including those with disabilities use the side entrance area. This is the aim of the Human Rights Commission Guidelines, that everybody uses the same entrance area.

The existing structure and staircases of the building meant that able-bodied people walk through these doors and then up a flight of stairs to reach the first floor while people with disabilities use a ramp at the rear of the building to reach the first level. Because the interpretation of the building starts at the first floor where everybody meets, disabled people experience the building in the same way as people without disabilities.

The George Brown House is an example of a project with severe structural constraints but the architects were able to maintain the historical integrity of the building while allowing for the needs of people with disabilities.

2. Central United Church, Sault Ste. Marie

A second example, of a historical addition which is accessible, is a design by Chris Tossel, Architect at the Central United Church in Sault Ste. Marie. The main door of the church is at the front of the building. The church decided to locate the barrier-free access at the rear of the building. Initially, one might think that the entrance at the rear might offend people with disabilities. However, the reason for this decision was that the parking lot is at the rear of the building and in many ways the location of the ramp at the rear, adjacent to the parking lot is a good one for people with disabilities, especially in the winter. This ramp is also a commonly-used entrance for all people who access the church.

The design of the ramp is beautifully detailed to match the historic building. The colour of the stone has been carefully selected to blend in *a* ith the original building fabric as does the profile of the mortar. The ramp is also well integrated with the surrounding landscape and does not appear out of place as part of this historic structure.

This addition at the Central United Church in Sault Ste. Marie is an example of barrier-free design which enhances the building both aesthetically and in terms of human needs.

3. Ombudsman Office
The Ombudsman Office is a classical building at the intersection of Avenue Road and Bloor Street in Toronto. The designers were fortunate to inherit a situation with space to install a ramp at the main entrance which was not the case in the previous two examples.

This ramp is integrated with the trees and flowers of the building and the stone used on the ramp matches the stone on the flower boxes and paving. The turning platform of the ramp has been designed with an attractive circular stone pattern and a very surprising but much appreciated tree to create a little oasis from the traffic and noise of Avenue Road. The next design step would have been to install a seat to enjoy the shade and eat lunch.

Although the railings have been painted a neutral colour in an attempt to blend in with the building facade, the double row of railings seems to detract from the historic appearance of the building. Nevertheless, this particular scheme has been successful in providing access for all people to the main door and is a good attempt at a creative and historically sympathetic design.

Solutions
The following are some suggestions to consider if you are planning accessible renovations to a historic building:

1. Form an Accessibility Advisory Committee
Before any construction is started, form a group of people to discuss and analyze accessibility issues and the historic structure. Try to attract people with expertise in different areas such as accessibility issues, architectural backgrounds, representatives of administration, and historians. The advantage of having a diverse group is that it can discuss accessibility from a variety of points of view to reach a well-informed decision.

2. Make a Plan

Develop a comprehensive plan for the building which deals with all accessibility issues. The plan should deal with all functional aspects for people with disabilities including telephones, drinking fountains, lever door handles, landscaping, fire alarms and accessible washroom facilities.

3. Understand the Positive Aspects of the Guidelines

We know that the negative aspects of accessible design are financial in nature. What are the positive aspects?

One positive aspect is that accessible entrances not only benefit the disabled but other groups of people as well. The Guidelines also assist people with children in strollers, access for senior citizens, people carrying heavy packages and allow for easier shipping of objects along the ramp.

The Guidelines are also a positive factor for disabled people because they are not excluded from society due to their disability. The aim is for persons with disabilities to lead a life similar to persons without disabilities.

However, the Guidelines have a further positive aspect. The Guidelines provide the opportunity for the larger society to be with people with disabilities. Our workplaces and organizations benefit by learning from people with a different experience and perspective on life than most of us.

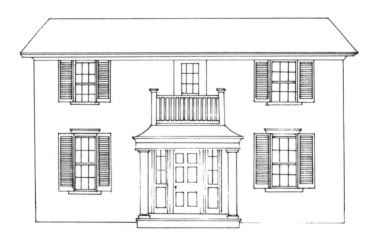

The Williamson House
238 Dublin Street

Handicapped Access to Historic Courthouses

Doug Wilson
Ontario Ministry of the Attorney General's Office

AS A TEAM MEMBER OF THE Ontario Ministry of the Attorney General's Office's Facilities Branch, I would like to take this opportunity to illustrate our current approach to "harmonizing" handicapped access into historic courthouses. Our use of the word "harmonizing" is deliberate, in that any solution to retrofit an existing historic building to fully accommodate facilities for the disabled is to walk an uncomfortable "sword edge" dividing two diametrically opposed factions.

The first faction is that of the "architectural heritage purists" whose highest goal is to attempt to restore a historic building as closely as possible to the original architect's intent, ultimately appearing as if it were just built. Items such as electric lights, gas mains, sprinkler systems, modern air conditioning and even thermopane windows are grudgingly accepted "nuisances".

The second faction believes that all architecture is not static, but must respectfully evolve to respond to changing needs and societal demands so that buildings will remain fully viable and refreshingly relevant. Denial that times have changed around these buildings has in some instances severely restricted their use and subsequent value. To avoid buildings becoming "white elephants" and closed because of difficulties in meeting current fire, building code, and accessibility requirements (if changes have to be undertaken within), or especially if a tenant's facility needs vary, "harmonizing" is the only practical way to achieve this adjustment.

Section 15 of the Ontario Human Rights Commission Charter could best be categorized as leaning to the second faction as guidelines forcing buildings to accommodate human needs. People with disabilities must be accommodated unless to do so would invoke "undue hardship" to the building owner. In today's present economic conditions, lack of adequate financing can be a common, legitimate impediment to this progress. From a practical standpoint, most private sector building owners would have to place tenant improvements above handicapped accessibility, simply catering to the majority in order to survive.

Courthouse buildings that our ministry occupies are usually government owned, or leased by the Ministry of Government Services for our use. The recent economic situation has been so severe that even the Ontario Government has had to slow down in realizing its mandate to uphold the Charter of Human Rights guidelines by upgrading buildings, as in many cases the money was simply not there. Currently, if a leased courthouse runs to the end of its term and the building that the facility is in has been deemed not to provide adequate accommodation for the handicapped, it is up to the landlord to provide full handicap accessibility, provide it in a reasonable time frame (due to local conditions), or we are forced to move the facility to alternate accommodations which provide full access to the handicapped. It is unfortunately a high cost of doing business passed on to the private sector to appease the second faction. "Pity the landlord" who must meet historic designation requirements as well, as it is a "double-whammy" business decision to make!

The "up"-side to all of this is that the forward thinking building owner can eventually recoup his investment over the long term (unless some incredible "space-age" prosthesis of the future renders handicapped accessibility alterations to buildings obsolete).

When dealing with valuable heritage properties, it is important not to damage any main historical features due to a tight budget or sudden rush to make the building accessible. It may be arguably better to install temporary ramps, etc. with a present long-term goal to integrate properly elements into an historic building than to haphazardly punch openings into significant features that future generations will regret. It is doubtful that the extremists of both factions will ever be completely satisfied when you have to make alterations to architectural "works of significance" by their definitions. Also, one cannot eliminate stairs between all building levels to remove distinctions between ambulatory and handicapped persons. No matter what, however, it is certainly worthwhile to achieve a general consensus "harmony" than to do nothing for fear of not pleasing everyone.

Most of us have seen or heard of "horror stories" - tarnished facades of heritage buildings with rough concrete ramps and steel railings imposed on once beautiful verandas, elevator shafts carved into magnificent foyers, wheelchair ramps next to receiving docks and "tradesmen-like" entrances singled out for the handicapped only. The list is endless.

The builders of these poor examples no doubt set out to simply allow handicapped persons to enter the building, but no further effort was expected to go beyond the immediate and treat all persons as equal. These "solutions" were not intended, but came-off similar to southern segregated entrances or the old "men's" and "ladies & escorts" doorways in small town bars.

The photographs shown at the conference of a Northwest Ontario Courthouse were merely intended as examples of a total lack of sympathy with either faction. User comfort (width of ramp, size of landings, door pull access, etc.) were considered far less important than getting the "chore" completed and not wasting any more valuable property than was absolutely necessary.

The engineer probably thought it would be a "nice touch" to put a plastic bubble roof over the ramp to make it easier to maintain. The structure says absolutely nothing about the heritage building to which it is attached and in fact insults everything around it. The steel bar door to the ramp cannot close in the winter and actually funnels snowdrifts down inside, making it impassable at times. Once the handicapped person parks their car at the exact opposite end of the building in the designated parking space, manoeuvres through the parking lot without a sidewalk, "squeezes" down the very narrow ramp and landing, they are greeted at the landingless bottom of the ramp with a solid steel door without a handle (or room to pull one if it was there). The victim has somehow to twist around in the wheelchair, reach up with their left hand over their right shoulder to hit an unmarked buzzer for an "attendant". Apparently, one individual had to wait in this manner for 6 hours one time; thankfully, it was not below freezing!

Our proposal to "harmonize" this building begins with filling the ramp and donating the plastic dome for a local bus shelter. If they will take it! Next, the front and side of the building should be landscaped to allow a gradually downward sloping driveway around the front of the building to create a dignified grade-level entrance that all the public can use. This will transform the previously "claustrophobic" basement into public space for court-rooms, hence upgrading the value of the building. Through this new entrance is proposed handicapped public washrooms, with the existing handicapped accessible elevator in line with the corridor. Handicapped parking is proposed directly outside this new entrance. A gradually sloping sidewalk curb is provided for wheelchair use. Everyone will benefit from this proposed landscaping as the "spin-off" advantages will be additional parking, renewed use of the originally intended main building entrance (largely unused for sixty years because the side door was open and all the parking was behind the building), and increased building security.

"Architectural heritage purists" might be upset that the architect never foresaw the public walking directly into the basement, or that a heritage facade may extend below grade, or that his intent might have been to pay homage to the "loftiness of the justice systems" by forcing the public to make a "pilgrimage" up the front steps. One answer to that would be that our society is much less formal, not everyone can climb steps, and the architect wouldn't be able to get a building permit today without providing the same facilities!

Another set of common accessibility problems in heritage buildings was illustrated by photographs of an Eastern Ontario Courthouse. The grade is a nuisance (being lower than the main floor all around the building) with stone steps leading into the building. There is a second floor and basement, with most of the important public activity occurring on the second floor.

A "solution" had been proposed but fortuitously was postponed due to a "hold" on funding. The previous proposal called for a large concrete ramp to start at the front entrance, over the stone steps and slope downward across the front of the building (with metal handrails to meet the building code). It was felt at the time that the only way to achieve a dignified entrance for the handicapped was to bring them in through the front door, regardless of what the building would look like. In this case, this is sort of like "bringing the mountain to Mohammed"! Handicapped washrooms, an elevator through the middle of the building, and extensive renovations were planned simply to accommodate the massive structural changes to the building as a result of the elevator installation. The "second faction" would have been satisfied after the renovations had been completed, but the "first faction" would have been "up-in-arms!" By-the-way, the initial location of the elevator would have resulted in an elevator bell ringing and door opening right beside the judge's dais (imagine this occurring in the middle of an intense trial!!).

Now here is where designers have to be given latitude to resolve creatively accessibility issues without "miring-down" with "red tape" piled up by proponents of the "first faction". To start with, the real problem is to convey people who may also be in a wheelchair throughout the building. The solution proposed may seem simple, but there is enough philosophy in it to engage even a "Zen Buddhist". The new proposal is to raise gently the grade to the side and rear of the building so that it would appear to be natural landscaping. The slopes must not exceed 1:12 for wheelchair circulation. This would preserve the front of the building, allow side and rear entry by all members of the public, and also provide a handicapped entrance to the adjacent law association building as well!

The rear of the courthouse building had already been "tampered" with years before when concrete block additions were added to the stone building. The new proposal calls for the construction of an addition to the building in the recessed courtyard, at the rear of the building, to "square up" the building. An elevator and exit facilities are proposed outside the original structure. In this new addition, it is intended to blend the old, new, and concrete block areas to appear as part of the original heritage construction, if approved by the local LACAC groups. Providing handicapped elevator accessibility to the courthouse may be more costly with this approach than installing an elevator inside the heritage structure, but instead of altering the original building framing, losing valuable interior space on all three levels and having to shut down the entire courthouse during construction, it will more than pay for itself over the life of the building, through its increased efficiency.

As outlined in this discussion paper, there is no "hard and fast" method to achieve accessibility within an historic building. In fact, it is highly desirable that there can be so many potentially creative solutions "tailor-made" to suit each individual building. Examples cited were more to illustrate an attitude towards solving accessibility issues than as a blueprint to follow. The goal is that all buildings should eventually permit full handicapped accessibility, but not through sacrificing our Canadian heritage.

676 Water Street

Archaeological Work

Archaeological Ethics

Susan Jamieson
Assistant Professor, Department of Anthropology, Trent University,
Peterborough, Ontario.
Susan is the Curator of Ontario Collections with the Department of
Anthropology at Trent University. She received her Ph.D. degree in
Anthropology from Washington State University in 1984. Her pri-
mary interests include the prehistory of the Ontario Iroquois and the
archaeological interpretation of small scale European Canadian
domestic sites.

ETHICS IS BOTH A SYSTEM OF MORAL VALUES which govern a profession
and of an individual's standards of behaviour as they relate to the
professional code. Because archaeology has developed and expanded
rapidly since the 1960s, traditional archaeological ethics, rooted in
academia, are no longer adequate to meet the needs of the new government and business practitioners. The result is a diversity in
archaeological objectives and in personal goals and values. Issues and
events of the last decade have demonstrated that there is a crisis in
archaeological ethics and that there are very few clear standards for
which there is general agreement. Decisions regarding right or wrong
have become a makeshift matter of personal judgement. Yet, values
do dictate that archaeologists have a responsibility both to the discipline and to other professionals. This has implications: when a
client's interests differ from or conflict with those of "good archaeology"; for the determination of site significance; and which dictate
the scope of work an archaeologist should undertake for a client.

References:

Fluehr-Lobban, Carolyn, ed. 1991 *Ethics and the Profession of
Anthropology*. University of Philadelphia Press, Philadelphia.

Green, Ernestene L., ed. 1984 *Ethics and Values in Archaeology*. Free
Press, New York.

King, Thomas A. 1977 Issues in Contract Archaeology. *Archaeology*
30 (5): 352-353.

McBryde, Isabel, ed. 1985 *Who Owns the Past?* Oxford University
Press, London.

Renfrew, Colin A. 1983 Divided We Stand: Aspects of Archaeology and Information. *American Antiquity* 48 (1): 3-16.

Smith, R. H. 1974 Ethics in Field Archaeology. *Journal of Field Archaeology* 1:375-383.

Thomas, C. 1971 Ethics in Archaeology. *Antiquity* 45:268-274.

Municipal Responsibilities for Archaeology

Heather Broadbent
Town of Caledon

Heather is the Heritage Resource Officer for the Town of Caledon. She is actively involved in many aspects of heritage preservation and is currently: the Chair of the Caledon Heritage Committee (LACAC); a member of the Conservation Review Board; Director, Ontario Heritage Foundation; Chairman, Albion-Bolton Historical Society & Caledon East & District Historical Society. Heather is also past-President of the Ontario Historical Society and the Peel County Historical Society.

Introduction

This article discusses municipal responsibilities for archaeology both in new planning and in Official Plan policies, as well as cultural and natural heritage in the context of environmental protection.

It reviews the methods used by the Town of Caledon to ensure that archaeological assessment undertaken by archaeological consultants are standard, meet the requirements of the Planning Act for subdivision of land, and are compatible with the Ministry of Culture and Communication guidelines.

Discussion

Many LACACs now have the benefit of a member or staff person who has some understanding of protection and identification of archaeological resources. My municipality just happened to be the first to have had such expertise since an archaeological assessment was undertaken by the University of Toronto in 1978. Since that time we have continuously had a licensed archaeologist on the committee. Not only do committee members constantly keep an eye and ear out for news of locally held collections of prehistoric material which may have been in family hands for dozens of years, but they alert the public to the destructive nature and dangers, both legal and social, of illegal archaeology. They also determine, where possible, the location of historic sites, be they former locations of mills, churches, log houses, or those other sensitive places known as unmarked burial places.

When subdivision or rezoning proposals arrive in the municipal office, among all the other assessments undertaken, the potential for evidence of early habitation and any existing historic sites is also explored. Although Caledon is a very large rural municipality, its proximity to Toronto and Mississauga make it very attractive for development, and so these applications are a frequent occurrence. As all applications are also circulated to the Development Review Unit at the Ministry of Culture & Communications, there is liaison and exchange of information between Caledon and the Unit.

It would seem appropriate to give a brief geographic description of the municipality. The Niagara Escarpment and the Oakridges Moraine meet in Caledon creating our dynamic scenery. We have the Watersheds of two principal rivers, the Credit and the Humber, containing several of both the minor and major tributaries of each. We also have a portion of the Nottawasaga Watershed. There is no part of Caledon that does not have some environmental or agricultural restraint as the streams that flow north and south from the escarpment and the moraine run through the good farm land of the Peel Plain where archaic sites (3 to 7000 years old) occur with great frequency. Unfortunately, the sub-divisions of massive homes in the northern parts of Brampton, where the streams run as they progress south, were built before assessment was required and even locally known sites were destroyed without evaluation.

As development occurs in Caledon, north of these homes, we hope to address this problem. Caledon's committee has been able to address the concerns of both Council and the development community about the cost and possible delays of approval if sites are located, by a report produced by Ogalvie & Ogalvie for the Ministry. I presume a copy can be obtained from the Ministry of Culture and Communications (MCC).

Many years ago, when I was quite small, my father told me that history and geography are really the same thing. As my favourite subjects at the time were just those, but two separate teachers were instructing my class about the mysteries of Egypt and the downs of southern England, the connections were quite lost to me.

Today, one has only to stand by the site of a native village looking at the spring on the land, the midden site way off on the other side, the ruins of a pioneer home, viewsheds and the remnants of the sugar maple copse to the north or north-west to realize that one cannot separate the two, and it is appropriate that environmental protection planning involves both cultural and natural heritage planning. To that end, Caledon is just embarking on the second stage of its Official Plan Review with a very progressive plan for environmental policies which include and interlock both.

As some developers make proposals for subdivisions which are outside areas already zoned for their purpose, they anticipate they may have to go the Ontario Municipal Board route. So often they take those items of subdivision approval which require little expense on their part but look good when their lawyers tell the OMB, "Look, my client did ALL this preparation and now these bad Councillors won't let him build a zillion houses (or a toxic waste site)".

Later, these assessments, or others undertaken for more regular approval, appear in Caledon and often do not match the M.C.C. guidelines for assessment. For example, they often have not even consulted the Ministry data base of registered sites, or they have an incorrect legal description so that you wonder just where they surveyed. On one occasion, the so-called "surveyed ploughed field" hadn't seen a plough in ten years. Caledon then realized that although M.C.C. had most comprehensive guidelines for surveying, they were not approved standards and created the potential for reports of various degrees of competence. I must state that 90% were excellent and up to standards but it was the rest which created problems and the delays that developers complained of.

Consequently, last year, the Town of Caledon adopted Standards for Archaeological assessment, based on Ministry guidelines which must be followed in Caledon. They are altered only slightly from the guidelines to include local references and requirements.

If your committee does not include someone with pre-historic interests perhaps it is time to do so. Someone with a licence, or the ability to acquire one, would be best. However, it is not essential to inventory what collections are held in your community, or by whom, or the location of historic sites. It is easy enough to locate them on a map which would be available to your planner when the dreaded developer walks in your municipal centre door. But never say these are the only sites, only the known sites.

Sources

Principally, the Heritage Resource Office, Town of Caledon, files.

Knapman-Turner House
604 George Street North

Other
Papers

Heritage and The School Room

Su Murdoch
Archival and Historical Consultant, Barrie, Ontario.

Formerly an archivist with Simcoe County Archives, Su has a wide range of experience in archives, local history publications, teaching, and architectural preservation. Recently, she prepared a Built Heritage In Schools resource kit for the Simcoe County Museum and the Simcoe County Board of Education.

IN MAY OF 1991 I WAS HIRED by the Simcoe County Museum for a one-year position sponsored by the Internship Training grant of the Ministry of Culture and Communications. The task was to prepare a **Built Heritage in Schools** teacher resource kit for the study of the built heritage of Simcoe County. The project was co-sponsored by the Ministry, the Museum, the Simcoe County Board of Education, and the Simcoe County Historical Association.

Built Heritage in Schools is a Ministry of Culture and Communications idea that is outlined in a manual prepared by Carol Chuhay and published in 1990. The program defines built heritage as works made by human beings and their effect on the natural landscape. With this broad definition, the topic spans a wide range including transportation, communications, architecture, the natural environment, monuments, machines, and any other "consultable record of past human activities". The bonus of this program to the heritage community is that it makes that critical link between built heritage education and Ministry of Education core curriculum guidelines. Failing to make that link often keeps heritage groups on the periphery of the school system. The Ministry of Education takes the approach that facts are "grist for the mill". The "mill" is the student's ability to learn and process information. As such, each classroom activity must meet the teaching objectives of providing the student with the opportunity to attain knowledge and to develop skills and attitude.

Looking Both Ways: A Resource Kit for the Study of the Built Heritage of Simcoe County is based on this approach. It is designed to meet the Ministry of Education core requirements for the History and Contemporary Studies, Geography, Visual Arts, Family Studies, Technological Studies, and Family Life Management curricula for Grades 7 to OAC. The Kit is divided into independent

Activities under the headings of Introducing Simcoe County, Architecture, Transportation and Communications Industry, Industrial and Commercial Development, Interiors, Heritage Planning, Researching a Property, and Community LACACs. As required by the Ministry of Education, each Activity is prefaced with the Educational Objectives of Knowledge, Skills, and Attitude. A teaching strategy, historical background, and list of additional resources are also provided with each activity. The Kit is a self-contained package with step-by-step instructions for the teacher.

For the heritage community, the challenge is to package all of our information and expertise into this educational approach. We need to devise a means by which we can get the information in and get the "mill" working. Well-researched information coupled with opportunities to analyze the issues and make judgements about heritage preservation, the environment, technology, and other quality of life concerns, is, I believe, the approach that will welcome us into the classroom. Simply instilling an **appreciation** of our heritage into today's students, although valid, does not necessarily say to them that maintaining the past is **important** to their future. This they must process, evaluate, and conclude for themselves. In the end, the students will gain the knowledge we want them to have about the past; and the ability to decide not only what is worth preserving but why.

Prepared under the guidance of a teacher advisory committee, **Looking Both Ways** should provide teachers with a means of introducing built heritage into the classroom. It also complies with the Ministry of Education curriculum requirements. Like any new project, it will take time to measure its success. For further information, contact the Simcoe County Museum, R.R. 2, Minesing, Ontario L0L 1Y0.

Motivating the Volunteer Committee

Georgette Houle
Regional Manager, Eastern Region, Field Services Branch, Ministry of Culture & Communication.

Georgette earned a Master's Degree in Education and Educational Administration and has had extensive teaching experience in areas of art, culture, leadership and management. A dedicated life-long volunteer, Georgette is particularly interested in the area of leadership and management problems and the needs of non-profit art organizations. A francophone born and raised in Saskatchewan, Georgette now lives with her husband Chuck in Ottawa and is an avid runner and skier.

Introduction

Volunteers are what make organizations such as LACACs work. Volunteers are the non-paid staff for the organization, its very lifeblood. These are the men and women of assorted ages, talents and backgrounds who will lend their time, energy and skills to encourage what they see as good for their community.

Your entire organization will stand or fall on how well you manage volunteer recruitment, orientation, training, placement, and supervision. Along with all of this goes the tasks of recognizing and thanking volunteers, promotions and the ever difficult task of moving an ineffective volunteer to a new task or out of the organization.

Today's volunteers are very discriminating and many approach the volunteer experience as a transaction, expecting something in return. In addition, those with a great deal of experience will often interview the organization rather than vice versa.

Who Are The Volunteers?

Statistics Canada recently did a study of volunteers in Canada and learned some interesting facts. For example, during the year November 1986 until October 1987, when the study was carried out, they found that 5.3 million Canadians aged 15 and older were volunteers. In addition, 3.2 million had volunteered in the past, and intended to volunteer again. In other words, 43% of Canadians are volunteers. They devote an average of 3.7 hours per week to their volunteer work and more than half of them volunteer for more than one organization.

One of the most interesting findings was that 62% of them started to volunteer because they were asked. Another 5% started because
of their work with related organizations and 5% helped start the
organization. Of those who volunteered, 28% had started to volunteer through formal channels; that is, either through a volunteer
bureau or an advertisement in the newspaper.

The higher percentage of volunteers are in the 35-44 year age
group. This is followed by those 45-54 and seniors. 25-34 year olds
also volunteer a lot. In Canada, 57% of women volunteer compared
with 43% of men.

The majority of volunteers have a high school education or less.
However, the tendency to volunteer increases with the level of education, and almost half of university graduates volunteer. The rate of
volunteering goes up with the level of household income.

Most volunteers are involved with fundraising, organizing activities, and working as board members. In addition, they also teach, do
office work, coach, and so on. Of those questioned in the Statistics
Canada survey, 93% responded that their volunteer activities were
very or quite important to them. Two-thirds of them considered
learning new skills an important aspect of their volunteer work.

Many volunteers expressed a great deal of satisfaction and enthusiasm for their work and 73% said they would volunteer more if
they were asked. 90% of volunteers said they were very or somewhat
satisfied with their experience as a volunteer. Only 2% were very dis-
satisfied.

In Ontario, there are over 1.8 million volunteers, or 25.5% of the
population. The averages of voluntarism follow very closely the
Canadian numbers.

Trends

Current trends in voluntarism have shown us that today's volunteers are much more discriminating than ever before. The volunteer
brings not only a willingness to serve but also expectations that, if
not met, will cause him or her to terminate the relationship. It is
much like the relationship between a company and a potentially
loyal customer. Organizations that understand this premise are
much more likely to match volunteers with the tasks that they find
satisfying and in which they are effective and to require solid performance from these members of the organization's work force.

There is a movement towards higher educated and more socially
conscious volunteers. Many are career professionals. From the career
professional's perspective, involvement as a volunteer can serve
many purposes. It can give a person visibility in the community and
expand one's contacts. This is beneficial to both the volunteer and

the organization. It can offer opportunities to improve skills in strategic planning, marketing, organizing, and fund raising that can be added to one's professional credentials. Volunteer work can also provide balance in one's life by offering social interaction and community service opportunities to offset the emphasis on career concerns in our culture.

There is a growing interdependence between volunteer agencies and organizations. While many organizations will recruit volunteers through their own members, they will also use the services of an agency to help recruit for special projects and events.

Organizations may also rely on a local volunteer bureau to assist them with training needs and other types of expertise. Most large communities have volunteer bureaus that have excellent resources available for non-profit organizations at a minimal membership cost.

Organizations, like business and government, are doing more with less in these times. With smaller budgets, organizations must depend on their volunteers to carry out much of their work. No wonder that fundraising was the primary activity for volunteers in the most recent Statistics Canada survey. An important resource to any organization in the present and the future will be the volunteer that has good community contacts and the ability to raise funds. Along with that, comes the ability needed to read, understand and manage budgets. No organization can afford to have surprises about its financial situation. Groups will have to ensure that their budget information and financial statements are presented in a format that can be understood and that all board and committee members take responsibility to ensure that these are viable and consistent with the goals of the organization.

The recession has presented organizations with an abundance of high quality volunteers. Consultants and contractors have less work and more time on their hands. For small business people, volunteering has become a way to drum up business. The market is also flooded with experienced people who may be unemployed or between jobs. A good way for some to get back into the job market may be through the contacts they make through their volunteer work. Students just completing post-secondary education continue to explore volunteer opportunities for these reasons, too.

Rights and Responsibilities of Volunteers

Volunteers have both rights and responsibilities. The Central Volunteer Bureau of Ottawa-Carleton suggests the following:

A volunteer has the right to:
• Be properly interviewed, selected and provided with a job description.
• A position that is worthwhile and challenging, that will promote learning and growth.

- Information on the organization's structures, insurance and funding.
- Expect his/her tasks have been planned.
- Orientation, initial and ongoing training.
- Receive support from a designated supervisor.
- Be treated as a non-paid staff member and given appropriate recognition.
- Be kept informed on what is happening in the organization.
- Be trusted with necessary confidential information.
- Be re-imbursed for expenses whenever possible.

A volunteer has the responsibility to:
- Choose an organization he/she can respect and support and be sincere in the offer for service.
- Only accept a volunteer position he/she believes in and feels will meet his/her skills, interests and available time.
- Ensure he/she understands the organization's policies and structures.
- Prepare for each work assignment: follow organizational guidelines and use time wisely.
- Acknowledge the need for training and participate fully.
- Consult with supervisor when unclear on policy or action and provide constructive feedback that will improve effectiveness.
- Work as a team member, understanding the function of paid staff and staying within the bounds of the volunteer position.
- Keep abreast of organizational changes.
- Respect confidentiality.
- Refuse gifts or tips from recipients of service.

Volunteer Management

Overall Policy

The purpose of volunteer policies is to provide overall guidance and direction to staff and volunteers. These could outline the definition of a volunteer, the role of the volunteer committee or volunteer management department, volunteer rights and responsibilities, and the scope of volunteer involvement.

Volunteer Procedures

Organizations should establish written procedures for the following: the maintenance of records, conflict of interest, representation of the agency, and confidentiality.

Volunteer Recruitment and Selection

Volunteers require a clear description of their duties and responsibilities. Prior to any volunteer assignment or recruitment effort, a position description must be developed for each volunteer position. All position descriptions should include a description of the purpose and duties of the position, a supervisor, a timeframe, a listing of job qualifications, and a description of the job benefits.

Recruitment should be done as much as possible in person, given the fact that most people volunteer because someone they knew asked them to. Prior to being appointed to a volunteer position, all volunteers should be interviewed to ascertain their suitability for, and interest in that position. The interview should determine the qualifications of the volunteer, their commitment to fulfil the job requirements, and should answer any questions that the volunteer might have about the position. At this time, standards of work should be discussed, as should policies and procedures.

Volunteer Training and Development

All volunteers should receive a general orientation on the nature and purpose of the organization. The orientation should be for present members, old and new, as well as staff. It is a good way to begin a new year - to discuss new directions for the year while making new members feel welcome. Each organization will handle this differently; successful ones I have been involved with went like this: an orientation package was prepared for each person and an orientation meeting was held. This was sometimes a two or three hour long meeting or a full day. The chairman and more experienced members covered basic information about the organization such as the mandate, goals, budget, how meetings would be conducted, when meetings would be held, and standards of performance. Generally, all the business of the organization was explained including policies and procedures. As well, it was an opportune time to discuss expectations on both sides, as well as to discuss the benefits of volunteer involvement. The orientation always included some form of socialization. After all, new people were being welcomed.

Additional training and educational opportunities should be made available to volunteers during their connection with the organization. Conferences and workshops are good vehicles for this and in fact, in the Statistics Canada survey, two-thirds of the volunteers considered learning new skills an important aspect of their volunteer work. And when volunteers holding paid jobs were asked whether their volunteering had provided them with new skills they could apply directly to their jobs, almost one-half replied "yes".

Volunteer Supervision and Evaluation

Each volunteer has a right to be supervised and his/her performance evaluated by a competent supervisor. Standards of performance should be well laid out and evaluations carried out professionally. In appropriate situations, corrective action may need to be carried out.

Examples of this would be additional training, re-assignment to a new position, review of expectations and procedures, or dismissal. This should be carried out by the appropriate person, i.e. the committee chairman or volunteer manager. Dismissing a volunteer is not easy to do, it takes wisdom and compassion, but sometimes it has to be done for the sake of the organization.

If and when volunteers leave, it is a good idea to carry out an exit interview. The interview should ascertain why the volunteer is leaving the position, suggestions the volunteer may have to improve the situation, and the possibility of involving the volunteer in some other capacity with the organization.

Volunteer Support and Recognition
After the initial welcome, the organization will need to work out ongoing methods of encouraging its members, of thanking them properly and recognizing them. You may consider acknowledging them publicly in the local newspaper once a year, on printed programs, or at community appreciation dinners in honour of community volunteers. If you do not already have a system in place for recognizing volunteers, a committee could be charged with developing means and ways to do this. Consider as well the Ontario Government's Volunteer Recognition Program through the Ministries of Citizenship and, Culture and Communication.

Support to volunteers should include the reimbursement of expenses, access to the organization's property and materials (i.e. the town office may set aside a space and equipment for you to use), and liability and accident insurance. Specific information about insurance should be available from the municipal clerk's office.

Summary
In this article, I can say only so much about volunteers. Additional materials are available which expand on each topic. I urge you to take advantage of the services offered through your local volunteer bureaus.

The importance of volunteer management can be summarized as follows: People want to contribute. They need to feel that their contribution has been appreciated. People need to feel that they have the skills, talents and time for the job or responsibility that is assigned. If matched carefully, they can succeed. Your LACAC will only be as good as the people in it. Help them and your organization succeed. Plan for success. Your efforts will be rewarded time and time again.

A Global Perspective: World Heritage Sites

John Marsh
Trent University

> *John grew up in England where he learned to appreciate its rich history and attractive countryside. He gained a Ph.D. from the University of Calgary with a thesis on the historical geography of Glacier National Park. He has since undertaken teaching, research and consulting on natural and cultural heritage conservation, tourism and interpretation in Canada and abroad. He is now Director of a research centre and graduate programme at Trent University dealing with Canadian Studies, and heritage management.*

Introduction

The aim of the illustrated presentation at the conference was to provide a global perspective on heritage, focusing on World Heritage Sites, and the aim of this paper is to do likewise. It will provide background on institutional aspects of World Heritage, describe various sites, in Canada and abroad, and identify problems and new directions requiring attention.

World Heritage

In 1972, UNESCO inaugurated a Convention concerning the World Cultural and Natural Heritage. It is intended to give international recognition and increased protection to cultural and natural sites generally deemed to be of global significance. By now, 134 states, including Canada, have signed the convention. Some 378 properties in 80 countries have been designated as World Heritage Sites and more are proposed. There are now 10 sites in Canada, and more are being considered for nomination (see Table 1). To date the World Heritage Committee has emphasized the designation of sites, but increasingly attention is being directed to their protection and management.

Examples of World Heritage Sites

Some examples of existing and proposed sites from six continents, selected to reveal their various characteristics and problems, and on the basis of their familiarity to the author, will now be discussed.

The Rocky Mountain National Parks of Canada
This area was accorded world heritage status because of its spectacular mountain landscape, already recognized by national park status. It retains much of its natural beauty and attracts increasing numbers of tourists from around the world. Unfortunately, it also exemplifies the problem of balancing protection and use. Road development, ski area expansion, the growth of town sites and tourist facilities are threatening the environmental integrity of the area. National Park planning and environmental impact assessments are intended to ensure the environment is protected but many would argue they have not been adequate. Public opinion, local, national and global, as well as political intervention will largely dictate the future of the area.

Quebec City
Quebec City gained world heritage status because of its historic core. The local authorities are striving to both protect this cultural heritage and derive the benefits of tourism from it. The integrity of the area has been threatened by various development proposals, including an IMAX theatre. Again, local and international vigilance will be necessary to ensure the values for which Quebec City was designated are retained.

Los Glaciares, Argentina
This national park features a spectacular portion of the southern Andes, with icefields and glaciers calving into lakes, as well as adjacent foothills with forests and grasslands. It is accessible by road and includes facilities such as hotels, restaurants and an interpretation centre. The persistence of cattle and horse grazing on former ranchlands is a management issue, as is the need to balance protection of the landscape and provision for tourism, which ranges from mountaineering to bus tours.

Machu Pichu, Peru
This site was designated to preserve the renowned Inca ruins and their spectacular forested mountain setting. Some reconstruction has occurred raising the question of how appropriate reconstruction is at World Heritage Sites. The visual and environmental integrity of the site was threatened by a proposed hotel but this development appears to have been averted. Access to the site from Cuzco by rail or hiking trail is somewhat problematic.

Ngorongoro Crater, Tanzania
The unusually large number of various wildlife species in a scenic extinct volcanic crater accounts for the designation, and tourist appeal of this area. Again, it is proving difficult to balance the

need for protection with the desire to provide for tourism, which involves numerous vehicles driving around the crater. As in many African parks, traditional native land uses, especially cattle grazing, and the need to ensure tourism benefits the local community, are also management challenges.

The Pyramids, Egypt
Few would argue with the designation of the pyramids outside Cairo as a World Heritage Site. However, world-wide awareness of such a site encourages tourism and can make management issues especially contentious. For example, the construction of an architecturally interesting and educational, but highly visible museum next to the Great Pyramid provoked considerable debate. The Sphinx was restored, for better or worse, prior to designation, but the question of how much restoration should occur in future remains. The spread of Cairo around the site is also changing its setting, many would argue, for the worse.

Fiordland National Park, New Zealand
This site was designated for its spectacular mountain and fiord scenery and associated natural values. It is accessible by road, boat and trails, such as the famous and very popular Milford Track. While some hydro-electric development has affected the area, a proposal for further development was defeated after a major national debate.

The Great Barrier Reef, Australia
The Great Barrier Reef gained designation because it is the largest such reef in the world, and, being now protected as a national park, is largely unspoiled. However, one area, Green Island, has suffered from environmental degradation and commercialisation. Being a very accessible part of the reef, tourists have flocked there and services and facilities have been provided for them. As a result, boating, scuba diving, the removal of shells and coral, as well as buildings and signs degrade the environment. While this seems undesirable, Green Island might be regarded as a "sacrifice area" that meets the needs of many visitors, and allows other parts of the reef to retain their natural integrity.

Taj Mahal, India
This is a renowned cultural site given world heritage status. It is readily accessible by road and train from Delhi. It receives numerous tourists throughout the year, requiring careful management, but providing economic and employment benefits. Like many heritage buildings there is an ongoing and expensive problem of maintenance, exacerbated here by the problem of acid rain.

The Giant's Causeway, Northern Ireland
This area is renowned for its unusual geological formations, of columnar basalt, located along a scenic coastline near Belfast. It indicates a willingness to recognize small natural sites as World Heritage Sites. The interpretive facilities and services demonstrate the educational potential of such sites for local citizens, school children and tourists. Unfortunately, as in the case of some other World Heritage Sites, terrorism is deterring many people from visiting the site.

Proposed Sites

Now, I would like to look at a few proposed World Heritage Sites in various parts of the world and some of the issues to be faced in designating and managing them.

While Chile has signed the World Heritage Convention, there are, as yet, no sites in that country. However, nominations are being considered for Easter Island, Juan Fernandez Islands, and Torres del Paine National Park. Easter Island has, of course, its famous stone heads (moai), but has also natural values, including species that link it to both South America and Polynesia. The Juan Fernandez Islands, while renowned for their association with the story of Robinson Crusoe, are more significant because of their unusual and highly indigenous plant species. The Torres del Paine are spectacular mountains, surrounded by glaciers and lakes, in the southern Andes. While the government has expressed some concern about potential loss of national sovereignty over such areas, it is expected they will eventually become world heritage sites.

The Lake District of England has been world renowned for over a century for its attractive mountains, lakes, farms, villages and literary associations, from Wordsworth to Beatrix Potter. Accordingly, it was nominated as a world heritage site. However, because it did not satisfy the criteria of a natural site, or those of a cultural site, it was not deemed eligible. It represents an appealing mix of natural and cultural elements, but, until recently there was no category of world heritage to recognise such attractive and valued cultural landscapes. Fortunately, recently after considerable debate, it has been agreed that such areas can be designated as world heritage cultural sites, so the prospects for the Lake District being so recognized are now good.

This new willingness to recognize cultural landscapes as World Heritage Sites should encourage us to identify such landscapes in Canada. Surely the Mennonite landscape of the Waterloo area, the Rideau Canal landscape, a prairie farm landscape, the orchard landscape of the Okanagan, or an outport landscape of Newfoundland deserve more attention and protection. Many recent initiatives, notably on the part of the Canadian Parks service, and more rural LACACs, to define and identify such landscapes should lead to national recognition, and perhaps world heritage recognition of some of these areas.

Finally, to complete the coverage of the continents, a brief comment on Antarctica as world heritage. As, by agreement, Antarctica does not belong to any nation, it cannot be nominated by any one nation for world heritage status. However, virtually everyone recognizes the natural magnificence and value of Antarctica, and many, notably Greenpeace and some countries, have suggested it be recognized as a World Park. The environmental protocol approved recently by the Antarctic Treaty nations has helped. However, scientific and tourism activities, while generally beneficial, do have environmental impacts that still require more control, and any renewed attempt to assert national claims must be resisted. Further, United Nations or World Heritage status seems desirable. Canada, as a signatory to the Antarctic Treaty, should support such world heritage status. Indeed, I would suggest that as Canadians concerned about the globe we should be taking a greater interest in the designation and protection of all heritage of global significance. In turn, we would welcome and expect other countries to take an interest in the welfare of our heritage that is of world significance. We have a mutual interest and responsibility here. We should again heed the words of Schumacher; let's act locally and think globally with respect to heritage.

Conclusion

An impressive array of natural and cultural sites, including a growing number in Canada, have now been recognized as World Heritage Sites. They possess enormous potential to enrich our lives, through local recreation, tourism, education, and inspiration. Their values require constant protection in the face of a variety of threats. These include external threats from activities in surrounding areas, and internal threats due to natural deterioration, inappropriate uses and excessive tourism. We must recognize that many cultural sites have some natural values, and some natural sites have cultural values, and manage them accordingly. Furthermore, there is merit in considering the recognition and protection of sites combining both natural and cultural values harmoniously in a cultural landscape. Finally, Canada has a role to play in encouraging the recognition and protection of heritage of world significance not only within Canada but also abroad.

Canadian World Heritage Sites

Name of Site	Location	Year Designated	Year Nominated	Nature of Site
Nahanni National Park	Northwest Territories	1978	1978	Natural
L'Anse Aux Meadows National Historic Park	Nfld.	1978	1978	Cultural
Dinosaur Provincial Park	Alberta	1979	1979	Natural
Kluane National Park Reserve	Yukon	1979	1979	Natural
Head-Smashed-in Buffalo Jump Provincial Historic Site	Alberta	1981	1981	Cultural
Burgess Shale	British Columbia (included in the 1984 Canadian Rocky Mountain World Heritage Site)	1980	1981	Natural
Anthony Island (Ninstints)	British Columbia	1980	1981	Cultural
Wood Buffalo National Park	Northwest Territories/ Alberta	1982	1983	Natural
Canadian Rocky Mountain Parks (Banff, Yoko, Jasper, and Kootenay National Parks)	Alberta and British Columbia (Mount Robson, Mount Assiniboine, and Hamber Provincial Parks designated in 1990)	1983	1984	Natural
Historic District of Quebec	Quebec	1983	1985	Cultural
Gros Morne National Park	Nfld.	1986	1987	Natural

References

Criteria for Cultural Landscapes under the World Heritage Convention." *APT Bulletin*, 24 (3-4), 1992, pp.79-80.

Masterworks of Man and Nature: Preserving our World Heritage. International Union for the Conservation of Nature and Natural Resources, and UNESCO. Harper MacRae Publishing, Australia, 1992.

May, J. *The Greenpeace Book of Antarctica*. Macmillan, Toronto, 1988.

Thorsell, J. "Twenty Years of World Heritage." *IUCN Bulletin*, 3, 1992, pp. 15-16.

304 Rogers Street

Biographies of Other Speakers

Unfortunately, not all presentations at the conference are available for publication; however, the following are the biographies of speakers not included earlier.

Cecelia Payne
Pre-conference Workshop: Cemetery Conservation
Cecelia is an Associate Professor in the School of Landscape Architecture, University of Guelph and is the principal of Cecelia Payne and Associates Inc., formerly situated in Ottawa, but recently relocated to Guelph, Ontario. Her teaching, research and practice specialization is in the area of historic landscape preservation. Cecelia has been involved in the preservation of numerous sites in Ontario, including the Billings Estate Cemetery, Beechwood Cemetery, and Notre Dame Cemetery, all located in the Ottawa area.

Allen Tyyska
A1: New Heritage Legislation
Allen was born and raised in Toronto. He first became involved in heritage conservation in 1963 as a student of archaeology at the University of Toronto. Since then, his archaeological studies have taken him to live and work in all parts of Ontario, and in the Canadian Arctic. Allen joined the Government of Ontario in 1972, holding positions with several ministries and with the Ontario Heritage Foundation. In 1981, he became Chief of Archaeology for the Ministry of Citizenship and Culture. Currently, Allen is Manager of the Heritage Legislation Project for the Ministry of Culture and Communications.

Dan Schneider
A1: New Heritage Legislation
Dan was born in Stratford, Ontario and raised in nearby Milverton. He holds a B.A. from the University of Toronto and a law degree from Queen's University. He has worked in the field of heritage conservation since 1979 when he spent the summer with the Stratford Local Architectural Conservation Advisory Committee. Since then Dan has been with the Ministry of Culture and Communications in Toronto. As a Senior Policy Analyst, Heritage Legislation Project, he

is currently working on a new heritage act for Ontario. On weekends, Dan spends his time fixing up an old stone house overlooking the Thames river north of St. Marys. He is also an avid architectural and landscape photographer.

Peter John Stokes
A2:The Dead Give-Away
Peter, born in England, graduated from the School of Architecture, University of Toronto in 1953, has, for over 20 years, been in private practice as a consulting restoration architect. A Fellow of the Royal Architectural Institute of Canada and a member of the Royal Canadian Academy of Arts, he has an honorary degree of LL.D. from Brock University. Involved with the Architectural Conservancy of Ontario, Inc., as President, 1976-1979, he originated the newsletter, Acorn. In 1983 he edited and contributed to Rogues' Hollow. His own publications include Old Niagara-on-the-Lake, Early Architecture of the Town and Township of Niagara, and The Settler's Dream. Peter makes his home in Niagara-on-the-Lake, Ontario.

Mary Lou Evans
A3: We Need a Reason to Designate?
Mary Lou is the local architectural conservation advisory committee, LACAC, Advisor in the Field Services Branch of the Ontario Ministry of Culture and Communications. She has held this position since 1988. From 1976 until 1988, she served as Assistant Curator (1976-1980) and Historian-Curator (1980-1988) for the City of Mississauga. She wore "many hats"in her work at the City, including that of LACAC Co-ordinator. Mary Lou received her Master's degree in History and Museum Studies from the University of Connecticut.

Judy Godfrey
A3: We Need a Reason to Designate?
Judy received her training in occupational therapy which restores people and she had applied the same principles to architecture. She is completing her term on the Conservation Review Board, on which she has served for six years. She and her husband, Sheldon, won the Heritage Canada Regional Award for the preservation of 49 Front Street East, Toronto, and the Heritage Canada National Award and the Credit Foncier Award for the preservation of the block (Bank of Upper Canada, Toronto's First Post Office, and the De La Salle Building) at 252 Adelaide Street East, Toronto. Judy has co-authored two books : Stones, Brick and

History; Burn This Gossip, the True Story of George Benjamin, Canada's First Jewish Member of Parliament; and is working on a third book looking at the development of civil and political rights for Canada's peoples.

Tamara Anson-Cartwright
A3: We Need a Reason to Designate?
Since 1988, Tamara has held the position of Grants Advisor in the Architectural Conservation Unit of the Ontario Ministry of Culture and Communications. Prior to her employment at the ministry, she was the Architectural Historian at the City of North York and the Town of Markham. As a Grant Advisor, she provides advice on the Designated Property Grants program to municipalities who are located in the Eastern and Northern part of the province. She also helps co-ordinate the various Commercial Rehabilitation Grants which are awarded by the ministry each year throughout the province of Ontario.

Marilyn Miller
A3: We Need a Reason to Designate?
Marilyn grew up in Kingston, Ontario, where she completed her schooling with an M.A. in History from Queen's University. She started working in the heritage conservation field for the provincial civil service upon graduation. Her work with the Ministry has evolved into heritage planning and architectural conservation work for other government ministries, local authorities, NGOs and individuals. Her region currently takes in the area south and west of Toronto bounded by Niagara, Haldimand Norfolk, Dufferin, and Peel, with some projects in Toronto.

Ivan Bateman
B2: Building Conservation and the 3R's
A graduate of Production Engineering at Bristol College of Technology (U.K.) and Marketing Management at the University of Western Ontario, Ivan's background includes 30 years in process engineering and marketing in business and industry. In 1989 he was appointed to the new position of Solid Waste Co-ordinator for the City of Peterborough. He is responsible for the planning and execution of programs for waste reduction and waste diversion from landfill. He has served as Chairman of the Public Liaison Committee for Peterborough City/County Waste Management Master Plan and serves on committees of the association of Municipal Recycling co-ordinators and Waste Reduction Advisory Committee. Ivan and his wife, Carol, make their home in Ashburnham, Peterborough.

John Blumenson

A6: ICOMOS Matrix System

John, author of Identifying American Architecture, a Pictorial Guide to Styles and Terms, 1600-1945, is presently a Preservation Officer with the Toronto Historical Board. He has been active in architectural conservation providing photographic recording, heritage building reports and architectural evaluations to both private and public sectors in Canada and the United States. Formerly a Heritage Planner with the City of Ottawa, John's most recent book, Ontario Architecture 2784-1984, was published by Fitzheny and Whiteside in 1990.

Jill Taylor

A6: ICOMOS Matrix System

Jill is a partner in the firm of Taylor/Hazell Architects. The office specializes in the conservation of heritage buildings, and is currently conducting restoration at the new Toronto Historical Board Headquarters in Toronto, the Bruce County Museum and Archives in Southampton, the Whithern and Dundurn Museums in Hamilton.

Dennis Carter-Edwards

AB12: Protection of Historic Landscapes and Buildings

Dennis has been the Project Historian with the Ontario Regional Office of the Canadian Parks Services since 1975. He is a graduate of Trent University and earned his Master's degree at the University of British Columbia. Dennis is also currently the President of the Ontario Historical Society and the former Chair of Heritage Cornwall (LACAC).

Jeremy Collins

A14: Heritage Easements in Ontario

Jeremy graduated with a B.A. Honours in History from the University of Toronto in 1981. He also holds a law degree from Queen's University. Jeremy is currently the Acquisitions Co-ordinator with the Ontario Heritage Foundation and has written numerous research papers dealing with heritage conservation. Prior to joining the Ontario Heritage Foundation three and a half years ago, Jeremy worked in private practice.

Peter Elliott

A14: Heritage Easements in Ontario

Peter is an Easements Advisor/Monitor with the Ontario Heritage Foundation's Conservation Easements Program. He is an architectural technologist specializing in the restoration of heritage buildings. He has been working with heritage property owners and monitoring heritage properties for the Foundation for nearly five years.

Brian Buchardt
B15: Preservation versus Demolition
As an employee with the City of Peterborough, Brian's primary responsibility is to work with developers to achieve a good standard of site and building design. This includes architectural expression, appropriate landscape treatments and site design to ensure the provision of parking, safe pedestrian and vehicular access and storm water control.Brian also acts as the municipal liaison with the Peterborough LACAC to ensure that development plans submitted for approval adequately address heritage conservation concerns. Brian has his Bachelor's degree in Landscape Architecture from the University of Guelph where there was great emphasis on design theory as it applied not only to outdoor environment, but other areas such as interior design and architecture. Brian has also gained a practical understanding of construction materials and building techniques from his background in the construction industry.

John Callender
B16: Sympathetic Renovations and Renewal
John is the President of Callender & Associates, Inc., an architectural design firm which began in 1971 in Perth, Ontario. The company has developed a reputation for restoration projects and in 1981, John's expertise in this field was recognized when he received the Heritage Canada Award of Merit for Ontario. This award specifically acknowledged his Main Street project of enhancing the commercial viability of a fire-gutted 1850's building while retaining its architectural history. John is equally interested in and proficient with modern structures. Over the years, design and construction projects have ranged from one-of-a-kind residences, clinic, prestigious offices to small public buildings. The dual nature of his design capacity was exercised during a two year assignment in London, England, where he converted a late Victorian mansion into four distinctive homes, two retaining the flavour of the building's exterior; the additional two were given a modern treatment. Along with his wife, Sandy, John runs his business in Peterborough and pursues other interests of choir singing and community involvement.

Others
Unfortunately, biographical information was unavailable at publication time for the remainder of our speakers:

Larry Sherman
Pre-Conference Workshop, Conflict Resolution

Gail Sussman
Pre-Conference Workshop, Cemetery Conservation

Fred Cain
B3: London's Talbot Block - What did We Learn?

Hamish Wilson
B7: Building Resources & Energies

Vanessa Brown
AB8: Cultural Tourism

A.K. Skulthorpe
AB8: Cultural Tourism

Doug Wilson
AB9:n Architectural Integrity vs Human Needs

John Lewis
AB10: Integrating natural and Cultural Heritage Protection

David McClung
AB10: Protecting our Rural Landscape Heritage

Bill Fox
A15: Pandora's Box or Panacea?

565 Harvey Street

Green Gutters & Gargoyles

The 1992 Provincial LACAC Conference

Conference Brochure and Programme

A Message from the Conference Chairman...

O N BEHALF OF THE CITIZENS and Council of the City of Peterborough, I am delighted to welcome you to our community.

I feel sure you will agree that the conference committee members have put together an interesting and challenging program with a first class array of speakers.

I would also hope that during your visit to the Kawarthas you will have time to enjoy the wide and varied amenities of the area and in particular, the numerous architectural features of the city. The Peterborough Architectural Conservation Advisory Board, developed initially by Martha Ann Kidd, has realized a number of outstanding achievements in architectural heritage preservation. To blend with these achievements, I also hope that you enjoy the more modern architecture of Trent University.

Paul S. Wilson
Conference Chair

An Introduction...

THE THEME OF THE 1992 LACAC* CONFERENCE, Green Gutters & Gargoyles, is to examine the relationship between our built and natural environments and the care of both. Conference delegates will be provided with the opportunity to explore this relationship and discover how a desire to retain our architectural heritage has had heritage preservationists Reducing, Recycling, and Reusing for many years. The location of the conference, Trent University in Peterborough, offers an especially beautiful and appropriate setting.

While the primary purpose of the conference is to provide an educational forum for LACACs, all interested persons are invited to attend. Developers, planners, municipal officials and interested citizens are sure to find the conference worthwhile and enjoyable. The conference program has been designed with a variety of needs and interests in mind. Several plenary sessions have been scheduled to address topics of interest to everyone. As well, concurrent workshop sessions allow the conference to be customized to the interest of each delegate. Among the workshops offered, long-time participants in heritage preservation will find a number of sessions that will allow exploration of new ideas as well as discussions of ongoing heritage issues. A number of workshops have been set up with the fledgling LACACs in mind, to help provide the basic information and details necessary to answer the "how do we do this?" questions. Novice LACAC delegates may find the workshops grouped in the "A" category will suit their needs, while others may find the "B" sessions more stimulating. The emphasis in all cases is on learning, sharing, and of course, having fun!

An Introduction to Peterborough...

PETERBOROUGH, A CITY OF 65,000 WITH AN ECONOMIC BASE set in manufacturing and tourism, is located approximately 130 kilometres northeast of Toronto. The region embraces the granite of the Canadian shield to the north of the city and to the south are the gently rolling hills and rich agricultural farmland of the St. Lawrence Lowlands. Founded early in the Victorian era, it has retained much of its architectural heritage and small-city charm on quiet, tree-lined streets. The city abounds with a wide variety of activities. In addition to the popular museum and art galleries, lively theatre groups and excellent recreational facilities, the city and district also boast a number of restaurants with traditional and specialized cuisine. Downtown, one finds shops that cater to virtually all interests.

The Otonabee River and the surrounding Kawartha Lakes provide a focus for both the city and for Trent University. The forests, lakes and gently rolling hills are the setting for the 1,500 acre Trent campus. The striking design of the buildings has won international awards and acclaim, and the combination of architecture and surroundings creates a setting of startling beauty, as aptly described by former Trent writer-in-residence Margaret Laurence... "I looked at the tall angularity of a few finely proportioned buildings, grey but not austere, standing castle-like in the diamonded snow of a clear January day, and at the river, crusted ice and darkly shining water, flowing so closely that it appeared almost to be winding in and through the buildings, a part of them, or they a part of it. That was my first view of Trent ... I realized I'd never before seen a campus which looked so beautiful...".

Other Important Details...

Special Requirements
Trent University is wheelchair accessible. If you have any special requirements, please contact the Conference Office.

Accommodations
Delegates are encouraged to make the most of this learning experience and stay where the action is - at the University! Accommodations in the University residence cost $40.00 per person per night. This includes a private room, linens, towels, maid service, shared washroom facilities and breakfast daily (what a deal!).

For those delegates who do not wish to reside at the University during the conference, a block of rooms has been set aside for conference delegates at the Holiday Inn, George Street. Reservations may be arranged by calling the hotel at (705) 743-1144. Delegates staying outside the University will be required to provide their own transportation to and from the conference.

Travel Arrangements
Peterborough is approximately 1.5 hours north-east of Toronto and 3 hours west of Ottawa. The area is easily accessible by a number of major surface routes and is also serviced by a local municipal airport. Detailed maps will be provided to all out-of-town delegates upon confirmation of registration.

Wednesday, June 10, 1992   **Pre-Conference Workshops**

PRIOR TO THE OFFICIAL OPENING OF THE CONFERENCE, delegates will have the opportunity to participate in one of two all-day workshops. These special workshops are sponsored by the Ontario Heritage Foundation and are offered to conference delegates free of charge.

The workshops will run from 10:00 a.m. to 5:30 p.m. Participants will have the choice of attending one of the following workshops:

Conflict Resolution
In a workshop setting, participants will be introduced to the field of conflict resolution. Learn how you and your LACAC can apply this technique to conflicts that arise in your municipality. Through simulation exercises you will have the opportunity to hone your negotiating skills on the types of conflict that often face LACACs.

To be presented by the Society for Conflict Resolution in Canada.

Cemetery Preservation
Municipalities throughout Ontario are faced with the increasing problem of the deterioration of their heritage cemeteries. This hands-on workshop will focus on both technical (stone conservation) and natural/environmental issues. Learn about the new Cemeteries Act and the issues arising from it. Then, join us in one of Peterborough's oldest and beautiful cemeteries for on-site participation.

To be presented by Gail Sussman, Technical Advisor, Ministry of Culture and Communications.

Lunch will be provided for all pre-conference workshop participants, courtesy of the Ontario Heritage Foundation (you can't afford to miss this!). At the end of the day, workshop participants and early-arriving conference delegates are invited to attend a reception to celebrate the opening of the conference Marketplace - an array of interesting exhibits offering various heritage-related items and services for sale and for display. The workshops have limited enrolment, so be sure to register early!

Thursday, June 11, 1992   **Conference Day 1**

9:00 a.m. (all day)
Conference Registration
Delegates may register and obtain their rooms. Refreshments will
be available and The Marketplace will be open.

10:50 a.m.
Welcome Address
Conference Committee Chair Paul Wilson, Mayor Jack Doris and
the Honourable Karen Haslam, Minister of Culture and
Communications.

Keynote Address
The Conference Committee is honoured to have Dr. T.H.B.
Symons address the delegates on the theme of the 1992
Provincial LACAC Conference. Dr. Symons, an internationally
distinguished conservationist, was the founding president of
Trent University, and is currently Chairman of the National
Historic Sites and Monuments Board.

12:00 p.m.
The "Strolling" Lunch
Delegates will be treated to a variety of buffet-style foods while
free to explore The Marketplace displays.

1:30 p.m.
Concurrent Sessions
Delegates may choose a topic of interest:

A1 *The New Heritage Legislation*
The province has undertaken to revise the 1974 Ontario Heritage
Act because of its serious deficiencies. This presentation will deal
with the Heritage Act and the anticipated new role that municipal advisory committees will play.

A2 *The Dead Give-away - Identifying Buildings*
Have you ever wondered exactly what makes an 1850's building
different from an 1890's building? With the help of slides, illus-
trations, and graphics, noted restoration architect, Dr. Peter John
Stokes, will show you exactly how you can identify and date a
building with the "dead give-away" clues.

A3 *We Need a Reason to Designate?*
This workshop will help novice and experienced LACACs alike to
examine the statutory requirements of designation, how to write

those difficult-to-put-into-words "reasons" for designation, and then, how to interpret the "reasons" for the purposes of grant applications and the altering of designated properties.

A4 *Counting Your Heritage*
Commissioned in 1990 by the Township of Uxbridge to prepare a comprehensive Heritage Inventory covering the time span from the First Nations to 1910, I.K. Woods & Partners Inc., Chartered Surveyors, will take you through the steps required to undertake such a mammoth project. Ian Woods, an enthusiastic professional, will also explain exactly what chartered surveyors are, their long and fascinating history and what they could do for your municipality.

B1 *Sustainable Development*
Sustainable development is the catchword of the '90s. How does it impact on heritage? How can heritage properties help the concept? Come and listen to former Peterborough Mayor Sylvia Sutherland and her passionate views on this issue.

B2 *Building Conservation and the 3 R's*
As society adopts the Reduce, Reuse, Recycle ethic, new criteria will be added to those governing the conservation of buildings. Future trends in waste disposal will also have an increasing impact on the design and execution of conservation projects. This workshop will discuss ways in which architects, planners, contractors, and municipalities must interact to achieve the overall goals of a conserver society.

B3 *London's Talbot Block - What did we learn?*
Although the Talbot Block in London was eventually demolished, a process was used in determining the fate of this building. Listen to the key players who were involved from the outset, and determine how other LACACs can benefit.

B4 *Heritage and the School Room*
It's well known that the future of heritage preservation is in the hands of children. There will be no preservation unless we educate children to appreciate their past. Simcoe County has undertaken a project with the M.C.C. to design a heritage program for grades 7 through O.A.C. that not only advocates heritage preservation, but links it to environmental issues.

2:45 p.m.
Refreshment Break

3:00 p.m.
Concurrent Sessions

Delegates may choose a topic of interest:

A5 *The Peterborough Approach to Designation*
Each municpality approaches the designation of properties and buildings differently. The Peterborough LACAC has issued three publications that are used either by the LACAC or sent to potential designated building owners. This session will outline Peterborough's approach to the designation process and the philosophies that have resulted in these publications.

A6 *ICOMOS Matrix System*
If all buildings were only four-sided cubes - wouldn't it be easy? How many times have you heard that line? It's not easy to describe a building - how many walls, how many windows, what does the brick look like? ICOMOS has come to our rescue and is developing the matrix System that will systemize the recording of buildings through drawings and photographs.

A7 *Motivating the Volunteer Committee*
The volunteer committee is essential to the success of every community, whether it's a LACAC or an after-school sports group. It's the responsibility of the entire committee to keep each individual feeling like he or she is a valuable member of the whole. This session is a "how to" - dealing with keeping a committee motivated, interested, and rewarded.

B5 *The New Heritage Legislation*
The province has undertaken to revise the 1974 Ontario Heritage Act because of its serious deficiencies. This presentation will deal with the Heritage Act and the anticipated new role that municipal advisory committees will play.

B6 *New Materials vs. Recycled*
How do recycled materials compare to new materials in terms of efficiency and cost? This session will address this and related issues to provide us with the opportunity to examine the "real costs" associated with the use and re-use of building materials.

B7 *Resources and Energies*
The materials of buildings and cities are a large bank of stored natural resources, always accompanied by embodied energy. Demolition usually wastes both. Repair, conservation and recycling of structures benefits the environment but there are some constraints upon recycling that must be considered as well.

4:30 p.m.
Community Heritage Ontario

This plenary session will feature reports from the Community Heritage Ontario Board of Directors and the Annual General Meeting of CHO.

6:30 p.m.

Barbecue and Evening of Entertainment

An opportunity for delegates and speakers to gather together and enjoy a leisurely dinner and evening of entertainment on the banks of the Otonabee River (nobody think rain!).

Friday, June 12, 1992   **Conference Day 2**

9:00 a.m.
Plenary Session
Community Heritage Ontario

10:30 a.m.
Refreshment Break

10:45 a.m.
Concurrent Sessions
Delegates may choose a topic of interest:

AB8 *Cultural Tourism*
This session will deal with sustainable development in communities where the economic base is primarily tourism-oriented. The approaches of Heritage Canada and various regions of Ontario will be discussed.

AB9 *Architectural Integrity vs. Human Needs*
Is architecture an art form? Does that mean it can never be changed? How does this meet the many needs of many different people? How can these buildings, old or new, be adapted for the disabled? Join the varied guest panelists to hear a lively debate on exactly what is architectural integrity.

12:00 p.m.
The Ontario Heritage Foundation Luncheon

1:30 p.m.
Introduction to the O.H.F. Concurrent Sessions
The afternoon workshops are sponsored by the Ontario Heritage Foundation. Dr. Gordon Nelson, Heritage Resource Centre, University of Waterloo, will provide an introduction.

2:15 p.m.
Concurrent Sessions
Delegates may choose a topic of their interest.

AB10 *Integrating Natural and Cultural Heritage Protection*
The aim of this seminar is to encourage the integration of natural and cultural heritage protection by examining the need to integrate such protection and concepts. Participants will have the opportunity to examine case examples of such integration.

AB11 *Protecting our Rural Landscape Heritage*
The aim of this session is to encourage the protection of our rural landscapes by examining their characteristics, the threats to this heritage, and the means to protect this heritage. Participants will have the opportunity to examine case examples of rural landscape protection.

AB12 *The Protection of Historic Recreation Landscapes and Buildings*
The aim of this session is to encourage the protection of our historic recreation landscapes and buildings by examining the heritage of recreation and tourism landscapes and buildings. Case examples involving the protection of historic recreation landscapes and buildings will be presented.

3:00 p.m.
Refreshment Break

3:15 p.m.
Concurrent Sessions
Continuation of the Ontario Heritage Foundation sessions which began at 2:15 p.m.

5:00 p.m.
Dedication Ceremony
The conference will move to the Peterborough Armouries to take part in the dedication of this historic building as a National Historic Site. The dedication ceremony will be followed by a reception, after which delegates will participate in a very special dining experience!

At Home ... in Peterborough
Delegates will have the opportunity to dine in one of several local heritage homes participating in this special event. Conference participants will board buses at the Peterborough Armouries and be welcomed by some very special Peterborough residents as their dinner guests. Afterwards, the chariots will return to whisk the delegates back to the University.

Saturday, June 13, 1992   Conference Day 3

9:00 a.m.
World Heritage Sites Display
Delegates are free to view an outstanding film and display which focuses on World Heritage Sites.

9:45 a.m.
Plenary Session

"Canada's built heritage has been harmed by acid rain...By the same token, some of the best architecture in the country is superior because it is fundamentally sensitive to the natural environs."

The Honourable Tom McMillan, Canadian Consul General, and former Canadian Minister of the Environment, responsible for both the federal anti-pollution efforts and its heritage programs, will address the delegates. Mr. McMillan will argue that the well-being of Canadians depends not only on clean air, pure water and healthy soil, but also on respect for the built environment.

10:30 a.m.
Refreshment Break

10:45 a.m.
Concurrent Sessions
Delegates may choose a topic of their interest:

A13 *A Purist Approach to Restoration*
There are few opportunities to completely restore a building. It happens frequently in living museums and less frequently in buildings used for modern living. But, when those few opportunities arise, we must be ready to tackle a restoration with the most stringent of accepted heritage restoration techniques.

A14 *Heritage Easements in Ontario*
The Ontario Heritage Foundation has been operating a successful Conservation Easements program in the areas of built, natural and archaeological heritage for the past 15 years. Foundation staff would like to share some excellent insights, gained during that period, into the issues.

B13 *Salvaging Heritage - The Non-Profit Way*
The Philadelphia Architectural Salvage Ltd. has long made the link between conservation and historic preservation. Not only does this innovative company salvage building materials because

of their beauty but because it saves landfill space and conserves dwindling natural resources. Hear firsthand about this interesting organization that manages to please everyone!

B14 *Facadism or Partial Retention*
This presentation will focus on the issue of facadism in the redevelopment of cities. The Toronto Policy on Facadism, developed by the Toronto Historical Board, will be presented as a case study. The session leader is of a view that facadism is not all bad - sure to be a lively discussion!

A15 *Pandora's Box or Panacea?*
A number of issues surround archaeological ethical and performance standards - an awareness of which should assist LACACs both in developing strategies and in meeting objectives when confronted with situations involving archaeological remains. The theoretical thrust of the presentation is enlivened by anecdotal reference to a recent case from Niagara-on-the-Lake.

A16 *Construction Management - The Team Approach to Restoration*
Restoration of Historic Buildings presents unique problems in the construction process. Work, once completed, is often irrevocable and the buildings may hold many surprises that will not be discovered until well after construction starts. This session will discuss the advantages of having the builder join the owner's team when the project is first initiated and how this leads to a healthier balance between quality and price.

B15 *Preservation vs. Demolition*
This session deals with the successful preservation of buildings that may have been slated for demolition. Using case studies from three municipalities, the workshop will illustrate alternatives to demolition that have been applied to saving buildings that appear to be redundant. Rather than advocating any one option as the ultimate solution, the goal of the session will be to present the results of these various approaches.

B16 *Sympathetic Renovations and Renewal*
Bridging the gap between "classical" restoration and simply re-working an older building is John Callender, award-winning designer and developer of unique properties. This presentation, through slides, lecture, and open discussion, will present a philosophy of building renewal that incorporates regulatory requirements, historical usage, financial restraint/opportunities, etc., within the context of respecting and enhancing the heritage value of the property.

12:00 p.m.
Luncheon

1:30 p.m.
The Big Bang! - Closing Address
The conference committee is pleased to present Mr. Michael Valpy from the Globe & Mail.

2:30 p.m.
Departure

More Fun Stuff!...
Along with the more "formal" conference proceedings, many other activities have been planned. Aside from a terrific way to meet new people and exchange ideas, these activities promise to be great fun! Here's a taste of what's in store:

Gargoyle of the Year Contest
Do you have any strange faces or creatures "hanging about" your municipality? LACACs are invited to submit an 8 x 10" photograph of a gargoyle, or any "gargoyle-like" decoration (green or otherwise!), from a building in their area. Delegates will have an opportunity to vote for their favourite creature. Submit your photos to the Conference Office before April 19, 1992.

Name the Gargoyle Contest
Your opportunity to come up with a name for our conference gargoyle...and win!

Building Balderdash for Breakfast
We'll let you wonder about this one - you will have to register and come and find out!

The Big Bang! Draw
All LACACs will be entitled to a chance in the Big Bang! Closing Draw - a chance to win a fantastic prize!

Chris Tossel Memorial Run
No Provincial LACAC Conference would be complete without this celebrated early morning run - a tradition started at the 1988 Conference in Sault Ste. Marie. This year, Conference Chair Paul Wilson will carry the torch and lead the troops.

Sunrise Bird-Watch with Fred
Trent Geography Professor Fred Helleiner will lead you early-risers on an interesting and informative bird-watching walk through the

beautiful Trent Campus.

* In case you were wondering (way back at the beginning of this booklet) what a LACAC is...a LACAC is a Local Architectural Conservation Advisory Committee. These committees exist in approximately 200 municipalities throughout Ontario for the purpose of advising Municipal Councils regarding built heritage issues.

Listing of Participants

Jim Alexander
Town of Niagara-on-the-Lake
Box 100
Virgil, ON L0S 1T0

Jim Anderson
MacAndrew Stratford Ltd
87 Nile Street
Stratford, ON N5A 4C7

Kathryn Anderson
16828 Baysview Ave
Newmarket, ON L3Y 3W8

Tamara Anson-Cartwright
Ministry of Culture &
Communications
77 Bloor St. W, 2nd Floor
Toronto, ON M7A 2R9

John K. Armour
Town of Port Hope
42 Bedord Street
Port Hope, ON L1A 1W3

Cathy Armstrong
6 Damascus Drive
Caledon East, ON L0N 1E0

Nancy Arthur
R. R. #1
Port Dover, ON N0A 1N1

Margaret Baily
28 Coronation Cr.
Cobourg, ON K9A 1T6

Frank Balint
Township of Hamilton
Box 138
Gores Landing, ON K0K 2E0

Tony Barake
City of Brockville
P. O. Box 1301
Brockville, ON K6Y 5Y6

Darlene Baronette
54 Canal Street
St. Catharines, ON L2N 4S9

Joan Barrett
Front of Escott Township
Box 842, R. R. #2
Mallorytown, ON K0E 1R0

Brian Basterfield
416 Chambers Street
Peterborough, ON K9H 3X1

Ruth Bell
Heritage Nepean Planning
Department
101 Centrepointe Drive
Nepean, ON K2G 5K7

Cliff Bennett
Lanark Heritage Regions Project
R. R. #1
Almonte, ON K0H 1A0

Leon Bensason
Dept of Planning &
Development
City of Kitchener
P O Box 118
Kitchener, ON N2G 4G7

Cindy Bergen
R. R. #1
Simcoe, ON N3Y 4J9

Janet Berton
30 Stegman's Mill Road
Kleinburg, ON L0C 1C0

Diane Bickley
R R #3
Huntsville, ON P0A 1K0

Dorie Billich
Corporation of the Town of
Markham
101 Towncentre Blvd
Markham, ON L3R 9W3

Martin Binkley
Township of Woolwich -
LACAC
69 Arthur Street South
Elmira, ON N3B 2Z6

Janet Black
316 James Street South
Hamilton, ON L8P 3B8

John Blumenson
Toronto Historical Board
Exhibition Place
Marine Museum
Toronto, ON M6K 3C3

Ann Bobyk
84 Sybella Drive
Oakville, ON L6K 2L8

Mark Boileau
340 Pitt Street
P O Box 877
Cornwall, ON K6H 5T9

Eric Brasus
Town of Whitby
575 Rossland Road East
Whitby, ON L1N 2M9

Heather Broadbent
Town of Caledon LACAC
200 Church Street
Caledon East, ON L0N 1E0

Celia Bronkhorst
Town of Pickering Civic Complex
One the Esplanade
Pickering, ON L1V 6K7

Ralph W. Brown
231 Dundas Street West
Napanee, ON K7R 2A9

Anita Brunet-Lamarche
Ministry of Culture &
Communications
10 Elm Street, 4th Floor
Sudbury, ON P3C 5N3

Michel Brykert
Corporation of the Town of
Carleton Place
273 Lake Avenue East
Carleton Place, ON K7C 1J4

Brian Buchardt
500 George Street North
Peterborough, ON K9K 1W8

Matalie Bull
115 Beechwood Avenue, #2
Ottawa, ON K1M 1L6

Bill Bullied
P O Box 400
Lakefield, ON K0L 2H0

Ruth Burkholder
251 Second Street
Stouffville, ON L4A 1B9

Elizabeth Burrell
225 St. Louis
Windsor, ON N8S 2K2

Chris Campbell
R R #3
Colborne, ON K0K 1S0

Douglas F. Campbell
R R #8
St. Thomas, ON N5P 3T3

Robert Cardwell
P O Box 966
Kingston, ON K7L 4X8

Greg Carrie
38 Isabel Street
St. Thomas, ON N5R 1J7

Dennis Carter-Edwards
1118 Edythe Avenue
Cornwall, ON K6J 1N9

Andrew Cavasin
Heritage Thorold LACAC
28 South Street South
Port Robinson, ON L0S 1K0

Ernie Chaplin
1209 Brimley Road
Scarborough, ON M1P 3G5

Ann Veronica Chesworth
131 York Street
Eden Mills, ON N0B 1P0

George Chipman
Welland LACAC
411 East Main Street
Welland, ON L3B 3X4

Betty Lou Clark
R R #5
Rockwood, ON N0B 2K0

Vernon Clark
1220 Wiltshire Drive
Sarnia, ON N7S 3W2

Lewis Coffman
Paisley LACAC
Box 217
Paisley, ON N0G 2N0

A.D.C. Cole
R R #3
Indian River, ON K0L 2B0

Dana Collins
Heritage Nepean Planning
Department
101 Centrepointe Drive
Nepean, ON K2G 5K7

Jeremy Collins
Ontario Heritage Foundation
10 Adelaide Street East
Toronto, ON M5C 1J3

Jack Connor
30 Doxsee Avenue South
Campbellford, ON K0L 1L0

Art Coose
R R #5
Port Perry, ON L9L 1B6

Paul Corriveau
180 Talbot Street
St. Thomas, ON N5R 2X7

Fiona Cowles
Heritage King - Municipal Office
R R #2
King City, ON L0G 1K0

Pamela Craig
Ministry of Culture &
Communications
Field Services Branch
Arthitectural Conservation Unit
2nd Floor, 77 Bloor Street West
Toronto, ON M7A 2R9

David Crozier-Organ
Ontario Restoration Limited
38 Skyline Drive
Dundas, ON L9H 3S5

John Curry
P O Box 610
Stittsville, ON K2S 1A7

Marcia Cuthbert
Toronto Historical Board
Exhibition Place
Marine Museum
Toronto, ON M6K 3C3

Cecelia M. Daley
40 Oak Street
Belleville, ON K8N 3S8

Hugh Davies
P O Box 1043
Southampton, ON N0H 2L0

Linda Davies
P O Box 1043
Southampton, ON N0H 2L0

Joy Davis
R R #1
Queensville, ON L0G 1R0

Harry Dawson
LACAC
Town of Niagara-on-the-Lake
Box 100
Virgil, ON L0S 1T0

Rosemary Dignam
P O Box 6
Grafton, ON K0K 2G0

Christine Dirks
172 Briscoe Street East
London, ON N6C 1X3

Ed Doering
Township of Woolwich LACAC
69 Arthur Street South
Elmira, ON N3B 2Z6

Allan Dracup
28 Albert Street South
Lindsay, ON K9V 3G7

Vaughn Dues
The Carpenter's House
69 Wellington Street East
Aurora, ON L4G 1H7

Dorothy E. Duncan
Ontario Heritage Foundation
10 Adelaide Street East
Toronto, On M5C 1J3

Jennifer Durkin
50 First Avenue
Uxbridge, ON L9P 1J7

Mark Earley
Town of Georgina LACAC
Civic Centre Road
Keswick, ON L4P 3E9

Alice Edgar
310 Fralick's Beach Road
R R #5 Port Perry, ON L9L 1B6

W. Eisenbichler
50 East Street
Sault Ste. Marie, ON P6A 3C3

Peter Elliott
Ontario Heritage Foundation
10 Adelaide Street East
Toronto, ON M5C 1J3

Jacqueline Ethridge
P O Box 966
Kingston, On K7L 4X8

Mary Lou Evans
LACAC Advisor
Ministry of Culture &
Communications
77 Bloor Street West, 2nd Floor
Toronto, ON M7A 2R9

Elaine Evoy
R R #4
Echo Bay, ON P0S 1C0

Marlene Fairbrother
Ministry of Culture &
Communications
114 Worsley Street
Barrie, ON L4M 1M1

David Falconer
Heritage Services
City of North York
5100 Yonge Street
North York, ON M2N 5V7

R.M. Farquhar
1050 Burnhamthorpe Road East
Mississauga, ON L4Y 2X6

Betty Farquharson
977 Weller Street
Peterborough, ON K9J 4Y3

Janet Fayle
17 Elizabeth Street North
Richmond Hill, ON L4C 4N4

Carolyn Davis Fisher
39 Lamar Street
Maple, ON L6A 1A5

Cindy Fisher
94 St. Patrick Street
Goderich, ON N7A 2L6

Jim Fisher
LACAC
Town of Niagara-on-the-Lake
Box 100
Virgil, ON L0S 1T0

Cynthia Flavell
P O Box 100
Bath, ON K0H 1G0

Steven Foster
37 Main Street South
Halton Hills, ON L7G 3G2

Kari Franx
Project Planning Ltd
55 City Centre Drive
Mississauga, ON L5B 1M3

Karen Frosch
Department of Planning &
Development
City of Guelph
59 Carden Street
Guelph, ON N1H 3A1

Roberta Fuller
Manvers LACAC
P O Box 63
Bethany, ON L0A 1A0

Sandra Fuller
Newmarket LACAC
127 Joseph Street
Newmarket, ON L3Y 4H3

Terrence Gallamore
36 Gunn Avenue
Cambridge, ON N3C 3J7

Wendy Gamble
City of Etobicoke
93 Seventh Street
Etobicoke, ON M8V 3B5

Dennis Gannon
86 Queen Street
St. Catharines, ON L2R 5H3

Susan Garossino
783 Rathbourne Avenue
Woodstock, ON L4N 4L8

Rob Garrard
32 Rathnelly Avenue
Toronto, ON M4V 2M3

William Gerrard
Ministry of Government
Services
25 Grosvenor Street, 13th Floor
Toronto, ON M6A 1R2

Jose I. Gill
Simcoe LACAC
114 Victoria Street
Simcoe, ON N3Y 1L6

Ann Gillespie
Regional Municipality of
Hamilton-Wentworth
71 Main Street West
Hamilton, ON L8N 3T4

Mark Gladysz
Heritage Planning, City of
London
300 Dufferin Avenue
London, ON N6A 4L9

Jim Gooch
Hope Township LACAC
Box 171
Port Hope, On L1A 3W3

Dorothy Gordon
Township of Elizabethtown
R R #2
Addison, ON K0E 1A0

Laurie Gordon
210 Richmond Street
Richmond Hill, ON L4C 3Y8

Melissa Gordon
77 Bloor Street West
2nd Floor
Toronto, ON M7A 2R9

Claire Grant
P O Box 29
Warkworth, ON K0K 3K0

William N. Greer
155 Hudson Drive
Toronto, ON M4T 2K4

Joan Grimes
P O Box 100
Bath, ON K0H 1G0

Daniel Guay
Ministry of Culture &
Communications
1 Nicholas Street, Suite 1105
Ottawa, ON K1N 7G7

William F.M. Haight
LACAC Cith of St. Thomas
38 Park Avenue
St. Thomas, ON N5R 4W1

Linda G. Harris
384 St. George North
Box 467
Dresden, ON N0P 1M0

John A. Harrison
Cavell School RT2
Owen Sound, ON N4K 5N4

Phil Haynes
68 Altadore Crescent
Woodstock, ON N4S 5E9

Ruby Heard
Hampton Place
1555 Taunton Road East
R R #1
Hampton, ON L0B 1J0

Brian Hern
Town of Pickering Civic
Complex
One the Esplanade
Pickering, ON L1V 6K7

Bruce & Carol Hodgins
7 Engleburn
Peterborough, ON K9H 1C4

Eric Hodgins
75 Cheritan Avenue
Toronto, ON M4R 1S7

Don Holland
27 Thornhill Ave
Toronto, ON M6S 4C6

Bill Hood
173 Angeline Street North
Lindsay, ON K9V 4X3

Louise Hope
Ontario Genealogical Society
R R #6
Claremont, ON L1Y 1A3

Stephan Hossbach
Heritage Sudbury LACAC
893 Notre Dame Avenue, #6
Sudbury, ON P3A 2T6

Mary Huffman
City of Etobicoke
Etobicoke City Hall
399 The West Mall
Etobicoke, ON M9C 2Y2

Barbara Humphreys
Rideau Township LACAC
Box 88
Manotick, ON K4M 1A3

Maureen Hunt
R R #4
Huntsville, ON P0A 1K0

Robert Hunter
400 Laurier Avenue East
Apt 9B
Ottawa, ON K1N 8Y2

Regan Hutcheson
Planning & Development Dept
101 Town Centre Blvd
Markham, ON L3R 9W3

Marilyn Hymus
Macaulay Heritage Park
P O Box 2150
Picton, ON K0K 2T0

Elizabeth Ingolfsrud
6 Strath Avenue
Etobicoke, ON M8X 1P9

Jane Irwin
526 Burlington Avenue
Burlington, On L7S 1R8

Debora Jackson
LACAC Prescott
Box 2235
Prescott, ON K0E 1T0

Ruth Zaryski Jackson
18725 7th Con. Road
R R #1
Mount Albert, ON L0G 1M0

Joan Johnston
R R #1
Martin Town, ON K0C 1S0

Al Junker
73 Peel Street, Apt 2
New Hamburg, ON N0B 2G0

Peter Kalogirou
9 Princess Avenue
St. Thomas, ON N5R 3V3

Deborah L. Karges
Box 38, R R #1
Vittoria, ON N0E 1W0

Michael J. Keefe
165 Toll Gate Road
Brantford, ON N3R 5AZ

Janet Kellough
McCaulay Heritage Park
P O Box 2150
Picton, ON K0K 2T0

Jane Kelly
R R #1
Grafton, On K0K 2G0

Eilene Kennedy
Town of Flamborough
P O Box 50
Waterdown, ON L0R 2H0

Paul King
Ministry of Culture &
Communications
77 Bloor Street West, 2nd Floor
Toronto, ON L1R 1W8

Mary Lou Kirby
136 Matchedash Street North
Orillia, ON L3V 1V1

Heather Konefat
Town of Caledon
P O Box 1000
Caledon East, ON L0N 1E0

Cheryl L. Kramer
MACAC
Box 307
Millbrook, On L0A 1G0

Tom Kuvlin
Macaulay Heritage Park
P O Box 2150
Picton, ON K0K 2T0

Eugene Kurzawski
Box 468
Smithville, ON L0R 2A0

Marg Lamb
14 Leeson Street
St. Catharines, On L2T 2R3

Paul Lanoman
c/o P O Box 842
Richmond, ON K0A 2Z0

John Leader
Box 479
Paisley, ON N0G 2N0

Rick Legault
P O Box 842
Richmond, ON K0A 2Z0

George F. Lewis
265 Lewis Road, Box 113
Winona, ON L0R 2L0

Mary J. Lewis
265 Lewis Road, Box 113
Winona, ON L0R 2L0

David Lienert
The Lienert Hobbs Partnership,
Architects
416 Chamber Street
Peterborough, ON K9H 3V1

Pauline Lyons
MACAC
Box 307
Millbrook, ON L0A 1G0

Cathy Macdonald
LACAC
Town of Niagara-on-the-Lake
Box 100
Virgil, ON L0S 1T0

Kathryn MacDonald
15 Kensington Pl
Chatham, On N7N 2X7

Sally MacEwan
316 Krohiner Drive
Goderich, ON N7A 4G5

Phyllis MacKay
R R #4 Echo Bay, ON P0S 1C0

Duart MacLean
R R #5
Campbellford, ON K0L 1L0

Sue Mansell
82 Albert Street
Waterloo, ON N2L 3S7

Quentin Martin
Township of Woolwich LACAC
69 Arthur Street South
Elmira, ON N3B 2Z6

David McClung
P O Box 382
Cayuga, ON N0A 1E0

Allan McGillivray
Box 1301
Uxbridge, ON L9P 1N5

Kathryn McHolm
Hope Township LACAC
R R #1
Port Hope, ON L1A 3V5

Thomas F. McIlwraith
University of Toronto
Erindale Campus
Mississauga, ON L5L 1C6

John McIntyre
Horton Place
15342 Yonge Street
Aurora, ON L4G 1N8

Norman McLean
Heritage Nepean Planning
Department
101 Centrepointe Drive
Nepean, ON K2G 5K7

Ian McMillan
Township of Elizabethtown
R R #2
Addison, ON K0E 1A0

Jeanette McPherson
106 Dawes Road
East York, ON M4C 5B6

Douglas McTaggart
20 Prince Arthur Avenue
Suite 8-G
Toronto, ON M5R 1B1

Janet Mehak
Town of Pickering Civic
Complex
One the Esplanade
Pickering, ON L1V 6K7

Kim Miggens
300 Broadway
Tillsonburg, ON N4G 3R7

Carol Millar
279 Kent Street West
Lindsay, On K9V 2Z8

Wayne L. Millard
334 Drew Street
Woodstock, ON N4S 4T9

Marilyn Miller
Ministry of Culture &
Communication
77 Bloor Street West, 2nd Floor
Toronto, ON M6P 2Z7

Gilles Miramontes
P O Box 1350
Picton, ON K0K 2T0

Bob Mitchell
LACAC Town of Parry Sound
52 Seguin Street
Parry Sound, ON P2A 1B4

George Mitchell
2260 Woodglade Blvd
Peterborough, ON K9K 1T9

Richard Moorhouse
10 Adelaide Street East
Toronto, ON M5C 1J3

Frances Moyle
4604 Jeanne Mance
Montreal, PQ H2V 4J4

Peter G. Mullen
Heritage Walkerton
P O Box 68
Walkerton, ON N0G 2V0

Su Murdoch
47 Rodney Street
Barrie, ON L4M 4B6

Gordon Nelson
Heritage Resources Centre
University of Waterloo
Waterloo, ON N2L 3G1

Ted Nicholson
Heritage Sudbury LACAC
City of Sudbury, City Clerks
Dept. Mailbag 5000, Station A
Sudbury, ON P3A 5P3

Pat Nixon
Rideau Township LACAC
R R #1
Kars, ON K0A 2E0

D.H. Graham Norcutt
P O Box 128
Castleton, ON K0K 1M0

Court Noxon
Box 69
Bloomfield, ON K0K 1G0

Gerry Lynn O'Connor
51 Toronto Street South
Box 190
Uxbridge, ON L9P 1T1

Lynda J. O'Krafka
85 Walter Street
Kitchener, ON N2G 1S3

Judith Ochalski
30 Hill Drive
Aurora, ON L4G 3A6

Connie Orr
P O Box 400
Lakefield, ON K0L 2H0

David Osborne
Algonquin College
7 Craig Street
Perth, ON K7H 1X7

John Ota
471 Gladstone Avenue
Toronto, ON M6H 3J1

Janet Oullahan
City of Kingston LACAC
216 Ontario Street
Kingston, ON K7L 2Z3

Cecelia Paine
University of Guelph
School of Landscape
Architecture
Guelph, ON N1G 2W1

Bruce Pappin
73 Pembroke Street West,
3rd Floor
Pembroke, ON K8A 5M5

Angela Pacchiarotti
2141 Major Mackenzie Drive
Maple, ON L6A 1T1

Susan Para
51 Toronto Street Sough
Box 190
Uxbridge, ON L9P 1T1

Ron Parlane
Scarborough LACAC
270 Timberbank Blvd
Unit #17
Scarborough, ON M1W 2M1

David M.J. Pearce
6808 Estoril Road
Mississauga, ON L5N 1N1

Harold Peets
252 Norfolk Street Sough
Simcoe, ON N3Y 2W4

Jim Peters
36 Front Street South
Box 1056
Campbellford, ON K0L 1L0

Donald Pineau
Heritage Planning
National Capital Commission
161 Laurier Avenue West
Ottawa, ON K1P 6J6

Nancy Pollock-Ellwand
14 Elora Street
Guelph, ON N1H 2X8

Betty Porrett
R R #1
Grafton, ON K0K 2G0

Sietza Praamsma
Box 400
Almonte, ON K0A 1A0

P. Kim Pratt
5 Thornton Avenue
London, ON N5Y 2Y1

M. Wendy Pritchard
287 Main Street
Ilderton, ON N0M 2A0

Pamela Pryjma
9 Vale Crescent
Ajax, ON L1S 5A4

Mary Purcell
Township of Pittsburgh
P O Box 966
Kingston, ON K7L 4X8

Tracy Quick
1037 Dominion Avenue
Midland, ON L4R 4V7

Amy Quinn
94 John Street
Port Hope, ON L1A 2Z6

John Quinn
Heritage Canada
P O Box 332
Cambridge, ON N1R 5T8

Roseanne Quinn
Box 40
Castleton, ON K0K 1M0

John Ralston
MACAC
Box 307
Millbrook, ON L0A 1G0

Ken Ramsden
508 Aylmer Street
Peterborough, ON K9H 3W5

Ruth Redelmeier
Box 90
Richmond Hill, ON L4C 4X9

Matt Reniers
City of Brantford Planning
Department
100 Wellington Square
Brantford, ON N3T 2M3

Mark Ridout
Box 316
Oakwood, ON K0M 2M0

Heather Rielly
#7 - 31 Keegan Parkway
Belleville, ON K8N 5N6

Jane Rigby
74 George Street
Hamilton, ON L8P 1C9

Rosemary Rowe
51 George Street
Waterloo, ON N2J 1K8

J. Grant Russell
Box 63, R R #1
Vittoria, ON N0E 1W0

Carlos Salazar
Heritage Sudbury LACAC
Planning Department
Mailbag 3700, Station A
Sudbury, ON P3A 5W5

Eva Salter
Ministry of Culture &
Communications
30 Duke Street West, #405
Kitchener, ON N2H 3W5

Peter Salter
LACAC
Town of Niagara-on-the-Lake
Box 100
Virgil, ON L0S 1T0

Thomas J. Salter
Salter Research Services
62 Carleton Street South
Thorold, ON L2V 2A1

Lloyd Sankey
37 Main Street South
Halton Hills, ON L7G 3G2

Andre Scheinman
36 Copperfield Drive
Kingston, ON K7M 1M4

Dan Schneider
Ministry of Culture &
Communications
Heritage Policy Branch
77 Bloor Street West
Toronto, ON M7A 2R9

Richard Schofield
24 Conlins Road
Scarborough, ON M1C 1C3

Anne Schrecker
P O Box 46
Arva, ON N0M 1C0

Matt Schultz
91 East Greenwood Avenue
Lansdowne, PA 19050

A.K. Skulthorpe
R R #3
Port Hope, ON L1A 3V7

Paul Sears
Bethany LACAC
Box 143 Bethany, ON L0A 1A0

Leonard Sharp
R R #5
Belwood, ON N0B 1J0

Greg Shinnie
Restore Store
55 Snyder's Road West
Baden, ON N0B 1G0

Beverley Simpson
City of Burlington
524 Emerald Street
Burlington, ON L7R 2N6

Keith Sly
Ellisville Road
Seeley's Bay, ON K0H 2N0

Eleanor M. Smith
290 St. David Street South
Fergus, ON N1M 2L5

Greig Smith
Box 400 Almonte, ON K0A 1A0

Kathy Smith
44 Laird Street
Sault Ste Marie, ON P6B 2R9

Nancy Smith
Conservation Review Board
Ministry of Culture &
Communications
77 Bloor Street West, 2nd Floor
Toronto, ON M7A 2R9

Renee Smith
Rideau Township LACAC
Burrits Rapids, ON K0G 1B0

Barbara Snyder
Township of Emestown LACAC
P O Box 70
Odessa, ON K0H 2H0

Alan Stein
Town of Parry Sound LACAC
52 Seguin Street
Parry Sound, ON P2A 1B4

Mary Stephens
763 Leroy Avenue
London, ON N5Y 4G8

Palmier Stevenson-Young
146 Main Street
St. Catharines, ON L2N 4V5

Peter John Stokes
244 King Street
P O Box 170
Niagara-on-the-Lake, ON L0S 1J0

James Strachan
Box 400
King City, ON L0G 1K0

Brian Stratton
Ministry of Culture &
Communications
280 Pinnacle Street, Ste 3
Belleville, ON K8N 3B1

Nancy Tausky
University of Western Ontario
288 St. James Street
London, ON N6A 1X3

John Theisen
Heritage Thorold LACAC
28 South Street Sough
Port Robinson, ON L0S 1K0

Kimberly Thompson
Town of Pickering Civic
Complex
One The Esplanade
Pickering, ON L1V 6K7

Suzanne Tissot
City of Orillia
334 Forest Avenue North
Orillia, ON L3V 3Y7

Janis Topp
534 Burlington Avenue
Burlington, ON L7S 1R8

Chas Tossell
524 Albert Street East
Sault Ste. Marie, ON P6A 2K4

Boxton Tosswill
R R #1
Bethany, ON L0A 1A0

John Towndrow
565 Joyce Street
Cornwall, ON K6J 1Y1

Marie Trainer
Town of Haldimand
P O Box 400
Cayuga, ON N0A 1E0

Ken Trevelyan
288 Park Street North
Peterborough, ON K9J 3W5

Edgar Tumak
Canadian Parks Service
Architectural History Branch
Ottawa, ON K1A 0H3

Louise Tyson
R R #1
Cardinal, ON K0E 1E0

Veronica Vaillancourt
Heritage Canada Foundation
Box 1358, Station B
Ottawa, ON K1P 5R4

Gerry Vanhees
29 Venison Street
Tillsonburg, ON N4G 1T8

Harry Verdun
308 N. Vidal
Sarnia, ON N7T 5Y6

Leslie Vyfhuis
231 Sydney Street
Cornwall, ON K6H 3H3

Mike Wagner, Alderman
City of Kitchener
P O Box 1118
Kitchener, ON N2G 4G7

Pat Wagner
LACAC City of Kitchener
P O Box 1118
Kitchener, ON N2G 4G7

Joanne Walters
Community Development
Office
5 North Street
Goderich, ON N7A 2T5

Mark Warrack
Planning & Development
300 City Centre Drive
Mississauga, ON L5B 3C1

Angelika Watson
39 Harland Crescent
Ajax, ON L1S 1K1

Jack & Wendy Watt
125 Main Street West
Apt 6
Grimsby, ON L3M 1S1

Laurie Wells
Summit Rest
121 Judge Road
Toronto, ON M8Z 5B8

Anne Westaway
128 William Street
Brantford, ON N3T 3L1

Isabel B. White
607 Euclid Street
Whitby, ON L1N 5B9

Alta Whitfield
R R 5 Peterborough, ON K9J 6X6

Irene Wigdor
P O Box 850
Uxbridge, ON L9P 1N2

Frank Williamson
Pickering LACAC
Town of Pickering Civic Complex
One the Esplanade
Pickering, ON L1V 6K7

Anna Willson
Town of Pickering Civic
Complex. One the Esplanade
Pickering, ON L1V 6K7

Dale E.A. Wilson
Heritage Walkerton
P O Box 68
Walkerton, ON N0G 2V0

Douglas Arthur Wilson
56 Three Valleys Drive, #2
Don Mills, ON M3A 3B5

Betty Wilson-Smith
118 Cumberland Drive
Mississauga, ON L5G 3M8

Hamish Wilson
78 Sussex Avenue
Toronto, ON M5S 1J9

Stephen Wohleber
Town of Parry Sound LACAC
52 Seguin Street
Parry Sound, ON P2A 1B4

Winston L. Wong
Heritage Policy Branch
Ministry of Culture &
Communications
77 Bloor Street West, 2nd Floor
Toronto, ON M7A 2R9

Ian K. Woods
I.K. Woods & Partners Inc.
112A Main Street
Markham, ON L3P 1Y1

Charles Wortman
City of Orillia
328 Delia Street
Orillia, ON L3V 1H2

David A. Worton
P O Box 198
Prescott, ON K0E 1T0

Ken Yates
602 Rubidge Street
Peterborough, ON K9H 4G8

Deborah M. Young
General Delivery
Bognor, ON N0H 1E0

Gordon Young
P O Box 400
Lakefield, ON K0L 2H0

Konrad Zeh
Town of Pickering Civic
Complex
One the Esplanade
Pickering, ON L1V 6K7

The Frost Centre for Canadian Heritage and Development Studies

The Centre

The Frost Centre for Canadian Heritage and Development Studies was established to promote interdisciplinary research on many aspects of Canadian society and heritage, past and present. The Centre works with, and includes faculty from various programmes and departments, including: Canadian Studies, Native Studies Environmental and Resource Studies, Cultural Studies, Geography, History, Politics and Sociology.

Research

Over forty faculty are involved in the Centre and actively engaged in research projects on such topics as: Canadian federalism, the development of native communities in the north, the protection of wilderness, northern sovereignty, regionalism in literature, conservation history, Canadian social policy, Indian policy, settlement geography, tourism history, and heritage management.

Graduate Studies

The Centre offers an interdisciplinary graduate program leading to an MA in Canadian Heritage and Development Studies. Research and teaching in the graduate program is organized around, and focuses on three distinct themes or clusters:

1. Community based native socioeconomic development, social impact of development, native history and policy.
2. Canadian culture and identity patterns of regional identity, disparity, development and interregional conflict.
3. Environment and heritage concerns, land use, parks and wilderness, environmental policy, northern issues, historical sites and resources.

Heritage Management Studies

A graduate course, under the Centre's Environmental and Heritage cluster, focuses to a large degree on heritage management themes. The Centre also offers conferences and publications, and is initiating professional short courses relating to the management of historical sites and resources.

For information contact:

On the Frost Centre, contact: Prof. Bruce Hodgins, Director, (705) 748-1749 or 1750.

On Heritage Management Studies, contact: Prof. John Marsh, (705) 748-1419 or 1409

Publications

PRICE

No. 1 1986 A BIBLIOGRAPHIC GUIDE TO UNPUB-
LISHED REPORTS: STUDIES OF COMMU-
NITY PATTERNS AND PLANNING IN THE
COUNTIES OF PETERBOROUGH, VICTO-
RIA AND HALIBURTON,
Roy T. Bowles, Rosemary Brand and Cynthia
Johnston $ 3.00

No. 2 1989 RECREATION AND TOURISM AT HISTORIC
SITES,
John S. Marsh, ed. Special issue of Recreation
Research Review 14 (4) 1989 $ 5.00

No. 3 1989 FEDERALISM IN CANADA AND AUSTRALIA:
HISTORICAL PERSPECTIVES, 1920-1988,
Bruce W. Hodgins, John Eddy, Shelagh Grant and
James Struthers, eds. Peterborough: Trent
University Frost Centre, 1989, 511 pages (Order
from: Broadview Press, P.O. Box 1243,
Peterborough, ON K9J 7H5 $19.95

No. 4 1990 BOOKS BY MEMBERS OF THE FROST CENTRE,
Bruce W. Hodgins and Shawn Heard Out of Print

No. 5 1991 FROST CENTRE MEMBERS: RECENT PUBLICA-
TIONS AND GRADUATE STUDENT THESES,
Bruce W. Hodgins and Shawn Heard $ 3.00

No. 6 1991 GREENWAYS AND GREEN SPACE ON THE
OAK RIDGES MORAINE: TOWARDS COOP-
ERATIVE PLANNING
ed. J. Fisher, F.M. Helleiner, K. Wehrenberg $13.00
(inclusive of postage)

No. 7 1992 CANADIAN PERCEPTIONS OF THE MILI-
TARY: A QUESTIONNAIRE ADMINISTERED
TO TRENT UNIVERSITY UNDERGRADU-
ATES. PART I. SUMMARY OF REPLIES TO
THE QUESTIONNAIRE,
F. H. Kim Krenz $ 3.00

List of M.A. Theses Available

	PRICE
LEONARD COHEN AND THE WORD MADE FLESH (1992) Marco L. Adria	$11.00
ELDORADO: LOCAL CITIZEN ACTIVISM AND THE NUCLEAR ESTABLISHMENT (1989) Donald H. M. Alexander	$17.00
SCIENCE, GOVERNMENT AND POLITICS IN THE ABOLITION OF THE COMMISSION OF CONSERVATION 1909-1921 (1988) James Robert Allum	$22.00
PUBLIC ACCESS TO PRIVATE LAND IN CAVAN TOWNSHIP, PETERBOROUGH COUNTY: INCENTIVES, AGREEMENTS AND ATTITUDES (1994) Martha C. Anslow	$21.00
"INDIAN CONTROL OF INDIAN EDUCATION": THE EVOLUTION OF PRIMARY AND SECONDARY EDUCATION FOR NATIVE STUDENTS IN ONTARIO, 1972-93 (1994) Kerry Ann Cannon	$30.00
LABOUR AND THE ENVIRONMENT IN CANADA TODAY (1989) Jennifer Myra Carter	$33.00
WE SHALL REMEMBER CANADIAN INDIANS AND WORLD WAR II (1993) Janet Frances Davison	$28.00
BORDER-CROSSING: DECONSTRUCTING A GENDERED REGION (1990) Joelle Marie Favreau	$14.00
PLANNING FOR ECOLOGICAL INTEGRITY ON A WATERSHED BASIS AROUND LAKE ONTARIO (1993) John R. Fisher	$16.00
TOWARDS A CANADIAN "CULTURAL MECCA": THE METHODIST BOOK AND PUBLISHING HOUSE'S PURSUIT OF BOOK PUBLISHING AND COMMITMENT TO CANADIAN WRITING, 1829-1926 (1994) Janet Beverly Friskney	$35.00

No. 8 1992   USING WILDERNESS: ESSAYS ON THE
               EVOLUTION OF YOUTH CAMPING IN
               ONTARIO,
               Bruce W. Hodgins and Bernadine Dodge, eds.
               Peterborough: Trent University Frost Centre,
               1992, 164 pages $

No. 9 1992   CO-EXISTENCE? STUDIES IN ONTARIO-
               FIRST NATIONS RELATIONS
               Bruce W. Hodgins, John S. Milloy and Shawn
               Heard. Peterborough: Trent University Frost
               Centre, 1992, 170 pages $

No. 10 1994   RAILS TO GREENWAYS: THE PROCEED-
               INGS OF A CONFERENCE AT TRENT UNI-
               VERSITY, PETERBOROUGH, ONTARIO,
               August 13-15, 1993 John Marsh, ed.
               Peterborough: Trent University Frost
               Centre, 1994, 202 pages $

The above publications are available from the Administ
Secretary, Frost Centre, Trent University, Peterborough, Ontari
7B8, Canada. Charges for postage and handling are as follows:
within Canada and $6.00 elsewhere. Please make cheques pa
to: *Frost Centre Publications.*

RECREATION RESOURCES, CONDITIONS AND USE IN
ONTARIO PROVINCIAL PARKS (1989)
Weihe Guan $24.00

THE "INDIAN POLICY" OF THE ANGLICAN CHURCH OF
CANADA FROM 1945 TO THE 1970s (1992)
Norman Andrew Gull $13.00

ECONOMIC PLANNING IN NORTHERN ONTARIO PRIMA-
RY RESOURCE TOWNS: A STUDY OF THE COMMUNITIES
OF TEMAGAMI, KIRKLAND LAKE, GERALDTON AND
ELLIOT LAKE (1993)
Shawn Robert Daniel Heard $28.00

THE STRUGGLE FOR FRENCH-LANGUAGE EDUCATION
IN STURGEON FALLS, WEST NIPISSING, ONTARIO: A
COMMUNITY OF CONTRADICTIONS (1989)
Tracy Jane Helm $24.00

VITAMIN A DEFICIENCY IN INUIT POPULATION USING
THE EYE AS A DEMONSTRATION ORGAN (1993)
Arthor Siksini Horn (Otskinau) $34.00

PATH TO PROTECTION: APPLYING THE ABC RESOURCE
INVENTORY METHOD TO LOCATE A HIKING TRAIL
ROUTE ON THE OAK RIDGES MORAINE (1994)
Kristine M. Keating $28.00

ECOLOGICAL REDEVELOPMENT IN FOUR FOREST-
DEPENDENT BRITISH COLUMBIA COMMUNITIES: SUS-
TAINING FOREST AND COMMUNITY (1994)
David MacKinnon $23.00

RELIGION AND SOCIAL CHANGE: ETHNIC CONTINUITY
AND CHANGE AMONG THE KAREN IN THAILAND WITH
REFERENCE TO THE CANADIAN INDIAN EXPERIENCE
(1993)
Chumpol Maniratanavongsiri $19.00

SUSANNA MOODIE AND ROUGHING IT IN THE BUSH:A
CASE STUDY IN CANADIAN LITERARY HISTORY (1991)
Thomas James Milburn $18.00

NATIONALISM IN CATALONIA AND QUEBEC COM-
PARED: POLITICAL AND ECONOMIC DEFICITS AND SUR-
PLUSES (1994)
Janice Anne Oliver $17.00

THE NECHI INSTITUTE ON ALCOHOL AND DRUG
EDUCATION:ILLUSTRATING THE USE OF A BI-CULTURAL TRAIN-
ING MODEL AND ITS EFFECT ON THE CULTURAL, PERSONAL AND
PROFESSIONAL DEVELOPMENT OF THE NATIVE TRAINEES (1994)
Busaba Paratacharya $20.00

DENE LEADERSHIP STYLES (1994)
Sarah Lynne Pocklington $20.00

RECREATION ACCESS AND ITS POLICY CONTEXT IN ONTARIO (1994)
John Paul Rexe $18.00

LOCATING LUKE (1993)
Margaret Mary Rodgers $24.00

STUDYING UNDER THE INFLUENCE: THE IMPACT OF
SAMUEL HEARNE'S JOURNAL OF THE SCHOLARLY LITER-
ATURE CONCERNING CIPEWYAN WOMEN (1994)
Heather Rollason $18.00

ONTARIO ABORIGINAL POLICY WITH AN EMPHASIS ON
THE TEME-AUGAMA ANISHNABAI (1990)
Fiona A. Sampson $22.00

THE EXPLOSIVE ISSUE OF LNG:A STUDY IN RURAL CONFLICT (1991)
Margaret Jennifer Sells $12.00

STANDING THE TEST OF TIME:A HISTORY OF THE
BEARDY'S/OKEMASIS RESERVE, 1876-1951 (1993)
Stephen George Sliwa $16.00

LITERATURE AS A MEANS OF HERITAGE INTERPRETA-
TION (1993)
Michael Brian Starr $15.00

LOCAL CONTROL OF EDUCATION AMONG THE
ATTAWAPISKAT FIRST NATION - THE PEOPLE'S VISION OF
A BAND-CONTROLLED SCHOOL (1994)
Norbert Werner Witt $26.00

VOICES OF EXCLUSION:ETHNICITY IN PETERBOROUGH,
A MID-SIZED ONTARIO CITY (1994)
Leslie Woolcott $20.00

The above publications are available from the Administrative
Secretary, Frost Centre, Trent University, Peterborough, Ontario K9J
7B8, Canada. Charges for postage and handling are as follows: $3.00
within Canada and $6.00 elsewhere. Please make cheques payable
to: *Trent University.*